Reconciling Rwanda: unity, nationality and state control

Jennifer Melvin

Critical Studies in Human Rights

This interdisciplinary peer-reviewed series investigates a wide array of human rights issues from diverse intellectual perspectives. It seeks to move beyond standard academic approaches to embrace critically engaged scholarship, creative non-fiction writing, and works that take positions on the issues. The series interrogates the human rights-related dimensions of phenomena such as colonisation, genocide, ecocide, reconciliation projects, racism, poverty, indigenous peoples' rights, corporate power and extractive industries.

Following Colin Samson's ground-breaking work *A World You Do Not Know*, this is the second book in the series. Jen Melvin's superb critical study of the Reconciliation project in Rwanda is a significant contribution to empirical and theoretical understanding and will be vital reading for students and scholars of post-genocide politics in Rwanda. More generally, it makes a significant contribution to wider debates on reconciliation projects and transitional justice, identity politics and difference and the sociology of human rights.

Dr Damien Short
Reader in Human Rights
Director: Human Rights Consortium
Series editor, Critical Studies in Human Rights

ISBN 978-0-9931102-0-7

Institute of Commonwealth Studies
School of Advanced Study
University of London
Senate House
Malet Street
London WC1E 7HU

Cover image: Rwandan flag

Contents

List of images

Abstract

In the 1990s, a number of countries including Guatemala, El Salvador, and Bosnia and Herzegovina implemented conflict resolution mechanisms to confront legacies of past violence. This 'paradigm shift' away from the traditional judicial methods of the Nuremberg and Tokyo Tribunals sought to engage directly with personal experiences of those who were affected by mass human rights abuses and violations (Kritz, 1996, p. 128). Growing academic interest in this approach to conflict resolution is evident in literature about truth commissions and the concepts of unity and reconciliation more broadly. This volume contributes a case-specific analysis of the National Unity and Reconciliation Programme in post-conflict Rwanda to the broad sociological study of reconciliation and human rights.

This book seeks to uncover and interpret how Rwanda's official reconciliation programme functions in social and political practice. It utilises a social constructionist framework to provide a nuanced, theoretical and empirical understanding of how the stated commitments, power dynamics and political interests of the Rwandan Patriotic Front (RPF) government inform this programme. Moreover, this book critically analyses the National Unity and Reconciliation Programme according to its own internal logic, international human right standards, and the theory and practice of reconciliation as a peacemaking paradigm. Rwanda's official programme is shaped by three major themes: justice; nation-building; and an interpretation of Rwandan history referred to in this work as the 'victor's narrative'. The volume examines how these themes reflect changing political interests and conceptions of unity, identity, and 'national reconciliation' as defined by the RPF. It argues that Rwanda's National Unity and Reconciliation Programme is far from an exercise in equality and engagement in the legacies of past violence. Instead, it promotes a singular national identity secured by a distorted narrative of the past and ambitious vision of future development. As such, this programme is best understood as a nation-building and state-legitimisation project that bolsters the political control of the current RPF regime.

Acknowledgements

I would like to thank Damien Short for guiding me through the process of writing this book. I am grateful for his immeasurable support, advice and encouragement. I would also like to thank Lars Waldorf, Paul Havemann, Leo Zeilig, and Colin Samson for reading early drafts of my work and providing constructive suggestions that helped to shape this volume.

I am indebted to Rwandan friends and research participants who took the time to share their experiences and perspectives with me. Their words gave life to this project.

My family deserves a special thank you for the encouragement and confidence to complete this book. I am also thankful for the support given to me by the Kent family.

I wish to thank the St John's Rotary Club and the Central Research Fund at the University of London for partially funding my fieldwork in Rwanda. I also wish to thank the *International Journal of Human Rights*, the *Journal of Human Rights in the Commonwealth* and the Commonwealth Advisory Bureau for the opportunity to publish papers that emerged from this book.

Finally, for your patience, advice, humour and love, thank you to Jack.

Acronyms and abbreviations

AFDL	Alliance des Forces Démocratiques pour la Libération du Congo (Alliance of Democratic Forces for the Liberation of Congo)
AI	Amnesty International
ASF	Avocats sans Frontières (Lawyers without Borders)
CDR	Coalition pour la Défence de la République (Coalition for the Defense of the Republic)
CHRI	Commonwealth Human Rights Initiative
CLADHO	Collectif des Ligues et Associations de Défense des Droits de l'Homme au Rwanda (Collective of Leagues and Associations for the Defense of Human Rights in Rwanda)
CNDP	Congrès National pour la Défense du Peuple (National Congress for the Defense of the People)
COPORWA	Community of Potters of Rwanda
DFID	Department for International Development
DRC	Democratic Republic of Congo
EAC	East African Community
EDPRS	Economic, Development, and Poverty Reduction Strategy
FAR	Forces Armées Rwandaises (Rwandan Armed Forces)
FARG	Fonds d'Assistance pour les Rescapés du Génocide (Fund for the Support of Genocide Survivors)
FDLR	Forces Démocratiques de Libération du Rwanda (Democratic Forces for the Liberation of Rwanda)
FHAO	Facing History and Ourselves
GNU	Government of National Unity
HRW	Human Rights Watch
ICTR	International Criminal Tribunal for Rwanda

ICTY	International Criminal Tribunal for the former Yugoslavia
IDP	Internally Displaced Persons
INGO	International non-governmental organisation
IRJ	Institute for Justice and Reconciliation
LIPRODHOR	Ligue Rwandaise pour la Promotion et la Défense des Droits de l'Homme (Rwandan League for the Promotion and Defense of Human Rights)
MDR-Parmehutu	Mouvement Démocratique Républicain – Party of the Hutu Emancipation Movement (see separate entry for Parmehutu)
MRGI	Minority Rights Groups International
MONUC	UN Peacekeeping Mission in DRC, now referred to as MONUSCO
MRND	Mouvement Révolutionaire National pour le Développement (National Revolutionary Movement for Development)
MSM	Mouvement Social Muhutu (Muhutu Social Movement)
NGO	Non-governmental organisation
NRA	National Resistance Army
NSGJ	National Service of Gacaca Jurisdictions
NUR	National University of Rwanda
Parmehutu	Parti du Mouvement de l'Emancipation Hutu (Movement for the Emancipation of Hutu Party)
PRI	Penal Reform International
RANU	Rwandese Alliance for National Unity
RDF	Rwandan Defense Force
RPA	Rwandan Patriotic Army
RPF	Rwandan Patriotic Front
RTLM	Radio et Télévision Libres des Milles Collines (Free Radio and Television of the Thousand Hills)
TNA	Transitional National Assembly
TIG	Travail d'Intérêt Général (Work of General Interest)
TO	Theatre of the Oppressed
TRC	[South African] Truth and Reconciliation Commission

UNAMIR	UN Peacekeeping Mission in Rwanda during the 1994 genocide
UNAR	Union Nationale Rwandaise (National Union of Rwanda)
UNDP	United Nations Development Programme
UNHCR	United Nations Refugee Agency
UNHRC	United Nations Human Rights Council
USAID	United States Agency for International Development

Rwandan Patriotic Front (RPF) government departments

Minaffet	Ministry of Foreign Affairs and Cooperation
Minaloc	Ministry of Local Government
Minecofin	Ministry of Finance and Economic Planning
Mineduc	Ministry of Education
Minijust	Ministry of Justice
MOD	Ministry of Defence
NCDC	National Curriculum Development Centre
NURC	National Unity and Reconciliation Commission
PBCM	Peacebuilding and Conflict Management Department of the NURC
RALGA	Rwanda Association of Local Government Authorities

Glossary of Kinyarwanda words

Banyarwanda	national identity shared by all Rwandans
Gacaca	community genocide courts
Ibigiye	value of hard work and pride
Igikingi	land contracts in pre-colonial Rwanda
Imidugudu	subsidised resettlement scheme for survivors and citizens living in rural areas after the 1994 genocide
Impuzamugambi	militia attached to the CDR party
Indongozi	participants at itorero ry'igihugu civic education camps who best reflect Rwandan social and cultural values
Ingando	mandatory live-in civic education camp
Inyangamugayo	gacaca judges
Inyenzi	term for 'cockroach' used to refer to Tutsi civilians and officials in 1994 genocide propaganda
Interahamwe	militia attached to MRND party
Intore	participants at itorero ry'igihugu
Imihigo	performance contracts publicly signed by district mayors and President Kagame
Itorero Ry'igihugu	mandatory live-in civic education camp mandated to teach the population about social values and development
Jenocide Yakorewe Abatutsi	Genocide against the Tutsi
Kugandika	action of interrupting everyday activities to reflect upon and find solutions to challenges facing the nation
Kwihutura	rare opportunity in pre-colonial Rwanda through which a Hutu individual who owned sufficient cattle could change their social status from Hutu to Tutsi
Rizabara Uwarirage	a statement in 1994 genocide propaganda that roughly translates to, 'The events, mainly negative, that occurred during the night will be narrated by the one who experienced them'

Rubanda Nyamwinshi/Bene Sebahinzi	the mass population
Ubuhake	cattle clientage system
Ubuletwa	forced labour system
Ubumwe bw' Abanyarwanda	the unity of Rwandans
Umuganda	mandatory community service one day per month for all Rwandan adults
Urugerero	mandatory national service for young people aged 18–35

Chronology of key events

1884	Germany takes possession of Rwanda and Burundi and governs them as a single state, Ruanda-Urundi.
1916	Ruanda-Urundi becomes a Belgian colony.
1933	Ethnicity is included in the national census for the first time.
1957	Nine Hutu intellectuals publish the 'Bahutu manifesto: notes of the social aspect of the racial native problem in Rwanda'.
1 November 1959	Group of Union National Rwandaise (UNAR) militants attack a Hutu sub-chief in Gitarama, central Rwanda, leading to the anti-Tutsi violence of the 'Social Revolution'.
1 July 1962	Rwanda becomes independent and Grégoire Kayibanda becomes the country's first president.
1972	Genocide in Burundi during which upwards of 200,000 Hutu are killed.
1973	Coup d'état results in Juvénal Habyarimana becoming Rwanda's second president.
1987	RANU, a group of Rwandan Tutsi in Uganda, renames itself the Rwandan Patriotic Front.
1 October 1990	The RPF invades Rwanda.
2 October 1990	RPF Colonel Fred Rwigyema is killed. He is replaced several weeks later by Paul Kagame.
October 1992	Habyarimana signs a power-sharing agreement with the RPF.
6 April 1994	President Habyarimana and Burundian President Cyprien Ntaryamira are assassinated by a missile attack on the plane in which they were travelling.
7 April 1994	The 1994 genocide begins. Hutu opposed to Habyarimana's regime are killed as are Tutsi civilians.

	Prime Minister Agathe Uwilingiyimana and ten Belgian peacekeepers are also killed.
Mid June 1994	French authorities launch Opération Turquoise.
4 July 1994	The RPF seizes Kigali and the 1994 genocide officially ends. This day is commemorated every year as 'Liberation Day'.
19 July 1994	The Government of National Unity (GNU) is formed as a transitional coalition government.
8 November 1994	The International Criminal Tribunal for Rwanda (ICTR) is officially launched in Arusha, Tanzania, to try cases of genocide and crimes against humanity.
1996	Rwandan Patriotic Army (RPA) soldiers attack refugee camps in Zaire with the stated mandate to 'flush out' genocide perpetrators.
1997	The RPF works in cooperation with Alliances des Forces Démocratiques pour la Libération du Congo (AFDL) to topple Zairian President Mobutu. The AFDL leader, Laurent Désiré Kabila becomes president of the newly renamed Democratic Republic of Congo (DRC).
August 1998–2003	The Second Congo War begins and ends.
2002	Rwandan troops officially pull out of DRC amid rumours of continued clandestine presence well into 2003.
2003	Paul Kagame is elected as Rwanda's president amid allegations of election irregularities.
2005	Gacaca courts begin hearing cases of genocide and crimes against humanity.
September 2008	The RPF wins the parliamentary election with a majority of 78.8 per cent.
November 2009	Rwanda joins the Commonwealth.
April 2010	Victoire Ingabire is prevented from registering for the 2010 presidential election and is arrested.
August 2010	Paul Kagame is reelected as the President of the Republic with a majority of 93 per cent.
October 2010	UN 'Report of the mapping exercise', describing human rights abuses in DRC 1993–2003, is published. It outlines crimes allegedly committed by RPA soldiers that may amount to genocide.

18 June 2012	Gacaca courts officially closed after trying more than 1.2 million cases.
7 April 2014	The 20th annual commemoration of the Genocide against the Tutsi begins.

Introduction

Rwanda is a small land-locked country in the Great Lakes Region of central Africa. Bordering Burundi, Uganda, Tanzania and Democratic Republic of Congo (DRC) (see image 1 below), it is the most densely populated country in sub-Saharan Africa with a population of 12 million in July 2015.[1] The Rwandan Patriotic Front (RPF) won the parliamentary election in 2003 and continues to lead the country under the presidency of Paul Kagame. Although the current RPF government promotes a national identity that supersedes ethnicity, the population can be roughly divided into three major ethnic groups: the Hutu

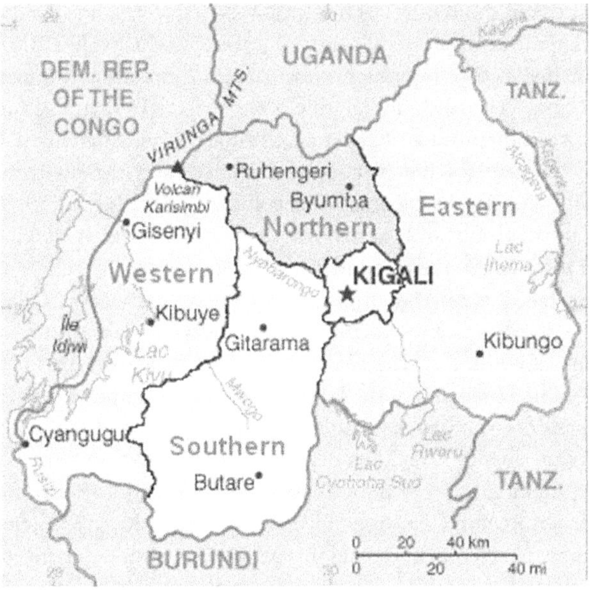

Figure 1.1. Map of Rwanda (source: Wikimedia Commons)

1 Rwanda's total land mass measures 26,338 square kilometres. This densely populated country is approximately 5,500 square kilometres larger than Wales. See Central Intelligence Agency, World Factbook: Rwanda (2015), https://www.cia.gov/library/publications/the-world-factbook/geos/rw.html (accessed 12 Mar. 2015).

majority, Tutsi minority and indigenous Twa community. Kinyarwanda is the language most commonly spoken by all three groups.[2]

Rwanda's colonial history began in 1884 under German rule (Newbury 1983, p. 257). Prior to the arrival of the German colonists, Rwanda was ruled by a *Mwami* or King of Bahindiro Tutsi lineage (Eltringham, 2004, p. 13). A small number of Tutsi chiefs held most of the political power. While opportunities were rare for Hutu to gain such power during this period. Hutu civilians could only do so either by becoming Chiefs of Landholdings, whose responsibility it was to watch over agricultural land and production, or through improving their socio-economic status by accumulating cattle through the *kwihutura* process to become Tutsi (Mamdani, 1996, p. 10). But under colonial rule, even these limited prospects were lost, particularly that of the Belgians which began in 1916 (ibid.).

As the colonial period progressed, the political, social and economic gap between the Hutu majority and Tutsi minority widened. Forced labour was a key factor in the subjugation of the majority of Hutu pastoral workers under Belgian rule. It became clear in 1928 how brutal the forced labour system was when hundreds of thousands of Hutu peasants fled to Uganda (ibid., p. 11). A short time later the process of ethnic stratification was formally institutionalised with the inclusion of ethnic identities in the 1933 census (Straus, 2006, p. 225). The final years of colonial rule were shaped by a transition towards independence and episodes of systematic brutality against civilians. The 1959 'Social Revolution' was the first major instance of anti-monarchic political upheaval and anti-Tutsi violence in the colonial period (Uvin, 1999, p. 256). It resulted in the deaths of hundreds of Tutsi civilians and an exodus of many more Tutsi into neighbouring countries (ibid.).

Rwanda faced further political change in late January 1961 when the 'Coup of Gitarama' resulted in Grégoire Kayibanda's seizure of power (Eltringham, 2004, p. 21). The Social Revolution ended shortly thereafter and Rwanda became independent on 1 July 1962. Violent attacks against civilians pushed more Tutsi out of Rwanda during the early years of independence and Kayibanda's presidency. The mass departure continued throughout the 1960s resulting in the migration of more than 100,000 Tutsi into other countries in the Great Lakes Region (Lemarchand, 1970, p. 172). However, these countries were not immune to conflict during this period. Burundi experienced genocide in 1972 when Tutsi soldiers in the national army attacked hundreds of thousands of Hutu civilians. Inside Rwanda, the political tide turned again when Juvénal Habyarimana seized power from Kayibanda's MDR-Parmehutu party in 1973 (ibid.; Newbury and Newbury, 1999, p. 299).

2 English and French are also official languages, although not as widely spoken as Kinyarwanda. In 2009, English became the official language of education for children above the age of nine.

As episodes of systematic brutality in Rwanda began to subside, Tutsi refugees in neighbouring countries faced forced expulsions and attacks. One such expulsion took place in 1982–3 when upwards of 40,000 Rwandan refugees were forced to return home or to flee to Tanzania following outbreaks of violence in Uganda (Mamdani, 1996, p. 25). These periodic conflicts in Uganda purportedly encouraged a group of Rwandan Tutsi fighting in the Ugandan National Resistance Army (NRA) to form the Rwandese Alliance for National Unity (RANU) to debate relevant issues – the Alliance was eventually abandoned and replaced with the RPF. The RPF's stated mandate included the repatriation of Rwandan refugees and the creation of a power-sharing agreement with Habyarimana's party, Mouvement Révolutionaire National pour le Développement (MRND) (ibid., p. 26).

The RPF later launched an invasion of Rwanda that changed the political landscape of the country. After allegedly growing impatient with Habyarimana's promises to repatriate Rwandan refugees, the rebel group set its attack in motion. The first day of October 1990 marked the beginning of what would become a four-year civil war in Rwanda. This bloody period included attacks against Hutu and Tutsi civilians as well as an aggrandisement of the anti-Tutsi propaganda machine that had built up steam throughout Habyarimana's rule. As the RPF advanced, militias attached to political parties, including the MRND, began to arm for further conflict (Melvern, 2000, pp. 44–5). Violence during this period took a severe turn for the worse on 6 April 1994. President Habyarimana and Burundian President Cyprien Ntaryamira were killed when the plane in which they were travelling was shot down near Kigali international airport. Within 24 hours of the assassinations, the systematic killing of Tutsi civilians and Hutu opposed to the Habyarimana regime had begun (Jones, 2006, p. 238). The 1994 genocide lasted approximately one hundred days and resulted in an estimated 800,000 fatalities. This death toll remains highly contested, however, with estimates ranging from 500,000 to one million (Des Forges, 1999, p. 1; NSGJ, n.d.(a), p. 1).

The RPF seized control of the capital city, Kigali, in early July and the genocide officially ended on 4 July 1994. The Government of National Unity (GNU), a transitional coalition government, was formed on 19 July 1994 and with that the period of post-conflict governance began. The GNU, under the leadership of Prime Minister Faustin Twagiramungu, began to conceive and articulate the transitional government's early commitments to justice and repatriation.[3] The National Unity and Reconciliation Commission (NURC)

3 The GNU identified the safe repatriation of refugees as paramount to the promotion of peace and social cohesion during the Nairobi Summit at the Bujumbura Conference, and during the trilateral agreements between Rwanda, the United Nations Refugee Agency (UNHCR) and neighbouring countries in January 1995 (UNSC, 1995, p. 2).

estimated in 2005 that the GNU facilitated the return of 'millions of Rwandan refugees' from DRC between 1994 and 1999 (2005, p. 13). With regard to justice, the sweeping arrests of suspected perpetrators shortly after the 1994 genocide prompted the commencement of criminal trials in the domestic justice system and the restoration of traditional *gacaca*[4] community courts in 2001 (Waldorf, 2007, p. 425). The reinvention of the gacaca system for genocide trials eventually facilitated the prosecution of 1.2 million cases of genocide and crimes against humanity (Bikesha interview, 20 July 2010).

Pierre-Célestin Rwigema replaced Twagiramungu in 1995 following the latter's exile in August of that year. This change of leadership coincided with the RPF's restructuring of Parliament and its establishment of an executive presidency (Reyntjens, 2004, p. 180). These actions ensured the dominance of the RPF within the transitional GNU, which oversaw the National Unity and Reconciliation Programme until the NURC was launched in March 1999. The official reconciliation effort in Rwanda does not have a formal name, as such. Instead, the NURC refers to it as a crosscutting programme that includes all projects with the stated mandate to promote unity and reconciliation. This book refers to this undertaking as the National Unity and Reconciliation Programme to indicate the connections between such government-led projects as gacaca, demobilisation and reintegration, the Vision 2020 development programme, and civic education as well as the stated mandates that guide them.

The NURC was created to act as an advisory body, research group and formal coordinator of government-level programming in unity and reconciliation across the country (MOD, 2003, p. 6). The NURC's stated mandate includes: coordinating the programme of national unity and reconciliation; restoring and consolidating reconciliation among Rwandans; educating the population about unity and reconciliation; proposing measures to eradicate divisions between Rwandans; denouncing discrimination; and making annual reports which reference the country's progress with regard to unity and reconciliation (ibid.). These responsibilities, as stated in Article 178 of the 2003 Constitution of the Republic of Rwanda, adopted on 26 May 2003, illustrate the scale of the NURC's mandate, but fail to define clearly the government's understanding of 'national reconciliation'.[5]

An official policy regarding the promotion of 'national reconciliation' was not formally adopted in Rwanda until 2007. The National Policy of Unity and Reconciliation (hereafter referred to as the 2007 Reconciliation Policy) formally defines the government's conceptions of unity and reconciliation.

4 Pronounced *ga-cha-cha*. Gacaca will be discussed in detail in chapter 3.

5 The term 'national reconciliation' appears in inverted commas to demonstrate the RPF's ownership of this complex term. The RPF's vision of 'national reconciliation' functions as both a theory and a practice guided by policy, legislation and stated commitments made by the Rwandan government.

Although relatively convoluted, it outlines some of the stated commitments that shape the government-led National Unity and Reconciliation Programme. They include: fighting 'genocide ideology' and 'divisionism'; prioritising citizenship and the common interests of all Rwandans over ethnicity, family relationships and religious groups; respecting the law and human rights; healing moral wounds by revealing the truth and asking and giving pardon; and preventing the recurrence of genocide (NURC, 2007, pp. 4–5).[6] These stated commitments to promoting 'national reconciliation' appear in various NURC documents, the 2003 Constitution, and the documentation outlining the Vision 2020 development programme. They are also repeated in official reconciliation discourse disseminated by the government during presidential speeches, radio programmes, and at genocide commemoration ceremonies.

The 'national' nature of the National Unity and Reconciliation Programme emphasises the participation of the entire population in the initiative. Official discourse does not specifically refer to the reconciliation of Hutu and Tutsi groups; instead, it depicts 'national reconciliation' as a collective process that requires the action of *all Rwandans*. This employs a theory shaped by a number of concepts the government has constructed to portray the rebuilding of relationships between individuals, groups and the state after the 1994 genocide. These include 'horizontal' reconciliation between citizens and 'vertical' reconciliation between civilians and the government. Other relevant concepts include 'genocide ideology', 'divisionism', ethnicity and unity. Alongside the de facto banning of ethnic identities from public discourse, the RPF's vision of 'national reconciliation' is put into practice through the pursuit of justice at gacaca; the reeducation of the population at mandatory civic education camps: *ingando* and *itorero ry'igihugu*; and development programming. The RPF's vision of reconciliation theory and practice, as depicted by the National Unity and Reconciliation Programme, is referred to as 'national reconciliation' throughout this book.

This short summation demonstrates the scale of the RPF government's official reconciliation programme. Its enormity and the absence of a clear definition of reconciliation creates a perception of the process being 'vague or messy' as described by Zorbas (2004, p. 29). The government's stated commitment to promoting what appears to be a curious mix of ideological and pragmatic goals also creates a sense of murkiness as it raises questions about how the programme functions in social and political practice. As this book progresses, these stated commitments and the specific projects with which

6 The terms 'genocide ideology' and 'divisionism', as well as 'good governance', 'bad governance' and 'sectarianism', discussed later in the book, appear in inverted commas to indicate that they are constructed by the Rwandan government. These terms appear in policy, legislation, the 'victor's narrative' and official reconciliation discourse.

they are associated will be examined. The government's vision of 'national reconciliation' and the logic that informs it will be analysed with reference to the themes that emerge from the programme: justice; nation-building; and the 'victor's narrative'. The entire National Unity and Reconciliation Programme will be analysed to determine its economic, social and political function in post-conflict Rwanda.[7]

Research questions

The research seeks to provide a nuanced interpretation of how the National Unity and Reconciliation Programme functions in social and political practice in post-conflict Rwanda. As such, this book is shaped by several broad questions. How does the government conceive and articulate 'national reconciliation'? How have the military and political roles of the RPF during the 1990 invasion, civil war, 1994 genocide and post-conflict period shaped the design and implementation of the official programme? The GNU restored gacaca with the stated mandate to promote justice and reconciliation. Did it in fact promote the government's conceptions of 'vertical' and 'horizontal' reconciliation? As the stated commitment to building a strong and united nation features heavily in official discourse, how has the RPF's nation-building agenda affected the promotion of 'national reconciliation'? What are the implications of the RPF's dissemination of a singular historical narrative, the 'victor's narrative', upon the promotion of its vision of unity and 'national reconciliation'? How does the National Unity and Reconciliation Programme function in social and political practice?

The analysis

This book defines 'reconciliation' as a peacemaking paradigm, a conceptualisation that draws on Lederach's description of reconciliation as both a theory and practice that extends beyond the mechanisms of traditional peacebuilding processes and statist diplomacy. For Lederach reconciliation is the 'meeting point between realism and innovation' (1997, p. 25). It creates a social space in which opponents may come together to acknowledge the past and build a shared future (ibid., p. 27). More specifically, this book analyses reconciliation in the context of Rwanda's official National Unity and Reconciliation Programme.

The research examines how the programme's 'internal logic', as defined by the RPF's stated commitments to 'national reconciliation', as well as related

7 This book uses the term 'post-conflict' rather than 'post-genocide' to describe Rwanda's social, economic and political landscape since the the genocide ended in July 1994. The term 'post-conflict' encompasses the influence on the construction of the National Unity and Reconciliation Programme of the October 1990 RPF invasion, and the civil war, as well as the 1994 genocide.

policy and legislation, promotes the current RPF regime's political dominance. The book also compares the programme against this logic in order to determine whether it meets its own goals. This particular examination sheds light on the gaps between rhetoric and reality in the post-conflict context. More generally, the research takes the post-conflict period, 1994 to the present,[8] as its primary period of study. This temporal parameter facilitates the in-depth analysis of formal commitments, official reconciliation discourse and pertinent legislation in the social, political and economic contexts in which they were made, stated or published, and those in which they continue to function. As the National Unity and Reconciliation Programme was created after the violence of 1994, the research considers historical events relevant to this period including colonisation, independence, civil war and the 1994 genocide.

This book views the official programme as a complex socio-political process. In its most basic form, it is an umbrella programme under which multiple state-sponsored projects seek to achieve the stated goal of promoting the RPF's vision of 'national reconciliation' in post-conflict Rwanda. Such promotion is complicated, however, by conflicting priorities and legal constraints; the inclusion of the loosely defined concepts of 'divisionism' and 'genocide ideology'; a highly restrictive education remit; and the absence of a clear definition of reconciliation in policy and official discourse. As such, the complex and often conflicting nature of the RPF's official programme requires an evaluative framework that facilitates the analysis of multiple priorities, commitments and concepts related to the RPF's vision of 'national reconciliation' in the post-conflict context.

David A. Crocker outlines a spectrum in which multiple concepts are defined according to their complexity. This framework of 'thin to thick' reconciliation formulations allows for the analysis of both theoretical and practical elements of post-conflict resolution programmes (2000, p. 108). Crocker describes the 'thinnest' version as consisting primarily of peaceful coexistence in which both survivors and perpetrators abide by local laws and refrain from killing each other (ibid.). Crocker's middle range of reconciliation includes the 'thinner' concept of non-violent coexistence, representation in national debate and public policy, and communication between conflict perpetrators and survivors. The 'thickest' version includes these practical elements and combines them with the promotion of 'a shared comprehensive vision, mutual healing and restoration, or mutual forgiveness' (ibid., p. 108).

Crocker warns that the latter form of reconciliation is not only difficult to achieve, but also difficult to defend in comparison with 'thinner' options. The 'thickest' version, commonly sought by truth commissions, is impractical because neither governments nor truth commissions can force agreement, forgiveness or love following mass human rights violations (ibid.). Short, who

8 The present is defined according to the date this book was completed, July 2015.

applies Crocker's spectrum to the analysis of the post-colonial reconciliation process between indigenous Australians and the settler state, also finds 'thicker' conceptions problematic. Short argues that the emphasis on mutual forgiveness and the creation of a shared vision of the future is inappropriate in the Australian context as it fails to deal with issues of sovereignty and colonial injustice (2005, p. 275).

Crocker's spectrum is well suited to the analysis of the RPF's vision of 'national reconciliation' in Rwanda since the National Unity and Reconciliation Programme is shaped by a number of stated commitments reflecting differing concepts and priorities that can be located across the spectrum. For instance, the GNU's stated commitment to repatriate citizens and end violence reflects the understanding of reconciliation as peaceful coexistence at the 'thinnest' end of the spectrum. This relatively narrow description is a far cry from the stated objectives of 'healing one another morally and edifying credibility among Rwandans based on recognising and proclaiming one's atrocities, asking and giving pardon, to reveal truth and to build hope of the future' as described in the 2007 Reconciliation Policy (NURC, 2007, p. 5). This commitment to moral healing, repentance and giving pardon resembles the 'thicker' conception as a process of mutual healing, restoration and forgiveness (Crocker, 2000, p. 108).

A social constructionist perspective also informs the analysis that shapes this book. Social constructionism is applicable to the study of post-conflict reconciliation processes for many of the same reasons that it is relevant to the study of human rights (Melvin, 2010, p. 934). The sociological study of human rights is a research field that has developed from the evaluation of rights within the citizenship framework to include contemporary debates regarding the social construction of rights (Morris, 2006; Short, 2008, p. 25). The latter analysis of human rights as socially constructed phenomena has questioned not only their meaning and use but also the intentions of social actors whose interests they serve and protect (Morris, p. 7; Short, 2009, p. 98). This form of inquiry engages with more than the legal conceptions of rights to analyse what Richard A. Wilson describes as the 'social life of rights' (2001, p. xvi; 1997, pp. 3–4). According to Short, the analysis of rights as socially constructed phenomena led to the conclusion that institutionalising human rights at the national level may in fact be detrimental to the realisation of particular rights within the context of an official reconciliation process. Short's evaluation engages with the colonial structures, commercial interests and power dynamics that inform the government-led reconciliation programme in Australia with particular reference to native land rights (2009, p. 107). He argues that the methods the Howard government used to institutionalise native land rights further dispossessed indigenous peoples in an attempt to maintain the status quo (ibid.). This argument builds on Freeman's assertion that institutionalising human rights may not lead to their full promotion, but to their protection in a way that does not jeopardise the existing power structures in society (2002, p. 85).

Wilson also uses a social constructionist approach to uncover the meaning and use of human rights within the reconciliation framework (1997). In a later work, he explores how and why South Africa's post-apartheid government applied human rights in promoting reconciliation at the South African Truth and Reconciliation Commission (TRC) (2001, p. 230). Wilson argues that human rights language was manipulated to promote a moral-theological discourse of reconciliation. This manipulation allegedly limited the ability of human rights to support the creation of lasting democracy and a non-prejudicial justice system (ibid.). Moreover, he argues that government interests in fostering state-legitimacy and nation-building were pursued at the expense of accountability, justice and procedural fairness (ibid., p. 224).

A social constructionist lens provides an analytical framework through which the actions, interests and dynamics that shape an official reconciliation programme can be interpreted. For instance, the National Unity and Reconciliation Programme was created, informed and institutionalised by its sponsor: the Rwandan government. The RPF formalised the official programme under the guise of the GNU until the party won the 2003 parliamentary elections. The GNU and subsequently the RPF's approaches to 'national reconciliation' continue to be top-down.[9] A social constructionist lens facilitates the investigation of power dynamics between the programme's authors and its participants within the social, political and economic contexts in which it was constructed and continues to function. Moreover, this perspective provides the tools necessary to transcend the formal definition of national unity and reconciliation as outlined in the 2007 Reconciliation Policy. It also makes it easier to investigate how the National Unity and Reconciliation Programme functions in social and political practice by determining whose rights it protects and whose interests it serves (Morris, 2006, p. 7).

International human rights standards are an important analytical tool in this regard. They provide a benchmark against which the impact of particular laws, projects and norms related to the National Unity and Reconciliation Programme may be analysed. This book recognises the implications of applying

9 The RPF's top-down approach to reconciliation reflects Wilson's interpretation of the South African government's vision of the TRC. Wilson refers to the predominance of the religious elite since vengeance was officially renounced in favour of a religious-redemptive approach to reconciliation. Vengeance, although still popular with many citizens, was invalidated and replaced with an emphasis on confession and forgiveness (2001, pp. 119–20). In the Rwandan context, the government's emphasis on justice for all those found guilty of acts of genocide and crimes against humanity, including those perpetrated against property, demonstrates a top-down approach to justice that greatly impacts on civilians through all social and economic levels of society.

what can be described as human rights' 'western imperialist values' to the analysis of conflict and reconciliation in an African context. These standards are applicable to the Rwandan case, as human rights language features in official discourse and equal rights are included in the list of attributes purportedly shared by all Rwandans outlined in the 2007 Reconciliation Policy (NURC, 2007, p. 3). Moreover, Rwanda has stated its adherence to pertinent human rights conventions and covenants including the (1948) Universal Declaration of Human Rights, the (1966) International Covenant on Civil and Political Rights, and the (1966) International Covenant on Economic, Social, and Cultural Rights (MOD, 2003).

This analysis of the National Unity and Reconciliation Programme in the Rwandan context also draws on a number of dominant responses to collective violence discussed in the broad body of literature: truth, justice and forgiveness. As will become clear in the next chapter, the study of reconciliation is shaped by numerous understandings of the concept. By drawing on the perspectives of multiple authors, this research identifies, compares and analyses the differing concepts, assumptions and priorities that underpin the RPF's promotion of 'national reconciliation' and the official programme more generally. The aim of this research is not to prescribe a more effective model, but to provide a rigorously analysed interpretation of how the RPF's official programme functions in the social, political and economic context of present-day Rwanda.

Scope of the book

The existing literature about the official reconciliation programme in Rwanda can be roughly divided into two categories. The first includes works that examine specific projects within the National Unity and Reconciliation Programme. Those whose work falls into this group employ a range of analytical frameworks in their interpretations. These authors include Waldorf (2007, 2009, 2010), Clark (2008, 2010a, 2014), Thomson (2011) and Mgbako (2005), who examine such projects as gacaca, ingando civic education camps, as well as the demobilisation and reintegration of convicted genocide perpetrators and ex-combatants. The second category includes literature that examines themes emerging from the programme such as memory, identity and ethnicity. Selected publications from relevant authors include those by Hintjens (2008), Zorbas (2009) and Buckley-Zistel (2009). This book falls into the second category of analysis, sharing a primary focus on themes that emerge from the programme while comprehensively examining, from a broad sociological perspective, the entire official programme.

The National Unity and Reconciliation Programme is shaped primarily by a stated commitment to address the wrongs committed during the 1994 genocide.[10] The 2003 Constitution's preamble states:

10 See Jones (2006), Shaw (2003), Melvern (2000), Uvin (2001), Gatwa (2005),

> We, the People of Rwanda,
>
> (1) In the wake of the genocide that was organised and supervised by unworthy leaders and other perpetrators and that decimated more than a million sons and daughters of Rwanda;
>
> (2) Resolved to fight the ideology of genocide and all its manifestations and to eradicate ethnic, regional and any other form of divisions;
>
> (3) Determined to fight dictatorship by putting in place democratic institutions and leaders freely elected by ourselves;
>
> (4) Emphasizing the necessity to strengthen and promote national unity and reconciliation which were seriously shaken by the genocide and its consequences;
>
> (5) Conscious that peace and unity of Rwandans constitute the essential basis for national economic development and social progress;
>
> (6) Resolved to build a State governed by the rule of law, based on respect for fundamental human rights, pluralistic democracy, equitable power sharing, tolerance and resolution of issues through dialogue;
>
> (7) Considering that we enjoy the privilege of having one country, a common language, a common culture and a long shared history which ought to lead to a common vision of our destiny;
>
> (8) Considering that it is necessary to draw from our centuries-old history the positive values which characterized our ancestors that must be the basis for the existence and flourishing of our Nation; (MOD, 2003, p. 1).[11]

Crimes of genocide and against humanity committed between 1 October 1990 and 30 December 1994 may be tried in gacaca community genocide courts. These include the murder and rape of Tutsi civilians and the destruction of their property. Official reconciliation discourse has a much wider scope, however, as it highlights the 'wrongs' of 'bad leadership' and 'negative ideology' in the colonial era, and the governments of Grégoire Kayibanda and Juvénal Habyarimana.

'Unworthy leaders', 'genocide ideology', and 'divisionism' are cited in the 2003 Constitution's preamble as the causes of the 1994 genocide (MOD, 2003). These political and ideological concepts represent the sources of conflict

Human Rights Watch (1994) and in particular Des Forges (1999) for analyses of the horrific events of the 1994 genocide. These texts, among others, will be discussed in chapter 2 regarding the context of the 1994 genocide and the development of the National Unity and Reconciliation Programme.

11 I have omitted the preamble's final four stated commitments from this quotation as they fall outside the National Unity and Reconciliation Programme's direct remit. These assurances include adhering to the principles described in key human rights statutes, promoting equal rights for all Rwandans, developing human resources and advancing social welfare. All four will be discussed in chapter 4 with reference to the RPF's nation-building agenda.

around which the RPF's official reconciliation programme is constructed.[12] This book endeavours to provide a nuanced interpretation of these concepts and how they relate to the broader structure of the RPF's vision of 'national reconciliation' in Rwanda. As such, its analytical scope extends beyond the 1994 genocide to include the social, political and historical contexts that informed the construction of these concepts. The widening of these parameters is particularly important given the role of historical narrative in the National Unity and Reconciliation Programme. This particular interpretation of Rwandan history is referred to herein as the 'victor's narrative'. Like the term 'victor's justice', used by authors including Tiemessen (2004), Sarkin (2001) and Waldorf (2010) to describe the RPF's impunity at gacaca,[13] the 'victor's narrative' denies RPF involvement in cases of genocide and crimes against humanity in Rwanda and DRC. Covering historical events from the pre-colonial era to the present day, this narrative includes a strong focus on unity, identity and social relations before, during and after the colonial period as interpreted by the RPF government. The 1994 genocide events and the concept of ethnicity (Hutu, Tutsi and Twa) are integral elements of the 'victor's narrative'.

The importance of genocide and ethnicity in how the government depicted the events of 1994 is evident in the name 'Genocide against the Tutsi'. This became the new official name of the Rwandan genocide in the run-up to the 15th Commemoration Ceremony of the 1994 genocide held on 7 April 2009. The RPF stated that newspapers, radio broadcasts and government documents would no longer refer to the 1994 events as 'the genocide', 'the Rwandan genocide' or 'the Tutsi genocide'. This change was allegedly made to prevent confusion about which group was targeted during the 1994 genocide (interview with son of returnee,[14] 6 April 2009). 'The Genocide against the Tutsi' will hereafter be referred as 'the 1994 genocide'.[15]

As the term 'Genocide against the Tutsi' indicates, genocide is defined as the attempt to destroy the Tutsi population in Rwanda, a description that

12 See Short (2009), Lederach (1998), Minow (1998) and Daly and Sarkin (2007) for discussions concerning the role of acknowledging sources of conflict in promoting reconciliation as a peacemaking paradigm.

13 The impact of victor's justice upon 'national reconciliation' at gacaca will be discussed in chapter 3.

14 The term 'returnee' refers to Tutsi refugees who fled during periods of violence in the 1950s and 1960s and returned to Rwanda after the 1994 genocide. Returnees are also referred to as 'old caseload' refugees.

15 The 1994 genocide was not the only one in the Great Lakes Region. To prevent confusion, the Burundian genocide will be referred to as the '1972 genocide in Burundi'. The relationship between the genocide in Burundi and violence in Rwanda will be discussed in chapter 2.

resembles the definition in the 1948 UN Convention on the Prevention and Punishment of the Crime of Genocide. The Convention states:

> genocide means any of the following acts committed with intent to destroy, in whole or in part, a national, ethnical, racial or religious group, as such:
>
> (a) Killing members of the group;
>
> (b) Causing serious bodily or mental harm to members of the group;
>
> (c) Deliberately inflicting on the group conditions of life calculated to bring about its physical destruction in whole or in part;
>
> (d) Imposing measures intended to prevent births within the group;
>
> (e) Forcibly transferring children of the group to another group (1948, p. 1).[16]

The inclusion of 'intention' and 'ethnical' group in the Convention presents several issues with regard to categorising the 1994 events as genocide. The fact that Hutu militias, local officials and civilians did not have a single motive for massacring enormous numbers of Tutsi civilians frustrates the definition of genocide relating to the intention to destroy the Tutsi group because of *who they are*. As will be discussed in chapter 4, the 'victor's narrative' emphasises the unity of all Rwandans and the non-existence of ethnic identities in present-day Rwanda. It points to the colonial era as the period during which ethnic identities were constructed in Rwanda and states that prior to the arrival of German and Belgian colonists, these identities reflected social status and were relatively flexible in nature (NURC, 2007, p. 4; Ingando lecture, 3 July 2009).

The emphasis on the shared history, language and culture of all Hutu, Tutsi and Twa in official reconciliation discourse raises questions about whether the Tutsi ought to be considered an 'ethnic group'. As Eltringham states, these identities do not meet the requirements of commonly accepted definitions of ethnicity (2004, p. 5). For instance, these groups are not culturally distinct from one another, nor are they distinguished according to a collective belief in a 'distinctive origin' as described by Banton (2000, p. 482). Weber also outlines criteria according to which an ethnic group may be defined, highlighting the role of a 'subjective belief' in common descent stemming from shared physical types, customs and memories of colonisation and migration (1968, p. 389). Although Hutu, Tutsi and Twa groups may not be easily characterised by distinct physical attributes, customs or memories, they may share a subjective belief or 'presumed identity' of ethnic distinctiveness (ibid.). As Fardon states, 'ethnic boundaries are between whoever people think they are between' (1987, p. 176, as cited by Eltringham, 2004, p. 8).

16 This definition of genocide is of particular importance in Rwanda. A very similar description is included in Law no. 33 'Repressing the crime of genocide, crimes against humanity and war crimes' (2003, pp. 1–2).

Abed also posits a form of subjective self-definition, which he describes as group members' consent to live a life in common. He stipulates however that consent alone is insufficient to determine whether a particular group is susceptible to genocide. Instead, he suggests three criteria according to which a group may be considered a *genos*: the group culture must be comprehensive, including customs and practices that are required for the culture to flourish; extracting oneself from the group must be difficult; and the group's members must consent to living a common life together (2006). Furthermore, Abed argues that genocide may occur when the group members are deprived of the culture and ethos that shape their particular community (ibid., p. 329). He builds on Claudia Card's conception of social death, which she defines as the loss of social vitality, identity, and the 'meaning for one's existence', as the characteristic distinguishing genocide from mass murder (2003, p. 63).

According to Abed's criteria, neither Hutu nor Tutsi may be considered capable of being genocide victims. Although exiting these groups was most certainly arduous, due to the assignment of identity cards[17] and insiders' and outsiders' continued perception of a person's identity as either Hutu or Tutsi, these groups are not culturally distinct from one another; which in itself could make the events of 1994 an example of so-called 'auto-genocide'.[18] Moreover, group membership is passed along patrilineal lines rather than consent of the group's members to live a life in common.[19] Abed's emphasis on the relationship between culture and genocide demonstrates the difficulties associated with analysing and categorising the type of violence that took place in Rwanda in 1994.

The trial of Jean-Paul Akayesu at the International Criminal Tribunal for Rwanda (ICTR) in 1996 attempted to clarify whether the massacres of Tutsi in 1994 constituted acts of genocide. Akayesu, the then mayor of Taba commune, was found guilty of nine counts of genocide and crimes against humanity (*The Prosecutor v. Jean-Paul Akayesu*, case no. ICTR-96-4-T). Akayesu's case was the first at the ICTR to interpret the definition of genocide as outlined in the 1948 Convention on the Prevention and Punishment of the Crime of Genocide (Scharf, 2008, p. 2). The court decided that Rwandan Tutsi did constitute a distinct group and that systematic brutality against this group met the crimes of genocide criteria. It cited the widespread nature of the violence against Tutsi, the use of ID cards to identify Tutsi prior to the massacres, the systematic nature of the murders, and the killing of newborn children and fetuses thought to be

17 The GNU ordered the removal of the request for ethnic identity from Rwandan identity cards in 1995 (Immigration and Refugee Board of Canada, 2001), p. 1.

18 In a theoretical paper, Dirk Moses uses the term 'auto-genocide' with reference to Cambodia. See Moses (2008) for more detail on his analysis.

19 See Eltringham (2004) for a discussion of the patrilineal descent of ethnic identities in Rwanda.

Tutsi as evidence of the intention to destroy the 'Tutsi group' (*The Prosecutor v. Jean-Paul Akayesu*, case no. ICTR-96-4-T, pp. 35–7).[20]

This judgment indicates that the ICTR sidestepped issues of ethnicity by considering the Tutsi to be a distinct group susceptible to genocide *because they were targeted as such*. If we assume that Tutsi are a distinct group, then we could reasonably assume that Hutu also qualify as one. As such, the systematic murder of Hutu 'moderates'[21] reflects the intention to destroy a distinct group's subset. This book recognises the complications and contradictions inherent in the definition of genocide and the rhetorical use of 'ethnicity' in official reconciliation discourse.[22] It does, however, refer to the 1994 anti-Tutsi violence as genocide, as per the Akayesu trial findings.

Central threads

The analysis of issues related to ethnicity and identity forms one part of this book's larger examination of the National Unity and Reconciliation Programme. More broadly, it seeks to provide a nuanced interpretation of larger thematic elements in order to understand how the official programme functions in social and political practice. These themes, which include justice, nation-building and the 'victor's narrative', are examined through the book's two central threads. The first focuses on the institutionalisation and dissemination of the RPF's 'national reconciliation' vision in Rwanda, which is the book's central focus since the programme is analysed as both a normative and legal framework through which the RPF promotes its own political interests. The institutionalisation of 'national reconciliation' is evident in how justice and repatriation are prioritised. These activities were facilitated through establishing gacaca courts and ingando civic education camps to demobilise ex-combatants and refugees returning from other countries in the Great Lakes Region after the 1994 genocide. 'National reconciliation' institutionalism is also evident in the formal establishment of the NURC and the National Service of Gacaca Jurisdictions (NSGJ). It is also apparent in the legal statutes that shape the RPF's official programme. These laws include the 2008 Law Relating to the Punishment of the Crime of Genocide Ideology and the 2001 Law on

20 Eltringham makes a similar point with regard to the ICTR's decisions in the Akayesu case. He criticises the ICTR, however, for ignoring genocide perpetrators' perception of Tutsi as a racially distinct group arguing that the tribunal missed the opportunity to uncover and grapple with the 'ideational nature' of 'genocide ideology' (2004, p. 30).

21 The term 'moderate Hutu' is used in official reconciliation discourse to describe Hutu who were targeted during the genocide because they opposed Habyarimana's regime. It is also used on occasion in relation to Hutu who refused to participate in anti-Tutsi violence before and during the 1994 genocide. See Des Forges (1999).

22 Chapter 2 discusses how ethnic identities have evolved in Rwanda and how they have been manipulated by colonial rulers and genocide propaganda.

Prevention, Suppression and Punishment of the Crime of Discrimination and Sectarianism.

Dissemination of the RPF's 'national reconciliation' vision is achieved through both overt and covert measures. In its most blatant form, 'national reconciliation' promotion is a stated mandate of the curricula taught in government-led mandatory live-in civic education, community service and demobilisation camps. The RPF's stated commitments to promoting unity and 'national reconciliation' are repeated in radio broadcasts, presidential speeches and commemoration ceremonies during the annual official mourning period (7–14 April). This vision and the concepts that shape it are promulgated in a covert fashion through the dissemination of *accurate* history. The RPF depicts the 'victor's narrative' as the only *correct* version of the nation's history, a narrative that is rife with concepts related to the government's interpretation of 'national reconciliation'. They include 'divisionism', 'genocide ideology', ethnicity and singular national identity. Presenting this narrative as historically accurate legitimises the government's aim of promoting what it deems to be the 'good' elements of unity and reconciliation and of eradicating the 'bad' elements of 'divisionism' and 'genocide ideology' that purportedly led to the 1994 genocide. The pervasive nature of the government's condemnation of these 'negative ideologies' is evident in the fear several interviewees expressed to me of being accused of acts of 'divisionism' or 'genocide ideology'. Those who mentioned such serious concerns did so in terms of publicly questioning the 1994 genocide's 'victor's narrative' and the government's approach to reconciliation. All these informants have been given anonymity in this research.

The second thread is that of the government's role in creating and monitoring the National Unity and Reconciliation Programme. Central to the book, it investigates the top-down structure of the RPF's official programme and the multiple roles the RPF plays in this project. The scope of this analysis extends beyond the post-conflict period. The RPF's actions as a rebel group that invaded Rwanda on 1 October 1990 and fought Habyarimana's forces during the ensuing civil war are integral to understanding the RPF government's stated commitment to 'national reconciliation' in the post-conflict context. Moreover, the RPF's transition from invading rebel group to political party when the 1994 genocide ended informs the ways in which its 'national reconciliation' concept has been institutionalised and promulgated in Rwanda. For instance, the RPF's roles as 'liberators of the nation' in 1994 and invading force in DRC in the late 1990s inform the post-conflict period's social and political landscape. The term 'liberator' refers to Liberation Day, 4 July 1994, commemorated every year on the 1994 genocide's final day during which the RPF seized the capital and ended the violence. With regard to the official programme, the party has played the roles of creator, monitor and disseminator of official reconciliation discourse.

Methodological issues

This book draws in part on qualitative research conducted in Rwanda throughout 2009 and the summer of 2010. I chose these particular time periods as they coincided with the 15th anniversary of the 1994 genocide and the run-up to the controversial 2010 presidential elections in which the incumbent President Paul Kagame won a 93 per cent majority. The book began as a deductive research project investigating whether the National Unity and Reconciliation Programme could be made more effective with the inclusion of Augusto Boal's Forum Theatre.[23] As a trained Forum Theatre practitioner, I endeavoured to test this hypothesis by using its techniques with a small group of Rwandan actors to investigate experiences of the government's efforts to promote 'national reconciliation'. At the same time, I began interviewing officials at the NSGJ and visiting gacaca trials in a suburb of Kigali and Butare in southern Rwanda. I realised that, although the participant observation and interviews I had conducted with actors and directors had been fruitful, no comprehensive sociological study had ever been made of the entire National Unity and Reconciliation Programme in Rwanda – a major gap in the research.

This realisation was confirmed as I attended more official reconciliation events including the 1994 genocide's 15th Commemoration Ceremony and further gacaca hearings. I decided to forgo my attempt to create Forum Theatre in order to focus on collecting detailed primary data about how the official programme functions in Rwanda. Through my contacts with officials and participants at gacaca, and with artists and performers in Kigali, I sought out government representatives and events related to the National Unity and Reconciliation Programme. I conducted semi-structured interviews with government officials directly involved in monitoring or leading projects including the Gacaca Sensitisation Programme, the development of curricula at mandatory live-in ingando and itorero ry'igihugu education camps, and the everyday operations of community service or Travail d'Intérêt Général (TIG)

23 Forum Theatre is a form of Theatre of the Oppressed (TO), devised and directed by the late Augusto Boal while living in Brazil during the 1970s dictatorship (Boal, 1998, p. 4). Like other TO forms, it is participatory in nature and tackles issues pertinent to the communities in which it is performed. Forum Theatre involves writing and performing a play about an issue to which the audience can relate. It is performed twice and, during the second run-through, the audience is invited to stop the action at any point and replace the protagonist on stage in an attempt to create a positive outcome or find solutions to the play's negative ending. There may be multiple stops and starts until many solutions have been found, or the actors and audience are exhausted. Boal's interest in community-level resistance to oppression was greatly influenced by Paulo Freire's *Pedagogy of the Oppressed* (1972). For more detail about Boal's work, see Boal (1979, 1995, 1998). For information about community theatre more generally, see van Erven (2001), Fisher and Shelton (2001) and Taylor (2003).

camps for convicted genocide perpetrators. I also interviewed a number of participants in these projects.

I used the purposive sampling technique to gather a variety of perspectives from officials and participants and to develop a nuanced understanding of each project's objectives. The iterative nature of this research strategy created flexibility to review and reshape research questions, follow emerging themes, and speak with a range of informants including government representatives, directors of, and participants in, specific reconciliation projects, and citizens taking part in grassroots reconciliation organisations. The latter projects included plays dramatising events related to the 1994 genocide, religious ceremonies and talks given by survivors. These interviews provided a wider breadth of perspectives to add to the analysis of the RPF's official programme.

I also collected further data through observing participants at major reconciliation events including multiple gacaca trials and appeal cases and ingando live-in civic education camp for students entering university, and through visits to TIG camps for convicted genocide perpetrators, commemoration ceremonies, demobilisation and reintegration camps and genocide memorial sites. The decentralised nature of gacaca courts and locations of TIG sites and ingando camps outside Kigali provided opportunities to conduct interviews and observe participants at events in both rural and urban areas. I selected these examples to provide a cross-section of the official programme. In many cases, I made several visits in order to gather a nuanced understanding of the scope and scale of the National Unity and Reconciliation Programme.

I triangulated the primary data collected through interviews and participant-observation with the textual analysis of relevant policy documents and legislation. These range from syllabi of ingando and itorero ry'igihugu education camps and NURC evaluation reports to legal texts related to genocide prevention and 'genocide ideology', as well as gacaca Organic Law. In addition to these texts, I conducted extensive documentary analysis of numerous state policies and reports including the 2007 National Policy of Unity and Reconciliation, Vision 2020 development programming and the 2003 Constitution of the Republic of Rwanda. I maintained its relevance by continually updating the project data. This includes recently published primary sources, such as government documents and presidential speeches, in addition to academic and policy literature.

The sensitive nature of research about conflict, 'national reconciliation' and government programming raised multiple ethical and pragmatic issues during my fieldwork. My interest in interviewing government officials required formal letters from the Institute of Commonwealth Studies and significant patience. In several instances, my attendance at events related to the National Unity and Reconciliation Programme including gacaca cases, ingando, demobilisation and community service camps required identification and formal letters of permission from government departments overseeing the projects. In many cases, I was obliged to state my research objectives and declare that I would not make 'divisionist' statements or participate in 'genocide ideology'.

With regard to ethical issues, many of my informants requested anonymity, particularly those critical of the RPF government. I was careful to comply and chose my interview questions conscientiously to prevent undue harm or being perceived as 'divisionist' or supportive of 'genocide ideology' in any form. More generally, I took a reflexive approach to the research in order to review my judgement regarding questions related to the 1994 genocide and government programming. This method was particularly important during 7–14 April 2009, the official mourning week, although I found the entire period of 7 April to 4 July to be a particularly sensitive time. It was also pertinent during my third fieldwork visit prior to the presidential election following the murder, on 14 July 2010, of André Kagwa Rwisereka, the Democratic Green Party's vice-president.[24]

Restricted freedom of speech in Rwanda impacted the data collection process on several occasions during my fieldwork. In three separate instances, interviewees retracted their statements in full, citing the risk of being accused of 'divisionism', and in one case the risk perceived to their own personal safety. These participants feared that anonymity would be insufficient to prevent them from being identified. The retractions relate to statements touching on negative experiences of the de facto banning of ethnic identities as well as freedom of press and political participation in the weeks leading up to the 2010 presidential election. In a similar vein, I did not include extended quotations from another research participant's statements, which criticised government programmes, President Kagame and political freedom in Rwanda. For instance in chapter 6, I included just one sentence from an entire interview transcript, as I feared a longer quotation would identify the speaker. Although the book does not include these extended quotations or retracted statements, the interviews from which they arose informed my analysis. The necessity to omit entire interviews speaks volumes about the restrictions facing not only research participants, but also researchers who engage with issues relevant to the current government and its programmes.

Organisation of the book

The next seven chapters of this volume are organised according to a thematic structure. Although at many points chronological, the book seeks to facilitate

24 André Kagwa Rwisereka was found dead on 14 July 2010. A dispute about money was initially rumoured to have been the reason for his murder. There was significant but quiet debate about the potential of political motives for his assassination. See BBC News, 14 July 2010, for more information. Rwisereka's murder followed that (on 24 June 2010) of Jean-Leonard Rugambage, editor of suspended newspaper *Umuvigizi* (BBC News, 25 June 2010).

the identification and analysis of the three major themes that emerge from the National Unity and Reconciliation Programme: justice, nation-building and the 'victor's narrative'. Chapter 1 engages with relevant literature in order to locate the book within past and current scholarship and demonstrate its contribution to the study of reconciliation and sociology more generally. It begins by identifying key concepts and theories that emerge in the literature. The chapter then critically evaluates the methodological assumptions that shape the relevant academic work about reconciliation, and assesses the strengths and weaknesses of these assumptions and publications more broadly. This analysis highlights pertinent gaps in the literature and specifies how this work seeks to fill those gaps.

Chapter 2 investigates the historical context that shaped the 1994 genocide and subsequently gave rise to the National Unity and Reconciliation Programme as devised by the GNU. It discusses the meaning of relevant themes including ethnicity throughout the eras of pre-colonial and colonial rule as well as after Rwanda achieved independence in 1962. The chapter engages with rising tension during the lead-up to the civil war and 1994 genocide, and analyses issues related to political dominance and exclusion during this period. It also considers the impact of events in eastern Zaire (now Democratic Republic of Congo) on the RPF's official reconciliation programme and Rwandan politics more generally. In conclusion it outlines the development of the programme. This discussion seeks to make connections between the social, economic and political landscape after the 1994 genocide and the construction of the government's vision of 'national reconciliation'.

Chapter 3 analyses justice: the first of this book's three key themes, which are also those of the RPF's official programme. Gacaca courts were mandated to prosecute all perpetrators accused of crimes of genocide and against humanity. They were also devised to promote the government's 'national reconciliation' vision. As such, this chapter applies the government's own definitions of 'vertical' and 'horizontal' reconciliation to analyse the potential of these courts to help rebuild relationships between individuals, groups and the state in the post-conflict context.

Chapter 4 examines the second theme of the National Unity and Reconciliation Programme – nation-building – by analysing the relationship between the RPF's conceptions of national unity, nation-building and 'national reconciliation'. The RPF's nation-building agenda is informed by two overarching priorities: uniting all Rwandans, and restoring the social and cultural values that allegedly promoted social cohesion prior to European colonists beginning to arrive in the late 19th century. This chapter investigates how the commonality and national identity concepts relate to the RPF's interpretation of national unity. It also examines the effects of this interpretation and the RPF's nation-building agenda on its own 'national reconciliation' vision.

Chapter 5 analyses the National Unity and Reconciliation Programme's third theme: the 'victor's narrative'. It builds on the preceding analysis to examine the ways in which mandatory civic education camps and the NURC's history book disseminate the government's conception of 'national reconciliation'. The chapter looks at the impact of the 'victor's narrative' on free speech and critical analysis at live-in education camps ingando and itorero ry-igihugu. It also analyses the role of the history textbook, *Histoire du Rwanda: des origines à la fin du xxe siècle,* published by the NURC in 2011, within the programme's overarching education remit.

Chapter 6 offers an analysis of the National Unity and Reconciliation Programme's social and political functions. It utilises a more holistic gaze to investigate the ways in which the RPF uses the official programme to project images of the nation and its leadership to different audiences. These interrelated images are disseminated both to the domestic population and to the international community of non-governmental organisations (NGOs), donors and foreign investors. This analysis seeks to uncover the ways in which the programme bolsters political support, promotes state-legitimisation and advances development programming among these different groups.

Finally, chapter 7 summarises the findings presented throughout this book. It suggests that the National Unity and Reconciliation Programme functions to bolster political support for the current regime and legitimise the state and people constructed by the RPF's nation-building and development programmes. It ends by describing this book's specific contribution to the broad sociological study of human rights and reconciliation.

Chapter 1

Contribution and engagement

> *[N]o response can ever be adequate when your son has been killed by police ordered to shoot at a crowd of children; when you have been dragged out of your home, interrogated, and raped in a wave of 'ethnic cleansing'; or when your brother who struggled against a repressive government has disappeared and left only a secret police file, bearing no clue to his final resting place. Closure is not possible. Even if it were, any closure would insult those whose lives are forever ruptured (Minow, 1998, p. 5).*

Martha Minow's assertion that closure is undesirable, inappropriate and ultimately impossible speaks to the devastation caused by mass violence and genocide. Although closure for those most deeply affected by mass human rights abuses and violations may not be possible, formal responses to conflict have developed throughout the 20th century (ibid., p. 1). In a later work, Minow traces the establishment of the international military tribunals of Nuremberg and Tokyo following World War Two; the International Criminal Tribunals for the former Yugoslavia (ICTY) and Rwanda (ICTR); and truth commissions such as that in South Africa (2001).

The development of the latter mechanisms, particularly truth commissions, reflects what Kritz refers to as a 'paradigm shift' (1996, p. 128). This shift represents a change in attitudes and priorities with regard to how nations deal with the violence of the past and its consequences in the present. Such changes are exemplified by the move beyond primarily punitive tribunals to commissions that focus on issues of forgiveness, accountability and rehabilitation following mass human rights violations (ibid., p. 127). Jean Paul Lederach captures the impetus to engage directly with experiences of violence following conflict:

> Contemporary conflicts necessitate peacebuilding approaches that respond to the real nature of those conflicts. While contemporary conflicts are indeed hard-core situations – the 'real politics' of hatred, manipulation, and violence – and require grounded political savvy, traditional mechanisms relying solely on statist diplomacy and realpolitik have not demonstrated a capacity to control these conflicts, much less transform them toward constructive, peaceful outcomes. Contemporary conflict thus demands innovation, the development

> of ideas and practices that go beyond the negotiation of substantive interests and issues. This innovation, I believe, pushes us to probe into the realm of the subjective – generationally accumulated perceptions and deep-rooted hatred and fear (1997, p. 25).

Lederach does not entirely forgo the traditional approaches of past conflict resolution mechanisms. Instead, he offers the notion of *reconciliation* as the meeting point between realism and innovation after mass violence (ibid.).

These changing priorities, as highlighted by Kritz and Lederach, reflect elements of Yaacov Bar-Siman-Tov's understanding of reconciliation as a peacemaking paradigm. Bar-Siman-Tov describes reconciliation as a process that engages directly with the emotional and cognitive obstacles which prevent the normalisation and stabilisation of peace following international conflicts (2004, p. 4).[1] Bar-Tal and Bennink examine reconciliation as both an outcome of peacemaking and a process through which conflicting parties build a peaceful relationship (2004). The authors briefly discuss the development of academic interest in the conception of reconciliation, which they argue is informed by a need to expand the study of peacemaking beyond issues related to conflict resolution. They contend that studying reconciliation from the political science and political psychology perspectives expands the scope of peacemaking to include the analysis of relationships between society members (2004, p. 11).

Reconciliation study is not limited to a single paradigm or discipline; rather, it is analysed from multiple methodological perspectives. Although multidisciplinary in nature, the literature is shaped by a major controversy: the lack of agreement about how reconciliation ought to be understood. Much of it engages with similar concepts including truth, justice and forgiveness. These discussions have produced what Hermann describes as 'theoretical fluidity', rather than consensus about how reconciliation ought to be understood, pursued or evaluated (2004, p. 41). Indeed, as the next sections will show, reconciliation study is shaped by a range of competing definitions and theories, some having been weakened by a lack of conceptual and contextual clarity.

Converging concepts

The reconciliation concept, as it applies to post-conflict contexts, has inspired an impressive body of literature from different perspectives and disciplines.[2] These

1 Bar-Siman-Tov qualifies this point by stating that not all international conflicts require reconciliation. Instead, he focuses on what he calls 'protracted and zero-sum' conflicts that more closely reflect civil war dynamics (2004, p. 4). The application of reconciliation processes to different forms of violent conflict will be discussed later in this review with reference to methodological assumptions and gaps in the literature.

2 I specify the post-conflict context in this review in order to clearly delineate between conceptions of reconciliation in the purely social realm, such as individuals reconciling after divorce or disagreement and that which takes place between

fields of study include philosophy, political science, theology, sociology, legal studies and psychology. Multiple perspectives and disciplines have influenced many authors in this review. Charles Villa-Vicencio's analysis of reconciliation as a political goal is influenced by both political science and theology (2000b), while psychology and political science shape Long and Brecke's assessment of the impact of reconciliation events on the development of future conflicts (2003). The literature's multidisciplinary nature has not led to the construction of a single comprehensive definition of the term 'reconciliation' in the post-conflict context. Instead, it has led to myriad competing concepts and images being created, ranging from reconciliation spectrums to webs of relationships, discussed in a later section of this review.

The literature, both case-specific and theoretical in nature, addresses reconciliation's connections with three main concepts: truth, justice and forgiveness. They are informed by an array of meanings, commonly shaped by the particular procedures through which they are pursued, such as amnesty processes at the South African Truth and Reconciliation Commission (TRC). Relationships between these concepts are, in some cases, fraught with conflict and contradiction. Forgiveness is the most contentious concern; some authors deem it vital to the pursuit of reconciliation between individuals, while others perceive it to be unattainable or unnecessary.

Truth

Truth played multiple roles in the pursuit of reconciliation after apartheid at the TRC. The commission included an amnesty process that was predicated on the act of full disclosure. Wilson argues that the exchange of 'truth' for amnesty favoured the pursuit of national reconciliation and nation-building over that of justice in the post-apartheid period (2001). This prioritisation raises issues related to truth's relative value with regard to justice and reconciliation.[3] Multiple conceptions of truth and the perceived roles of truth-seeking procedures in the post-conflict context complicate the relationship between justice and reconciliation. Clark identifies the processes of 'truth-telling', 'truth-hearing' and 'truth-shaping' as being related to the discovery of truth (2010a, p. 34). He argues that truth-telling and truth-hearing constitute one half of a dialogue between individuals after mass conflict (ibid.). The other half includes truth reception and reshaping by persons who did not participate in

individuals and/or large groups following mass human rights abuses and violations. The latter context includes intrastate and interstate wars and genocide, as described by Adelman (2005), and colonial dispossession as analysed by Short (2008).

3 Hayner clarifies that many truth commissions acknowledge truth about events rather than discover it. She argues that the population commonly knows the facts of what happened to whom, but does point to the value of officially recognising and recording truth that may previously have been denied (1994, p. 607).

the original exchange. These individuals may reshape the truth to serve their own interests (ibid., p. 35).

The differing processes used to uncover the truth may influence the *type* of truth produced. For instance, as Wilson argues, truth delivered through testimony may be 'forensic' in nature as it focuses on legal evidence, whereas truth shared through emotional expression outside a legal setting may have a narrative quality (2001, p. 36–7). Borer builds on Wilson's two 'truth paradigms' in order to draw attention to the potential implications of how truth is gathered and reported (2006, p. 24). Borer warns that the types of truth revealed, whether forensic or narrative, and the ways in which they are manipulated may negatively impact victims' healing, contending that multiple types of truth ought to be collected in order to promote lasting peace (ibid.).

The potential for truth to delay or prevent healing raises the question: is truth-telling appropriate in the post-conflict context? Rigby acknowledges the importance of remembering victims, but raises a concern about the impact of 'too much memory' on existing divisions in society and the ability of victims to heal (2001, p. 2). Daly and Sarkin also warn that revealing the truth may prevent reconciliation between victims and perpetrators if the facts presented intensify social divisions and impede forgiveness (2007, p. 6). If we take this concern seriously, what are the alternatives to telling the truth? Govier discusses the ability of individuals and groups to deny the truth, warning that self-deception most commonly results from collusion among individual or groups. Purposely avoiding the truth in this way may include denying or ignoring unpleasant details about one's own history (2003, p. 75).

Whether we deny the truth to avoid acknowledging harm or to prevent further social divisions, the refusal to tell or hear the truth negatively impacts the pursuit of justice. General agreement about the past is vital to correctly identify and prosecute individuals suspected of having committed human rights abuses or violations. It is also integral to providing compensation to victims (Crocker, 2003, p. 45). Incentives to lie in court and the narrow parameters of criminal trials make independent investigation and due process all the more important following mass human rights abuses.

Acknowledging truth at criminal trials, truth commissions and other public events is a particularly salient concept in the literature. Authors including Allen (1999), Borer (2006), Lederach (1997) and Minow (1998) argue that truth is also vital to reconciliation procedures. Lederach considers acknowledgement of the past through telling and hearing the truth integral to the reconciliation process after conflict, arguing that the act of listening to the truth acknowledges and validates emotions and represents the first step in rebuilding relationships damaged by the conflict (1997, p. 2). The act of *granting* acknowledgement adds another step to the process as it includes admitting one's complicity in the harmful act and committing oneself to positive change (Govier, 2003, pp. 71, 81).

> In cases of past wrongs, there is much to be acknowledged. That those wronged are human beings with human dignity and moral worth. That these things did happen and were wrong. That the people in question deserved better. That their feelings of hurt, anger, or resentment are natural and legitimate. That those who harmed them or who have been complicit in these harms should feel guilt and shame about such things. Significantly, such acknowledgement carries with it an implied commitment that these and similar wrongs should not be perpetrated again (ibid., p. 79).

Hayner contends that officially acknowledging and recording the truth at a commission can support healing (1994, p. 607). Although multiple conceptions of the truth may exist, she argues in a later work that truth commissions can successfully debunk lies and foster the acceptance of a 'generally accurate' narrative informed by fundamental facts of the conflict (2011, p. 189).

The notion of apology merges those of acknowledgement and truth with forgiveness. Apologising includes personally acknowledging the transgression and one's responsibility for it, expressing genuine sorrow and regret, seeking forgiveness and agreeing to abide by social norms (Tavuchis, 1991, pp. 8, 121). The 'painful re-membering', as Tavuchis describes it, sees the perpetrator become aware of his or her own membership in the moral community (ibid., p. 8). The act of apologising, whether between individuals, groups, or individuals and groups, culminates in granting forgiveness. Tavuchis contends that in this context forgiveness symbolises reconciliation between the perpetrator and victim and facilitates the return to normal social relations (ibid., p. 121).

Justice

There is general consensus in the literature that some form of justice is necessary following mass human rights abuses or violations. The type necessary and its compatibility with reconciliation is less clear, however. This lack of clarity stems primarily from differing understandings of both concepts and the perceived roles of justice and reconciliation procedures in post-conflict contexts. Daly and Sarkin suggest that retributive justice, democracy and reconciliation ought to be perceived as mutually reinforcing values (2007, pp. 15, 30). Other authors understand justice as a process that may result in reconciliation. Biggar argues that retributive justice will result in reconciliation between the victim and wrongdoer if the process eradicates advantages acquired by those who committed crimes and expresses the community's condemnation of the wrongdoing. Biggar's conception of justice also includes repentance, reparations and reassuring the victim (2001, pp. 13, 18). Villa-Vicencio concedes that criminal trials are often necessary following mass conflict, but argues that they are insufficient to prevent future human rights abuses or violations in politically driven conflicts (2000a, p. 70).

Restorative justice is commonly posited in opposition to retributive justice as it includes what could be considered elements of reconciliation processes such as dialogue and relationship rebuilding. Villa-Vicencio and Llewellyn both assert that restorative justice can be a comprehensive and viable alternative to retributive justice following conflict (Villa-Vicencio, 2000a, p. 69; Llewellyn, 2006, p. 91). Kiss's conception of restorative justice merges elements of reconciliation and retributive justice. She emphasises the opportunities facilitated by restorative justice for victims to tell their stories, hold perpetrators accountable and receive compensation for emotional and material losses (2000, p. 83). Graybill and Lanegran offer a slightly different configuration of restorative justice when they argue that it favours reconciliation between former enemies over punishment (2004, p. 2). This prioritisation can be identified in its emphasis on restoring relationships between victims and perpetrators and between communities affected by the conflict (Llewellyn, 2006, p. 91). Villa-Vicencio argues that the opportunity to rebuild relationships fostered by restorative justice processes will prevent human rights abuses recurring (2000a, p. 70). As truth commissions have pursued this form of justice, it raises the question: do material redress and relationship rebuilding reflect a sufficient form of justice for survivors?

> Survivors of violence often ache for retribution against identifiable perpetrators, and for public acknowledgement of what happened. Some want financial redress; psychological or spiritual healing seems crucial to others. Some survivors, and their fellow citizens, place higher priorities on moving ahead with life, building or rebuilding trust across previously divided groups, and establishing or strengthening democratic institutions. Many believe that the entire society needs to stand behind efforts to punish the wrongdoers, and to deter any such conduct in the future. People understandably may have great trouble sorting out priorities among these possibilities (Minow, 1998, p. 4).

Compensation and reparations may support victims' abilities to move forward following restorative or retributive trials. Providing material support, returning stolen property, or enabling access to medical and educational services may help to restore the status quo that was transformed during the conflict (Crocker, 2003, p. 51). Nesiah contends that reparations have an emotional element as they symbolise a public declaration of the perpetrator's guilt. Moreover, reparations look to both the past and future as they acknowledge harm and increase opportunities for the future (2005, p. 276). Both Crocker and Galtung posit reparations as a way of 'righting' past wrongs (Crocker, 2003, p. 51; Galtung, 2001, p. 6). Galtung warns however that reparations are only appropriate following harm that can be reversed or 'undone' by restoring the material circumstances of the past (2001, p. 6). He contends that offering financial or material restitution would insult survivors of mass violence or deep trauma (ibid.). The TRC did not heed the potential insult inherent in reparations as the Reparations and Rehabilitation Committee sought to facilitate national reconciliation by compensating apartheid victims. Wilson states that Reparations and Rehabilitation was the weakest of the TRC's three committees as its lack of funds left it able to do little more than make recommendations about compensation to the President's Fund (2001, p. 22).

Forgiveness

The relationship between reparations and forgiveness is unclear in the literature. Although Bar-Tal and Bennink state that accepting compensation may indicate a survivor's readiness to forgive, the connection between compensation and forgiveness is not a common theme in the field of study (2004, p. 30). In fact, there is little agreement about the relationship between the forgiveness and reconciliation processes more generally. Literature about forgiveness can be roughly divided into two groups. The first considers it to be critically important following collective violence. The second understands its benefits but deems it to be either unattainable or unnecessary for reconciliation promotion. Hannah Arendt wrote in *The Human Condition*,

> Without being forgiven, released from the consequences of what we have done, our capacity to act would, as it were, be confined to one single deed from which we could never recover; we would remain the victims of its consequences forever, not unlike the sorcerer's apprentice who lacks the magic formula to break the spell (1958, p. 237).

Arendt captured the perceived power of forgiveness to release perpetrators from the cycle of guilt and free victims from the grip of suffering. Its value in this context is immense as it may *undo* the wrongs of the past. Abu-Nimer stipulates that elements of forgiveness, although vital to the process of rebuilding the relationship between the wrongdoer and the victim, need not result in forgetting the violence of the past. Instead, remembering victimhood experiences and sharing history will help to address the conflict and promote equality between both parties (2001, pp. 245–6).

Arendt posits forgiveness as the opposite of vengeance (1958, p. 240). This forgiveness/vengeance dichotomy reflects what Minow describes as an 'implicit pair of goals' following collective violence (1998, p. 10). Minow warns that vengeful responses ought to be constrained and recast as retributive justice used to administer punishment proportional to the crime committed (ibid., p. 12). Like Minow, Arendt depicts vengeance as an automatic and natural reaction to violence, arguing that the freeing quality of forgiveness is born out of its unpredictability. The highly personal and unexpected act of forgiveness relies on the harmed individual's willingness to change his or her mind and start again (1958, pp. 240–1).

The particular form of reconciliation pursued after mass violence affects how relevant forgiveness is in the post-conflict context. Political reconciliation, for instance, forgoes forgiveness yet demands more than whatever can be achieved by state diplomacy alone (Villa-Vicencio, 2005, p. 60). Villa-Vicencio's approach to political reconciliation advocates creating a process that prioritises justice and facilitates discussion between former enemies (ibid.). Morever, reconciliation conceived as the rebuilding of trust may not require forgiveness. Worthington Jr. concedes that although forgiveness may smooth the path to reconciliation, it is not necessary to rebuild relationships damaged by conflict (2006, p. 221). Forgiveness is not fundamental to Dwyer's understanding of reconciliation as constructing coherent and mutually tolerated conflict narratives. She advocates for a realist understanding of reconciliation that is not dependent upon forgiveness (2003, p. 108).

Images and models of reconciliation

Forgiveness may be located at the 'thick' end of David A. Crocker's spectrum of 'thin to thick' reconciliation conceptions after violent conflict. He places non-violent coexistence at the 'thinnest' end (2000, p. 107). The 'middle' of the spectrum adds discussion and requires former enemies to participate in public policy decisions as well as compromise on areas of mutual concern. He compares the 'thickest' end, which includes forgiveness, healing and creating a shared future, with the stated mandates of truth commissions in Chile and South Africa. Crocker rejects the 'thickest' conception in favour of political reconciliation, a multidimensional concept, which more closely resembles the 'middle'- range description (ibid., pp. 60, 107).

Adelman also uses the notion of the 'thick' end to describe and advocate for his 'modern-liberal' reconciliation model, applicable to the resolution of intrastate conflicts (2005, p. 288).[4] Wilson applies the range of 'thin to thick' conceptions to describe the transformation of the South African TRC's stated mandate over time. This progression was shaped by a shift away from a predominantly religious or 'thick' understanding of reconciliation, advocated by Archbishop Tutu, towards a 'thinner' conception that sought to promote nation-building and national identity. Wilson, like Crocker, includes forgiveness in the 'thickest' vision but adds confession, sacrifice and redemption to what he calls a 'religious-redemptive approach' to reconciliation (2001, pp. 121–2).

Govier and Verwoerd reject using a spectrum to analyse relationships in the post-apartheid context. They argue that a spectrum's linear arrangement

4 Adelman argues that this 'thick' form relates to the 'polis' in which the conflicting parties are included after war (2005, p. 304). Modern-liberal reconciliation includes systematic recognition of conflict events through testimony, restorative justice, redress for victims and reconstruction or healing. Adelman argues that this model is not appropriate following genocide, an issue that will be discussed later in this review.

is too simple to grapple with the nuanced intersections between interpersonal reconciliation (among individuals) and national reconciliation (between large groups). Instead, they suggest a web of connections to accommodate the complex network of relations between individuals, groups and communities in post-apartheid South Africa (2002, pp. 178, 187). Contrary to Govier and Verwoerd's conclusion, a spectrum is still a valuable evaluative framework for analysing reconciliation programmes after collective violence. Crocker's spectrum, in particular, facilitates the analysis of a wide array of conceptions, stated commitments and changing priorities over time. As in the case of Rwanda, these commitments reflect both 'thinner' and 'thicker' understandings of reconciliation after genocide.

Like Govier and Verwoerd, Lederach emphasises the role of relationship rebuilding between former opponents after conflict. His book, *The Moral Imagination: the Art and Soul of Building Peace*, published in 2005, builds on his influential work, *Building Peace: Sustainable Reconciliation in Divided Societies* (1997), to focus on human beings' capability to transcend violence in the peacebuilding context. Lederach describes this capacity as the 'moral imagination' through which we envision ourselves in a web of relationships with our former enemies (2005, p. 34). He contends that the web concept is vital to the moral imagination because it involves everyone taking personal responsibility for their own role in the violence and acknowledging the connection between conflicting groups and individuals (ibid., p. 35).

Methodological assumptions

Much of the multidisciplinary literature concerning reconciliation after mass conflict is shaped by similar methodological assumptions. These are broad in nature and affect the literature in a variety of ways. Most prominent is, first, that reconciliation is achievable following violent conflict and, second, that it is desirable in this context. A smaller proportion of literature is informed by a third assumption that reconciliation can be prescribed to a nation or nations that have experienced mass violence.

The sense of urgency in the quotation, 'Reconciliation is not a luxury or an add-on to democracy. Reconciliation is an absolute necessity' (Bloomfield et al., 2003, p. 12), is predicated on the notion that reconciliation procedures are vitally important after conflict. This assertion is reflected in the authors' assurance that 'effective reconciliation is the best guarantee that the violence of the past will not return' (ibid.). Underlying this assertion is the supposition that this process is achievable after conflict. Bloomfield et al. (2003) are not alone in this expectation; see Villa-Vicencio (2000a; 2000b), Govier and Verwoerd (2002), Lederach (1997) and Nesiah (2005). This assumption raises questions about what is to be achieved when we discuss reconciliation. Is it the end goal of a process? Alternatively, is reconciliation a process that will result in benefits for society after it has been completed successfully?[5]

There is no consensus in the literature more generally, about whether reconciliation ought to be viewed as a process or end goal. For instance, Rigby describes it as a process that includes what he deems to be conflicting values including truth, justice, mercy and forgiveness (2001, p. 184). Clark takes a different approach, seeing reconciliation as both a process and an end goal. He argues that both these configurations seek to address the causes of past violence and the emotions surrounding it as well as to create a positive future for all (2010a, pp. 44–5). Villa-Vicencio contends that reconciliation ought to be understood as a political goal (2000b, p. 199). He stipulates that although the prerequisites for reconciliation often change, the paradigm still includes building or rebuilding trust, respect for human rights, and democracy (ibid., p. 208).

The assumption that reconciliation as a process, end goal, or both, is achievable is bolstered by a lack of retrospective analyses about how particular reconciliation programmes functioned or continue to function in social and political practice. Achievability, in this sense, refers to the particular reconciliation concept on which the programme is centred. For instance, the TRC initially employed a religious-redemptive approach to reconciliation that emphasised truth and forgiveness between individuals; see Wilson (2001). Wilson's work and that carried out by Hayner (1994; 2011) are rare exceptions to the general dearth of analyses about how specific programmes have functioned. Hayner directly questions the possibility of achieving reconciliation in the context of the TRC. She contends that although forgiveness and reconciliation were achieved between some individuals, the TRC did not meet public expectations in this regard (2011, p. 185). This belief had allegedly been fostered by the TRC's stated commitment to achieve 'full' reconciliation, at both the interpersonal and national levels, in two-and-a-half years (ibid., pp. 183, 185).[6]

The notion that reconciliation either nationally or between individuals is achievable is also supported by the absence of systematic criteria against which to judge whether it has in fact been achieved. The comparative nature of Hayner's analysis of 15 truth commissions is helpful here as she suggests three criteria against which a truth commission's success can be measured. These conditions include the process, product and eventual impact of the truth commission (Hayner, 1994, as cited by Graybill and Lanegran, 2004, p. 4).

5 Chapter 4 analyses the implications of this form of conceptual ambiguity in the context of 'national reconciliation' in Rwanda.

6 Hayner contends that the TRC's failure to achieve this stated goal led to Archbishop Tutu's suggestion that the commission's objective be changed to the promotion of reconciliation rather than the achievement of it (2011, p. 184).

> The degree to which the commission's work contributes to long-term reconciliation, healing, and reform will be determined in large part by whether perpetrators or state officials acknowledge and apologize for wrongs, whether and how the commission's report is distributed and put to use, and whether its core recommendations are implemented (ibid.).

Although Hayner's comparative evaluation provides insight into what she deems important for the success of long-term reconciliation, its scope is limited to truth commissions (1994). Further retrospective studies, comparative or individual in nature, that clearly define 'successful reconciliation', explicitly state the criteria against which they measure this success. They also expect the asssumptions shaping these criteria to shed light on reconciliation's achievability in contexts other than those related to truth commissions.

The supposition that reconciliation is achievable is also supported by the lack of differentiation between post-conflict contexts. Although some authors analyse the meaning of reconciliation after specific events such as apartheid, see Villa-Vicencio (2000a; 2000b), Govier and Verwoerd (2002), Van der Merwe (2001) and Daye (2004), many others suggest more general conceptions without reference to specific circumstances, see Lederach (1997) and Gloppen (2005). Neither group considers the multitude of post-conflict contexts nor the potential implications of differing forms of mass violence on the achievability of reconciliation as an end goal of a process. For instance, failing to differentiate between distinct forms of violent conflict implies that societies recovering from interstate wars face the same pressures, constraints and needs as those attempting to rebuild after genocide.

Adelman is the only author in this review to state explicitly that his understanding of reconciliation is inappropriate following some types of mass violence. He distinguishes between three forms of conflict that may lead to social divisions: interstate wars, intrastate or civil wars, and wars, such as genocides, sponsored by governments against their own people (2005, p. 287). Adelman argues in favour of a form of modern-liberal reconciliation that seeks to replace violence with peaceful coexistence (ibid., p. 288). This vision includes officially recognising wrongdoers as civil society members after interstate or intrastate war. Adelman stipulates that recognising genocide perpetrators as equal members of society legitimises their crimes. Moreover, including genocide perpetrators in the process of modern-liberal reconciliation would render it unsuccessful as perpetrators and survivors could not peacefully coexist with 'proper respect for each other' (ibid., p. 301).

This inability to coexist peacefully raises the question: is reconciliation appropriate or desirable in all post-conflict contexts? Works such as those by Bloomfield et al. (2003), Villa-Vicencio (2000b), Bar-Tal and Bennink (2004), and Long and Brecke (2003) envision the positive outcomes of reconciliation as a process or end goal after conflict. These descriptions sound appealing in theory, but little consideration is given to their desirability in practice. Minow touches upon this issue in the long quotation earlier in this review in which she outlines survivors' various interests including financial redress, acknowledgement of the truth and rebuilding trust (1998, p. 4).

Authors ought to consider more seriously whether governments and/ or civilians perceive reconciliation to be a worthwhile pursuit. For instance, as Reyntjens and Vandeginste argue, political leaders' and survivor groups' aversion to the notion of national reconciliation following the 1994 genocide in Rwanda resulted in the concept being considered taboo until the end of 1998. They contend that constructing a formal national reconciliation programme was undesirable in the years immediately after the 1994 genocide because the transitional government viewed it as promoting power-sharing with the Hutu majority (2005, p. 102). The authors argue that the government did not deem reconciliation to be advantageous until the perceived threat of internal opposition and military action by former members of the national army and genocide militias based in DRC was eradicated (ibid., p. 103).[7]

Multiple works portray reconciliation as being both achievable and desirable after conflict. Several of these contributions suggest frameworks or steps through which 'successful reconciliation' may be achieved. They are informed by the methodological assumption that reconciliation processes can be prescribed. Prescription, in this context, refers to a range of recommendations varying from specific solutions in response to perceived deficits in existing strategies to proposed models seeking to achieve the end goal of 'successful reconciliation'. Although many authors such as Bar-Tal and Bennink include the caveat that reconciliation is never assured, they press on with suggested approaches to achieving it after mass violence (2004). Several commentators, including Gloppen (2005), Bloomfield et al. (2003) and Van der Merwe (2001), argue that no single strategy will bring about reconciliation following mass human rights violations. Instead, each writer suggests a different set of key elements that must be present if reconciliation is to be achieved. For instance, Gloppen contends that although every post-conflict context is different, several minimum requirements must be met for a programme to achieve its goals. They include addressing the conflict's context, introducing institutional support at the appropriate time, encouraging local ownership and legitimacy of the project, and applying multiple strategies such as justice, truth, restitution and reform (2005, pp. 18, 45).

Van der Merwe suggests a different set of key elements in his analysis of the legislation and strategies that sought to promote national reconciliation at the TRC. He argues that a single national programme is insufficient

7 Literature analysing reconciliation as a peacemaking paradigm in post-conflict Rwanda has not been included in this review as it will be discussed in detail in later chapters.

following mass human rights violations (2001, p. 102). Instead, he frames his recommendations around the inclusion of communities in designing and leading multiple projects that are informed by needs at the local level. Van der Merwe also outlines several key features that ought to be implemented at the national level in order to facilitate community projects focused on reconciliation. They include stated commitments to political transparency, support for survivors and criminal prosecution of those accused of having committed human rights violations (ibid., p. 104). Both Gloppen (2005) and Van der Merwe (2001) make practical recommendations for constructing reconciliation processes in separate contexts. These suggestions are informed by different objectives and reconciliation concepts. Although these contributions differ in many ways, both raise questions about the relationship between theoretical interpretations of the concept and the practical implementation of reconciliation programmes. For instance, how generalisable are the suggested approaches? Do analyses of specific strategies have any practical implications for other nations seeking reconciliation following mass violence?

Bloomfield et al. outline practical suggestions for policymakers seeking to design and implement reconciliation programmes in post-conflict contexts. Bloomfield et al. reject a universal model as they argue that processes must always be specific to the context in which they are invoked. Instead, they suggest basic requirements that will support policymakers in developing a programme that is appropriate for a specific post-conflict context.

> Basic principles which should underpin the design of every reconciliation process, and which may assist readers as they work through the handbook:
>
> – Begin early, when attitudes are most receptive to change and challenge.
>
> – Stick to the commitment and deal with the hard issues; they will only get harder with time.
>
> – Give it sufficient time: it cannot be rushed.
>
> – Be transparent about the goals, the difficulties, the time span and the resources (2003, p. 17).

The practical nature of Bloomfield et al.'s *Reconciliation after Violent Conflict: a Handbook* is evident in the suggested three-stage process outlining the 'essential ingredients for lasting reconciliation' (2003, p. 19). These stages include replacing fear with peaceful coexistence, building confidence and trust between survivors and perpetrators, and fostering empathy between victims and offenders (ibid., pp. 20–2). The authors maintain that every post-conflict context requires a new reconciliation process to be designed that includes more than one mechanism such as healing, justice or truth-telling. Moreover, they argue that national reconciliation projects should be understood as part of larger peacebuilding and democratisation procedures and must be implemented alongside constitutional reforms (ibid., p. 167).

Bloomfield et al.'s recommendations can be located in the suggested approaches to reconciliation that emerge in the literature ranging from basic requirements to explicitly recommending specific models. Bloomfield et al.'s suggestions include both minimum requirements and a full process. Authors, among them Daye (2004), Bar-Tal and Bennink (2004) and Adelman (2005), propose specific models or list recommendations that they argue will promote particular reconciliation concepts. These are in conflict with Gloppen (2005) and Bloomfield et al.'s (2003) assertions that no single model is sufficient to bring about reconciliation. For instance, Daye proposes a working model of political forgiveness or 'deep reconciliation' at the socio-political level (2004, p. xiii). This is partly shaped by research conducted in South Africa, but is designed to be applicable in other contexts including societies implementing truth commissions and nations recovering from civil war or mass violence (ibid., p. 172). Daye's suggested model includes five acts: truth-telling; apologising and claiming responsibility; building a transitional justice framework; finding ways to heal; and embracing forgiveness (ibid., p. 9). Although the sequence of several acts is flexible, Daye contends that the process must begin with truth-telling and end with embracing forgiveness (ibid.).

The entire range of prescriptive works begs questions related to generalisability and how appropriate suggested approaches to reconciliation are as a process or end goal. For instance, how do key elements or suggested models account for the varying constraints, pressures and needs of different post-conflict societies? The generalisability issue is diminished somewhat by the flexibility of certain suggested approaches. For instance, the basic recommendations put forward by Van der Merwe and Gloppen do not prescribe how minimum requirements, such as encouraging local ownership and supporting survivors, should be accomplished. The relatively open-ended nature of these suggestions creates the leeway necessary for the approaches to be adopted in societies facing different constraints after mass violence. In contrast, the relatively inflexible methods described by Daye and Adelman present problems with regard to their applicability in different post-conflict situations. As discussed above, Adelman states that his model of modern-liberal reconciliation is not appropriate following genocide. Daye suggests the application of his own model of political forgiveness to any and all societies in transition following mass conflict. The absence of contextual specificity in the work of both authors is worrying. This concern stems from the notion that the nature of violence and the social, economic and political landscape it creates will most certainly affect the ways in which reconciliation processes are constructed and pursued.

Prescriptive notions of reconciliation are also at risk of appearing implausible when applied in differing post-conflict societies. The recommendations put forward by Van der Merwe largely escape this concern due to the case-specific nature of the analysis (2001). For instance, his suggested inclusion of community-level projects relates directly to perceived deficits in the TRC's promotion of reconciliation outlined in his analysis. Van der Merwe's evaluation of the TRC and community reconciliation processes in South Africa support these suggestions. Conversely, the models proposed by Daye and Adelman are not related to perceived deficits in specific programmes. Daye discusses the influence of field research conducted in South Africa on his proposed model of political forgiveness, but presents no empirical evidence to support it. Adelman does not state the empirical foundations of his proposed model of modern-liberal reconciliation or provide evidence of its potential effectiveness, thus limiting its plausibility. The lack of empirical evidence and sufficient plausibility limits Daye and Adelman's highly prescriptive models to purely theoretical interpretations of reconciliation.

Weaknesses, gaps and alternative solutions

The breadth of interest in reconciliation as a response to mass violence has yielded many understandings of the concept. As we have seen, numerous disciplines, theoretical frameworks and methodological assumptions have shaped these interpretations, creating the problem that 'seldom is anyone talking about the same thing when using the term' (Borer, 2006, p. 31). Many authors including Borer (2006), Hermann (2004) and Nesiah (2005) raise the issue that consensus has yet to be reached regarding the meaning of reconciliation in the post-conflict context. Although its 'theoretical fluidity' has facilitated interesting debates, it has the potential to negatively affect the implementation of reconciliation programmes in post-conflict contexts (Hermann, 2004, p. 41).

A great deal of the difficulty of putting the theory into practice stems from disagreement and conceptual confusion in the literature. Some elements have been touched on earlier in this review including disagreement about whether reconciliation ought to be conceived of as a process or an end goal. This issue raises significant questions with regard to construction and implementation. For instance, how can reconciliation be brought about if there is no consensus about what form it should take? Should it be supported as a long-term process as suggested by Bloomfield et al. (2003)? Or can we expect it to be promoted from the work of mechanisms such as ad hoc criminal tribunals or truth commissions, as Archbishop Tutu suggested with regard to the TRC? Although some authors argue that reconciliation ought to be conceived of as both a process and an end goal, see Clark (2010a) and Bar-Tal and Bennink (2004), the fact that there is no general agreement about what the term means could make the pursuit of reconciliation more difficult.

The notion that reconciliation can be understood as either a process, end goal, or both, implies that it requires some form of intervention to take place (Bar-Siman-Tov, 2004, p. 5). Although several writers, including Van der Merwe (2001), Bar-Tal and Bennink (2004) and Bloomfield et al. (2003), agree that procedures ought to include participation from the bottom-up and top-down simultaneously, each author outlines how this is achieved differently. For instance, Van der Merwe describes the bottom-up approach to reconciliation as one led from the community-level that prioritises individuals' health and wellbeing and their relationships with each other (2001, p. 90). The top-down vision, he argues, seeks to foster conditions of reconciliation that will filter down through all levels of society (ibid., p. 91). Bar-Tal and Bennink argue that top-down and bottom-up approaches ought to spread the notion of reconciliation at the community level. They contend that disseminating the reconciliation message among the grassroots will support positive changes in individuals' beliefs, motivations, goals and emotions following mass violence (2003, p. 27).

The notion of processes operating in opposite directions fails to answer some important questions related to desirability and achievability. If the reconciliation paradigm is perceived to be inappropriate or undesirable at either the community or the governmental level, is the process doomed to fail? Moreover, can reconciliation be forced in either direction in the hope that it will become more attractive to its opponents over time? Bloomfield et al. argue that reconciliation cannot be imposed from the top-down alone and that authorities can never force individuals to trust, feel empathy, or forgive those who have harmed them (2003, p. 26). This assertion is confounded by the distinctions made in the literature between the interpersonal and national forms of reconciliation.

Borer sees interpersonal reconciliation as taking place at the individual level either with oneself or between two persons such as a survivor and a perpetrator (2006). She contends that such procedures are commonly guided by either a religious narrative emphasising forgiveness or a therapeutic narrative prioritising healing and the restoration of relationships (ibid., p. 32). Borer goes on to describe national unity and reconciliation as taking place at the political level between socio-political institutions and processes; the end goal of which amounts to little more than peaceful coexistence (ibid., p. 33).

Donna Pankhurst depicts this distinction differently. She outlines five different meanings most commonly associated with the verb 'to reconcile' including: establishing or reestablishing friendly relations between two or more people; settling a quarrel; making oneself or another no longer opposed to something; acquiescing to something unpleasant; and making two conflicting things compatible with each other (1999, p. 240). Pankhurst argues that these definitions are most commonly associated with reconciliation between individuals (interpersonal reconciliation). They are, however, increasingly being transposed to political contexts following mass conflict. At the political or national level, these definitions take on different meanings including peaceful coexistence (making two things compatible with each other) and political compromise (making oneself no longer opposed to something) (ibid.). Pankhurst contends that applying these conceptions of reconciliation to political contexts transforms what was once an effort between individuals into a collective process (ibid., p. 241).

The distinction between interpersonal and national reconciliation raises questions about individual agency in pursuing the latter. For instance, must all individuals participate in the 'collective process' of national reconciliation? This question is particularly pertinent with regard to national programmes imposed from the top-down. It also raises questions about interpersonal reconciliation. Should this be led by the individuals directly affected by the damaged relationship as Bloomfield et al. (2003) suggest, or can it be encouraged by a religious-redemptive narrative disseminated by religious or political leaders? Also can a single process promote both understandings of reconciliation, interpersonal and national? If we are to assume that the former ought to be pursued by individuals, who should be expected to lead it? Should perpetrators initiate the process and apologise or should those affected negatively by the violence be the first to act?[8]

These unanswered questions complicate implementation of the programmes in a number of ways. Firstly, they contribute to confusion about the type of reconciliation that ought to be pursued, be it interpersonal, national, or both. Secondly, these questions neglect issues related to agency and the roles of individuals and groups in pursuing reconciliation as a process or end goal. Thirdly, they fail to get to grips with the potential obstacles posed by issues related to desirability and achievability of these procedures. Part of this problem may relate to what Wilson identifies as an overemphasis of philosophical discussions about elements of the reconciliation process.

> The study of transitional truth and justice has been too dominated by philosophical discussions abstracted from specific texts, and we should instead examine how the politics of punishment and the writing of a new official memory are central to state strategies to create a new hegemony in the area of justice and construct the present moment as post-authoritarian when it includes many elements of the past (2001, p. xvi).

Wilson's interest in *how* the creation of a new official memory and act of punishment relate to state strategies refers to the *function* of truth and justice in the socio-political context of post-authoritarian rule in South Africa. The themes of power and political dominance detectable in this quotation point

8 See Tavuchis (1991) for a sociological investigation of the meaning and function of apology at the individual and community levels.

to understanding reconciliation as a strategy that ought to be examined with reference to the regime seeking to pursue it. Short also analyses the political function of reconciliation processes in his work about the Australian programme under the Howard and Keating governments. Short argues that during Keating's leadership, the official reconciliation programme functioned to construct a new 'ethical' image of the non-indigenous population's promise of future social justice for aboriginal communities (2008, p. 317). He states that during Howard's time as prime minister, the programme functioned to encourage cultural assimilation and the 'sanitisation' of the country's colonial past (ibid., p. 319).

Some authors including Van der Merwe (2001), Hayner (1994; 2011) and Villa-Vicencio (2000a; 2000b) locate their analyses in the context of the TRC or truth commissions more generally; further context-specific analyses are necessary to understand reconciliation programmes' theory and practice within the socio-political realms in which they are pursued. Analyses of this type may potentially uncover how social, economic and political contexts inform how these programmes function.

The fluid nature of theoretical understandings of reconciliation, as discussed by Hermann (2004), makes analysing how it is conceived by those invoking it all the more pertinent. Similarly, Nesiah argues that its meaning ought to be uncovered by 'concrete political tasks' rather than 'tautological' exposition (2005, p. 271).

> Reconciliation is a difficult and ambiguous concept – often stripped of any meaning by the fact that it is invoked by so many people, to justify so many different goals. In giving value and dimension to the notion of reconciliation we need to have a more historically grounded sense of the tasks that specific truth commissions typically address (ibid., p. 280).

Although Nesiah specifically refers to truth commissions, the impetus to understand the ways in which reconciliation programmes are pursued in relation to different political goals is similarly relevant in other post-conflict contexts. Vital to this investigation is the analysis of reconciliation as a process or end goal informed by the interests, relationships and power dynamics of those involved in it. As such, the case-specific study of reconciliation as a socially constructed phenomenon may be a particularly helpful alternative to purely philosophical discussions of the subject.

Social constructionism is appropriate in this context as it makes it easier to investigate the historical and cultural specificity of concepts we use (Burr, 2003, p. 4). Moreover, it facilitates a critical understanding of our knowledge of the social world, a perspective that assists the investigation of the actions, interactions and power relations informing how we understand the world in our everyday lives (ibid., pp. 5–6).[9] It also allows us to be critical of the interests, objectives and power dynamics that inform particular phenomena, including reconciliation. Hacking presents six grades of social constructionism that facilitate the investigation of the meaning of different phenomena. They range from relatively uncritical historical analyses to those that actively seek to change phenomena identified as being unnecessary or detrimental to society (1999, pp. 19–21).[10] Hacking employs Karl Mannheim's (1952) conception of the 'unmasking of the mind' to demonstrate how the social constructionist perspective can expose the *function* of particular phenomena.

Social constructionist analyses of the ways in which particular phenomena function have the potential to find solutions to many questions left unanswered by the literature discussed in this review. For instance, social constructionism's critical perspective of the status quo facilitates in-depth analyses of the political interests and dynamics that inform reconciliation programmes in different post-conflict contexts. These interests and dynamics relate directly to the desirability of formal reconciliation procedures following mass violence.

Social constructionism also facilitates the analysis of the objectives, interests and relationships that shape the construction and implementation of reconciliation projects in specific post-conflict contexts. This form of analysis not only investigates whether reconciliation is conceived as a process, end goal, or both, but also why it is understood this way. Social constructionism's emphasis on historical and cultural specificity makes it easier to investigate how the social, economic, political and cultural context informs the construction of particular phenomena. This form of contextual specificity is particularly important with regard to the differing pressures, constraints and needs of individuals and groups following mass violence. It also facilitates the analysis of why particular individuals and groups participate in the process or seek to support the end goal of reconciliation.

More generally, these analyses seek to uncover the discourses, narratives and official definitions that shape how reconciliation programmes are constructed and put into practice. As outlined in the introduction, Wilson uses a social constructionist framework to explore how and why South Africa's post-apartheid government applied human rights to promoting reconciliation at the TRC (2001, p. 230). Wilson argues that the manipulation of human rights language to promote moral-theological reconciliation discourse limits rights' ability to support the creation of lasting democracy and a non-prejudicial justice system (ibid.). Moreover, he argues that government interests in

9 See Berger and Luckmann (1966) for an in-depth analysis of knowledge as socially constructed in everyday life.

10 Hacking's grades of constructionism include: historical; ironic; reformist; unmasking; rebellious; and revolutionary (Hacking, 1999). Revolutionary constructionists refer to activists who attempt to radically change or eradicate the phenomena they deem to be harmful to society (Marshall and Scott, 2005).

fostering state-legitimacy and nation-building after conflict are pursued at the expense of accountability, justice and procedural fairness (ibid., p. 224).

Social constructionist analyses of reconciliation's meaning and function in different post-conflict contexts uncover details that may be useful in evaluating individual programmes. Although there is no consensus in the literature about how to evaluate the success of a reconciliation process, the inclusion of data about interests, objectives and power dynamics may reveal who does and does not benefit from it. Bloomfield et al. argue that it is inappropriate to judge the success or failure of entire programmes. Instead, they suggest the evaluation of the progress of individual processes and initiatives that operate as part of the overall reconciliation project (2003, p. 167). This investigation may also facilitate the analysis of why a programme promotes the interests and rights of some individuals and groups more than others.

In the chapters to come, a social constructionist framework is used to analyse how Rwanda's National Unity and Reconciliation Programme functions in social and political practice. This investigation includes analyses of the social, political and historical contexts in which the programme was constructed and implemented. It also includes analysis of the political interests, actions and power dynamics that shape the government's vision of 'national reconciliation' as well as discussions about who does and does not benefit from the programme. As such, the book seeks to provide a detailed interpretation of how 'national reconciliation' is envisioned, constructed and put into practice in post-conflict Rwanda.

Conclusion

The multidisciplinary nature of the literature reveals myriad understandings of reconciliation after violent conflict which are expressed using different images including relationship spectrums and webs. Although there is no consensus as to the definition of reconciliation, there is general agreement that justice and truth are important following mass violence. The connections between justice, truth and reconciliation is complicated however, by different understandings of justice – retributive and restorative – as well as different processes of telling, hearing and manipulating the truth. Methodological assumptions that reconciliation is achievable and desirable also inform the literature. The lack of context-specific analyses of existing programmes supports these suppositions. Other analyses in this review are shaped by the methodological assumption that specific reconciliation models can be prescribed and it is one that appears in the recommendations related to the perceived deficits in specific programmes and to models of how the procedures ought to be pursued. The latter prescriptions do not provide the flexibility or contextual specificity necessary for their application in varying post-conflict contexts.

Overall, the most significant gaps in knowledge relate to nuanced understandings of how specific reconciliation programmes are constructed and implemented and how they function in different post-conflict contexts. This book provides a comprehensive theoretical and empirical study of the National Unity and Reconciliation Programme in Rwanda that will help to fill this gap. Informed by a social constructionist perspective of reconciliation, it examines the context, political interests and power dynamics that shape the RPF's official programme and how it functions in social and political practice.

Chapter 2

Conflict in context

On the morning of 7 April 1994, members of the national army, the Forces Armées Rwandaises (FAR), and the pro-government Interahamwe militia began firing at the homes of Tutsi living in the Kigali neighbourhood of Kimicanga.[1] A ten-year-old girl named Angélique and her older brother Emmanuel survived the attack but their parents and siblings were killed.[2] Angélique was struck on the head with a machete and repeatedly clubbed by neighbours who had joined in the growing violence outside the house. They dragged her through the street by her legs to a mass grave that had been dug nearby. A passing group of Red Cross volunteers spotted the bodies and rescued the young girl. She was brought to a clinic but fled after being threatened by another patient. Eventually Angélique found her way to a house belonging to a member of the church she attended with her family, a woman named Claudette and her husband, a Chief of the Interahamwe in a Kigali district.

Angélique remained uneasily in the house for many weeks until the family decided to flee to Zaire in an attempt to escape the approaching RPF rebels. She was taken across the border to Goma, eastern Zaire, where the family gave her no food or water. The young girl eventually fled from Goma and the Interahamwe and walked across the border into Gisenyi, western Rwanda. Once there, RPF rebels approached her and gave her shoes, clean clothes and cake. They returned with her to Kigali where she was reunited with Emmanuel and continues to live today.[3]

Angélique's experience of the 1994 genocide highlights several themes that are pertinent to understanding how the violence took place. In discussion, Angélique pointed to the deliberate search for Tutsi civilians in her neighbourhood. She described the weapons the militia members carried and the efficiency with which they attacked the area. The second theme is the participation of civilians in the attack. She talked about her neighbours' use of

1 Pronounced *Ki-mee-chon-ga*.

2 All names and locations have been changed.

3 This story is paraphrased from Angélique's experience of the 1994 genocide. I met her during the 15th Annual Commemoration Ceremony at Amahoro Stadium in Kigali.

machetes and clubs in their assault against her family and in looting her home. The third theme concerns issues of identity and group membership. Angélique claimed that the neighbour who owned her family's house identified them as Tutsi prior to the attack. This public naming of Tutsi transformed Angélique and her family into targets of violence. Lastly, Angélique's story emphasises the perceived heroism of the RPF rebels, whom she lauded for her rescue in Gisenyi. Official reconciliation discourse promoted by the current RPF government also emphasises the rebels' role as heroes after the 1994 genocide ended. Although Angélique's account focuses solely on events between April and July 1994, themes of violence, popular participation and identity can be traced throughout Rwanda's history (interview, 9 April 2009).

Identity from the pre-colonial era to independence

In Mahmood Mamdani's words, 'the Batutsi were like a layer of cream spread over the entire society, administering a subject peasantry, the Bahutu' (1996, p. 5).[4] His observation concerning the administrative relationship between Tutsi and Hutu refers to the development of a hierarchical social, political and economic structure during the pre-colonial period in Rwanda in the latter part of the 19th century[5] (ibid., p. 5; NURC, 2011a, p. 85).[6] This system was initiated in conjunction with the expansion of the central kingdom ruled by a Mwami or King of Bahindiro Tutsi lineage. With the centralisation of power came the establishment of clientage systems led by chiefs appointed by the Mwami. The control of resources including land and cattle became increasingly concentrated in the hands of a small minority of individuals who held or were given 'Tutsi status' (Eltringham, 2004, p. 13). Access to political power and natural resources was further restricted with the introduction of the

4 The prefix 'Ba' indicates the plural form of Hutu, Tutsi and Twa identities. The prefix 'Mu' refers to the singular form, such as 'Mutwa' or 'Mututsi'. The ethnic identities of Hutu, Tutsi and Twa will be referred to without the prefixes throughout this book.

5 This chapter focuses primarily on relations between Hutu and Tutsi civilians and political groups throughout Rwanda's history. The experience of Twa civilians during the 1994 genocide and post-conflict period is closely examined in chapter 4 with reference to nation-building and the RPF's construction of a singular national identity.

6 The pre-colonial period is described in the history textbook, published by the NURC, as having begun in the 14th century (2011a, p. 85). Although official reconciliation discourse states that 'social cohesion' thrived during the entire pre-colonial period (14th century up to 1884), particular emphasis is placed on the purportedly 'positive relations' between the Hutu and Tutsi during the 19th century. This emphasis on the end of the pre-colonial era may be due in part to the absence of historical data about how Hutu, Tutsi and Twa identities were understood prior to 1860 (Pottier, 2002, as cited by Eltringham, 2004, p. 13).

ubuletwa forced labour system and the expansion of land contracts referred to as *igikingi* (Prunier, 1995, p. 21). This concentration of power did not take place consistently across the country. By the end of the 19th century, the majority of the population, both Hutu and Tutsi, had become impoverished and dependent on the highly inequitable clientage system (Vidal, 1974, as cited by Prunier, 1995, p. 22; Eltringham, 2004, p. 14).

The development of this system and the hierarchy it represented reflects several important themes that began to emerge during the pre-colonial period, the first being political exclusion. As the clientage system became more restrictive, political power was limited to those with 'elite' Tutsi status – a small minority of Tutsi chiefs who had significant political influence during this period. Gérard Prunier, a French historian who has written extensively about countries in central Africa and the Horn of Africa, identifies this shift as a precursor to violence as it created 'a centre versus periphery affair' (1995, p. 21). Prunier differentiates this understanding of political dominance from that of '*Tutsi versus Hutu*', as many Tutsi were also repressed by the clientage system (ibid.; author's italics).

Mamdani offers a different understanding of political relations during this period. He refers to a 'double domination' in which Hutu were repressed by a pastoralist aristocracy and by the Tutsi minority as a whole (1996, p. 8). Mamdani points to the political distinction between subjects and non-subjects as well as that between Hutu and Tutsi. He clarifies that although many Tutsi did not have elite status, they maintained a favoured relationship with the state (ibid.). The second theme is that of ethnic exclusion since Hutu and Tutsi identities became more restrictive towards the end of this pre-colonial period. Eltringham argues that no distinct meaning was uniformly attributed to Hutu or Tutsi during that time (2004, p. 14). This began to change, however, with the arrival of first German and then Belgian colonists, who built a formal state apparatus upon the Tutsi minority's perceived dominance (Mamdani, 1996, p. 10).

The colonial period began in 1884 when Germany took possession of Rwanda and Burundi and governed them as a single colony, Ruanda-Urundi (Newbury, 1983, p. 257). German colonial rule was maintained by 96 German officials, creating the need for indirect rule.[7] Colonial leadership relied heavily on the Mwami and Tutsi with elite status to enact its administrative responsibilities, resulting in the further stratification of political power in Rwanda (Prunier, 1995, p. 25). Germany lost the colony to Belgium in 1916.

Belgian colonial rule brought about additional institutional changes that further concentrated power in the hands of Tutsi chiefs. This hierarchical system was built upon a hypothesis of ethnic origin defined and promulgated by German anthropologists (Mamdani, 1996, p. 11). The 'Hamitic

7 This number includes missionaries and officials (Prunier, 1995, p. 25).

Hypothesis' states that the Tutsi had travelled from Ethiopia to Rwanda where they conquered the indigenous Hutu agriculturalists and Twa hunter-gatherers prior to the arrival of European colonists (ibid., p. 6). The Tutsi or 'African Hamites' purportedly brought with them 'higher forms of African civilisation' and German and Belgian colonists considered them to more closely resemble Europeans (Miles, 2000, as cited by Eltringham, 2004, p. 186).[8] Although this theory has since been discredited, Mamdani (1996) and Eltringham (2004) agree that little consensus exists about the origins of Hutu, Tutsi and Twa people.[9]

Social and political disparity during Belgian colonial rule was reinforced by the continuation of the forced labour system,[10] which was so harsh that in 1928 hundreds of thousands of Hutu peasants fled to Uganda to search for work as coffee farm labourers (Mamdani, 1996, p. 11). The Belgians formally institutionalised the ethnic stratification system upon which the state apparatus functioned during the 1933 census. Every citizen was issued an identification card on which with his or her ethnicity was printed (Straus, 2006, p. 225). The recording of ethnic labels reflected ethnicity's early 'racialisation'.

The evolution of ethnic identities into status-based ethno-racial divisions relates closely to the development of anti-Tutsi violence associated with the 1959 Social Revolution and Rwanda's movement towards independence in 1962. From the early 1950s, the UN pressured Belgium to support Ruanda-Urundi's transition into separate independent states (Van de Meeren, 1996, p. 254). The impetus to prepare Rwanda for independence coincided with what French political scientist René Lemarchand describes as 'a decisive heightening of expectations among Hutu intellectuals' (1970, p. 146). These alleged expectations resulted in this group's frustrations being publicly articulated with regard to the social and political conditions the Hutu in Rwanda were enduring (ibid.). This grievance was published in the 1957 'Bahutu Manifesto: notes of the social aspect of the racial native problem in Rwanda', written by nine

8 Miles states that German and Belgian colonists identified these purportedly 'non-African' qualities as intellectual and political sophistication, and physical attributes such as narrow noses, thin lips and significant height (2000, as cited by Eltringham, 2004, p. 186).

9 The exception to this statement is agreement among certain authors including Lewis (2000) and Jackson (2003) that the Twa were the first inhabitants of Rwanda. The implications of the Twa community's efforts to be officially recognised as an indigenous people are discussed in chapter 4.

10 As political control and financial resources were stripped away from Hutu and Twa people and given to the minority of elite Tutsi controlling the country, 'non-elite' Tutsi received no noticeable financial gain for their shared Tutsi identity. Moreover, towards the end of the 1950s, non-elite Tutsi, 90 to 97% of those called Tutsi, earned the same family incomes as Hutu across the country (Linden and Linden, 1977, as cited by Eltringham, 2004, p. 226).

Hutu intellectuals who had studied in Catholic seminaries. The text disputed the clientage system and sought an end to the perceived social, economic and political injustices created by the Tutsi's political monopoly. In its place, the authors suggested such initiatives as promoting Hutu individuals to public office, expanding educational opportunities for all Hutu children, and eradicating prejudice related to social class (ibid., p. 149). Grégoire Kayibanda's political party the Mouvement Social Muhutu (MSM), established in June that year, outlined similar proposals.

The relationship between Tutsi elites and Belgian authorities began to sour following the manifesto's publication. Lemarchand contends that the Belgian authorities sought to maintain control over what they perceived to be an impending social transformation with regard to rising tension between Hutu and Tutsi groups. He states that Tutsi elites greatly underestimated the breadth of support within the Hutu population for social and political change. Instead, they sought to retain political control of Rwanda through pushing for independence from Belgium (1970, p. 153). In this pursuit, a monarchist party called the Union National Rwandaise (UNAR) was officially launched on 15 August 1959 (ibid., p. 158). On 1 November 1959 a small group of UNAR militants attacked a Hutu sub-chief in Gitarama, central Rwanda. Within several days, violence had spread across the country (ibid., p. 162). Spontaneous uprisings and localised anti-Tutsi violence continued under the guise of the Social Revolution, resulting in the deaths of hundreds of Tutsi civilians, while many more fled into neighbouring countries (Uvin, 1999, p. 256).

The so-called 'Social Revolution' was a major factor in the proliferation of later violence in Rwanda for several reasons. Firstly, it represented the first episode of systematic anti-Tutsi violence. The 1957 'Bahutu Manifesto' had challenged the monarchy and feudal system, but the violence of the revolution was targeted at Tutsi civilians. Secondly, this period transformed the political power dynamic. Masses of Hutu civilians, long excluded from political authority through the 'double domination' of pastoral and minority rule were now one step closer to power (Mamdani, 1996, p. 5). Thirdly, the ideological impetus from which the violence sped became an integral element of genocide propaganda. The desire to protect the supposed 'social gains' made in 1959 by Hutu civilians became a rallying call against the RPF invasion in October 1990 (Eltringham, 2004, p. 45).

A radical shift in political structure took shape in Rwanda less than two years after the Social Revolution began with Grégoire Kayibanda's party, MDR-Parmehutu, taking control of the country during the 'Coup of Gitarama' on 28 January 1961 (ibid., p. 21).[11] The revolution ended nine months later with a

11 Kayibanda converted the Mouvement Social Muhutu into a new party called the Parmehutu on 19 October 1959.

referendum held in September. Rwanda was officially awarded its independence from Belgium on 1 July 1962 and Kayibanda was installed as the country's first president (Mamdani, 1996, p. 16). The birth of an independent Rwanda and Kayibanda's inauguration did not abate the exodus of hundreds of thousands of Tutsi from Rwanda into neighbouring countries, where many continued to live as refugees until after the 1994 genocide concluded (ibid.).

Rwanda's history from the pre-colonial era to independence spans several years, yet these periods are related by the emergence of several themes. The pre-colonial period saw inequity and inequality proliferate in the form of clientage systems. Even at this early stage, the majority of the population, Hutu, Tutsi and Twa, were excluded from political power (ibid., p. 8). Access to political control became increasingly restricted throughout the colonial era. This exclusion erupted in violent anti-monarchist upheaval in 1959 that continued until independence in 1962. The narrowing understanding of the ethnic identities of Hutu and Tutsi exacerbated the reaction of some Hutu to this history of exclusion. By 1962, the ethnic identities had become race-like.[12] It would not be long before these identities, and the political power associated with them, would again become embroiled in mass violence.

Refugees and the October 1990 invasion

Violent attacks against Tutsi forced large groups to flee Rwanda between 1960–7. Lemarchand estimates that by April 1960, the number of Tutsi refugees who had fled the violence reached 22,000. Three years later that number had risen to 130,000 (1970, p. 172). While exiled Tutsi refugees launched attacks against Kayibanda's regime, Tutsi civilians inside the country faced the consequences of violent retaliation.[13] One such attack took place in 1963 when several hundred Tutsi refugees launched what Mamdani refers to as the 'Cockroach' or '*Inyenzi*' invasion (1996, p. 15).[14] This attempt to seize political power from Kayibanda was thwarted in violent clashes with the Gendarmes National Rwandaises and resulted in thousands of deaths (ibid.).[15] Tutsi-led violence outside the country

12 The massacring of civilians during the 1994 genocide – both Hutu and Tutsi – because assailants deemed them to look like Tutsi, demonstrates the race-like distinction that had developed between both groups. Des Forges described the deliberate disfigurement during this period of women who allegedly looked Tutsi. As well as the amputation of breasts and mutilation of sexual organs, Des Forges pointed to how genocide perpetrators would cut off body parts that looked 'particularly Tutsi' including long fingers and thin noses (1999, pp. 17, 164).

13 Kuperman estimates that between 1959–67 upwards of 20,000 Tutsi were killed inside Rwanda (2004, p. 64).

14 *Inyenzi*, the Kinyarwanda word for cockroach would come to feature heavily in anti-Tutsi propaganda during the civil war and the 1994 genocide.

15 The estimated number of deaths following this invasion range from the UN's calculation of between 1,000 and 3,000 to that of the World Council of Churches,

reached an apex during the 1972 genocide in Burundi when Tutsi soldiers in the Burundian national army killed up to 200,000 Hutu.[16]

Burundi shares a similar colonial history with neighbouring Rwanda as it also achieved independence from Belgium on 1 July 1962. Although Burundi's population is divided along the same ethnic lines as its neighbour, Hutu successfully deposed the Mwami in 1965. Tutsi members of the military seized political control in 1966 and maintained it until 1993. The exclusively Tutsi army launched numerous attacks on Hutu civilians between the mid 1960s and early 1990s. An invasion of Hutu refugees from Tanzania, intra-Tutsi tension and an internal Hutu insurgency culminated in genocide in 1972. Like the 1994 genocide in Rwanda, ethnic conflict fuelled the violence. In Burundi members of the national army targeted Hutu government officials, civil servants and students (Klinghoffer, 1998, p. 9).

The Burundian genocide had violent implications for both Hutu and Tutsi inside Rwanda. Lemarchand argues that the systematic killing of Hutu men throughout 1972 bolstered an anti-Tutsi backlash in Rwanda. This hostile response in turn facilitated Juvénal Habyarimana's coup d'état in 1973 (Newbury and Newbury, 1999, p. 299; Lemarchand, 1998, p. 6).[17] Lemarchand contends that the 1972 genocide against Hutu in Burundi also informed the extreme nature of anti-Tutsi violence following the assassination of Burundi's President Melchior Ndadaye in 1993, which was so brutal that it resulted in the migration of 300,000 Burundian refugees across the border into Rwanda (1998, p. 6).

A reprieve from the violence inside Rwanda eventually came in 1974; a year after Habyarimana successfully deposed Kayibanda as president. Outside Rwanda, however, Tutsi refugees who had fled violence in Rwanda in 1959 and 1967 faced periodic attacks in Uganda (Sibomana, 1999, p. 38).[18] Anti-Tutsi prejudice was allegedly encouraged by the state and accepted by much of society. In April 1979, a group of Tutsi refugees founded the Rwandese Alliance for National Unity (RANU) with the stated mandate to facilitate debate and discussion. The Alliance's creation preceded the growing suspicion and xenophobia in Uganda that led to the expulsion of Rwandan refugees in 1982–3, a violent eviction that forced 40,000 refugees back into Rwanda before the borders were shut. A further 19,000 were expelled from Uganda in 1983 (Mamdani, 1996, p. 25). Tutsi refugees faced further violent expulsions in 1986, which were not well received by Rwandan Tutsi fighting alongside

which was between 10,000 and 14,000 (Mamdani, 1996, p. 15).

16 The number of estimated Hutu deaths between April and November 1972 ranges from 100,000 to 200,000 (Lemarchand, 1998, p. 6).

17 Habyarimana's Mouvement Révolutionaire National pour le Développement (MRND) became Rwanda's single political party in 1973.

18 Mamdani estimates that the total number of Tutsi refugees living in Uganda reached 200,000 in 1990 (1996, p. 25).

Ugandans in the National Resistance Army (NRA). The Rwandan Patriotic Front (RPF) cites the ongoing violent intolerance of refugees as the motive for RANU's disbandment and the RPF's creation in 1987 (ibid., p. 26).

The RPF's official mandate included the repatriation of Rwandan refugees and the establishment of a new power-sharing arrangement with Habyarimana (Kuperman, 2004, p. 68). Habyarimana attempted to avoid an impending RPF invasion by a joint agreement with Uganda to facilitate refugees' safe return to Rwanda (ibid., p. 69). The RPF allegedly cited Habyarimana's failure to repatriate 60,000 Rwandan refugees as the reason for its invasion (Sibomana, 1999, p. 39). The rebels chose 1 October 1990, Ugandan Independence Day, to start what was purportedly planned as a swift attack.

At the time of the October 1990 RPF invasion, President Habyarimana was facing increasing pressure from the United Nations Development Programme (UNDP), the US, the World Bank and International Monetary Fund (IMF), as well as international aid organisations to adopt a multiparty democratic system (Andersen, 2000, p. 447). This pressure reflects a trend among peacebuilding missions at the time, which promoted democracy as a form of conflict management in countries that had experienced civil war. Democratisation, demonstrated by periodic elections, constitutional reforms limiting government control, and increasing respect for civil rights, were prioritised in the 'liberalisation' efforts of these missions in the 1990s. Liberalisation also included neoliberal economic reforms that championed market-oriented economic systems, minimised government intervention in the economy, and significantly increased investor and consumer freedom. Political scientist Roland Paris contends that these reforms were shaped by the assumption that rapid liberalisation would foster lasting peace (Paris, 2004, p. 5).

In 1990, Habyarimana agreed to enact political reforms. In July of that year, the president formally announced the legalisation of multiple political parties. A commission was also established in September 1990 with the stated mandate to write a new constitution (Klinghoffer, 1998, p. 19). Following continued pressure from the UNDP, the World Bank, the US and multiple international aid agencies, Habyarimana signed power-sharing agreements with the RPF in October 1992 and January 1993 as a further condition of aid (Andersen, 2000, p. 447). Andersen states that aid conditionality served as an important leverage tool with regard to democratisation and power-sharing agreements during this period (ibid., p. 451). In 1993, the US terminated most of its aid programmes in Rwanda and capped the remaining aid at US$6 million when Habyarimana's government failed to comply with conditions of rapid democratisation, human rights protection and improved rule of law. At the same time, several European states and the World Bank threatened to suspend aid (Chossudovsky, 1996, as cited by Andersen, p. 451). This political pressure created what Andersen describes as a 'virtual economic stranglehold' which compelled Habyarimana to compromise with regard to the power-sharing agreement with the RPF at the Arusha Accords (2000, p. 451).

While participating in the Arusha Accords with RPF representatives, Habyarimana allegedly pursued a militarisation programme against the rebels. The arming of Hutu civilians was purportedly motivated by fear that Habyarimana's MRND party would lose political control to the RPF (Klinghoffer, 1998, p. 20). By 1992, the MRND's militia, the Interahamwe and the Impuzamugambi militia, affiliated with the Coalition pour la Défense de la République (CDR), were armed and ready to fight the RPF (ibid., p. 21).

Pressure from foreign aid donors and multilateral organisations to create a multiparty system exacerbated ethnic and political tensions in Rwanda. As Paris states, liberalising Rwanda's political system promoted the rise of political parties that were associated with anti-Tutsi militias such as the CDR. Moreover, liberalising media outlets created more opportunities for anti-Tutsi propaganda to be spread across the country in magazines and radio broadcasts. Paris goes so far as to say that the democratisation process provoked Hutu extremists to organise and launch the 1994 genocide (2004, p. 78).

The RPF invasion in October 1990 and the civil war that followed took place amid economic decline in Rwanda. As civil war violence destroyed arable land, displaced civilians and increased military spending, the country plunged further into economic strife. Habyarimana's government agreed to implement a Structural Adjustment Programme (SAP) as prompted by the World Bank and the IMF (Andersen, 2000, p. 447). The programme included privatising public programmes, salary freezes, and decreased government spending (Waller, 1993, as cited by Klinghoffer, 1998, p. 23). It also included significant cuts to the funding of health and education initiatives (Klinghoffer, p. 24). These neoliberal economic reforms coincided with famine and plant disease that devastated coffee production, Rwanda's main export. Coffee prices fell in 1989, as did farmers' income. The SAP exacerbated this problem as the government cut state subsidisation and marketing for coffee and devalued the currency (ibid.).

Hunger and poverty increased, particularly in the country's southern regions, while military expenditure continued to rise. Foreign aid rolled in, yet was siphoned off by the military to fund the purchase of arms (Chossudovsky, 1994, as cited by Klinghoffer, 1998, p. 24). According to the African Rights NGO, civil war, rapid economic liberalisation and famine severely limited the economic opportunities available to young Hutu men (1995, p. 18). Militias profited from young men's desolation when recruiting Hutu civilians to fight the RPF.

Despite the context of economic deterioration and political instability, Habyarimana made several concessions regarding the return of refugees to Rwanda in 1990. Contrary to the RPF's assertion that the MRND would not repatriate exiled Tutsi; Habyarimana actively negotiated the return of refugees who would be allowed to enter the country in November 1990 (Kuperman, 2004, p. 69). Had the RPF delayed its attack, the repatriation programme could have been successful, thus negating the rebel group's primary stated reason for invading (Sibomana, 1999, p. 40). Alan J. Kuperman explains that RPF officials have since confessed privately that they would still have continued their invasion if Habyarimana had allowed the return of all Tutsi refugees, but not offered the rebel group a significant amount of political control (2004, p. 69).

The Habyarimana regime reacted swiftly to the attack with a wave of mass arrests following a reportedly 'staged' shoot out against the RPF in Kigali on 4 October 1990 that left no casualties (Des Forges, 1999, pp. 42–3). The government reportedly used this 'staged' attack to justify imposing an official curfew in the city and cracking down violently on those accused of supporting the RPF (Gatwa, 2005, p. 123). The notion of Tutsi civilians as RPF supporters or accomplices became a particularly salient concept during this period, featuring prominently in anti-Tutsi propaganda and reflecting the growing contention that all Tutsi were 'the enemy'. As the civil war progressed, members of Habyarimana's government began to refer to supporters of his regime as 'Rwandans' while Tutsi and Hutu opposed to his rule became known as '*ibyitso*' or 'accomplices of the enemy' (Des Forges, 1999, p. 8).

Shortly after the RPF's initial invasion, the rebel group met significant resistance from the Rwandan government army, FAR. The RPF leader, Colonel Fred Rwigyema, was killed on 2 October 1990 and replaced several weeks later by a fellow Tutsi refugee, Paul Kagame, a major in the NRA who was participating in a command training course in Kansas during the invasion (Kuperman, 2004, p. 71). While the RPF pressed forward with its military and increasingly political campaign, anti-Tutsi propaganda was surging not only in Habyarimana's party, but throughout the country. *Kangura* newspaper published statements comparing the 'biological' distinction of Hutu and Tutsi ethnicities to that of gender (Chrétien et al., 1995, cited in Eltringham, 2004, p. 50).[19] One such doctrine was the Hutu 'Ten Commandments', which it printed in December 1990.

> 'The Ten Commandments'
>
> 1. Every Hutu male should know that Tutsi women, wherever they may be, are working in the pay of their Tutsi ethnic group. Consequently, shall be deemed a traitor:
>   – Any Hutu male who marries a Tutsi woman;

19 In March 1993, *Kangura* repeated the supposed 'biological' quality of ethnicity in Rwanda by stating that, '[s]pecialists in human genetics tell us that the small population of Tutsi is due to the fact that they only marry one another … a cockroach cannot give birth to a butterfly. A cockroach gives birth to another cockroach' (Chrétien et al., 1995, p. 155, quoted in Eltringham, 2004, p. 22).

- Any Hutu male who keeps a Tutsi concubine;
- Any Hutu male who makes a Tutsi woman his secretary or protégée.

2. Every Hutu male must know that our Hutu daughters are more dignified and conscientious in their role of woman, wife and mother.

   Are they not pretty, good secretaries and more honest!

3. Hutu woman, be vigilant and bring your husbands, brothers and sons back to their senses.

4. Every Hutu male must know that all Tutsis are dishonest in their business dealings. They are only seeking ethnic supremacy.

   'RIZABARA UWARIRAYE'[20]

   Shall be consequently considered a traitor, any Hutu male:

   - Who enters into a business partnership with Tutsis;
   - Who invests his money or State money in a Tutsi company;
   - Who lends to, or borrows from, a Tutsi;
   - Who grants business favours to Tutsis [granting of import licenses, bank loans, building plots, public tenders...]

5. Strategic positions in the political, administrative, economic, military and security domain should, to a large extent, be entrusted to Hutus.

6. In the Education sector, (pupils, students, teachers) must be in the majority Hutu.

7. The Rwandan Armed Forces should be exclusively Hutu. That is the lesson we learned from the October 1990 war. No soldier must marry a Tutsi woman.

8. Hutus must cease having any pity for the Tutsi.

9. - The Hutu male, wherever he may be, should be united, in solidarity and be concerned about the fate of their Hutu brothers.
   - The Hutus at home and abroad must constantly seek friends and allies for the Hutu Case, beginning with their Bantu brothers.
   - They must constantly be firm and vigilant towards their common Tutsi enemies.

10. The 1959 Social revolution, the 1961 referendum and the Hutu ideology must be taught to Hutus at all levels.

Every Hutu must propagate the present ideology widely.

20 The Kinyarwanda words *Rizabara Uwariraye* loosely translate to, 'The events, mainly bad, that occurred during the night will be narrated by the one who faced them'.

> Any Hutu who persecutes his brother for having read, disseminated and taught this ideology shall be deemed a traitor (pp. 46–7).[21]

The 'Ten Commandments' clearly identified *all Tutsi* as *the enemy* during the four-year civil war. It also served as a rallying call for *all Hutu* to unite against the common foe. The Social Revolution of 1959 and the subsequent referendum are posited as social and political achievements that ought to be protected from the encroaching RPF rebels who were depicted in propaganda as wanting to reestablish a Tutsi regime (Mamdani, 1996, p. 30).

In light of the civil war's growing violence and the pressure from international aid agencies to adopt a multiparty democracy, Habyarimana was left balancing the RPF's demands for a power-sharing agreement and the frustration that was purportedly growing within a Hutu wing of his own party. This 'Hutu Power' faction within the MRND was an extremist power base whose identity developed as an offshoot of the Hutu 'counter-elite' in the run-up to the Social Revolution (Mamdani, 1996, p. 14).[22] Extremism in this context refers to the active propagation of what Des Forges described as the 'determined' slaughter of Tutsi and Hutu opposed to Habyarimana's regime (1999, p. 9). Irrespective of these competing pressures, Habyarimana intensified Arusha Accords negotiations with the RPF in 1992 (Waugh, 2004, p. 54).

As the RPF offensive continued through 1993, Habyarimana signed the Arusha Accords that would provide the rebels with the majority of seats in the interim cabinet and legislature prior to the upcoming elections (Kuperman, 2004, p. 75). The extremist members of Habyarimana's government gave a poor reception to these concessions. The Hutu Power Alliance brought together factions that were prepared to take radical measures to prevent the RPF and its Tutsi allies from controlling the country (ibid., p. 76). They included establishing Radio Télévision Libres des Milles Collines (RTLM), a privately owned radio station that actively encouraged brutality against Tutsi civilians (ibid., p. 77). As the RTLM spread genocide propaganda, the RPF armed and trained local militias of Tutsi civilians to withstand the growing retaliatory violence (ibid., p. 78).[23]

The conflict's retaliatory nature demonstrates the civil war's deterioration into what sociologist Martin Shaw describes as 'degenerate war' (2003, p. 5). It differs from civil war in that it includes systematic attacks against unarmed

21 'The Ten Commandments' were cited in *The Prosecutor v. Ferdinand Nahima, Jean-Bosco Barayagwiza, Hassan Ngeze*, case no. ICTR-99-52-T. In 2003, the International Criminal Tribunal for Rwanda convicted Hassan Ngeze, *Kangura*'s chief editor, of genocide and crimes against humanity, sentencing him to 35 years' imprisonment.

22 The term 'counter-elite' refers to Hutu who challenged the political domination of the Tutsi elite during the Social Revolution (Mamdani, 1996, p. 12).

23 See Chalk (1999) for detailed discussion of the RTLM's role in promoting violence against Tutsi civilians.

civilian groups (ibid.). In the Rwandan context these included retaliatory assaults against Tutsi civilians, one of which, in northern Rwanda, resulted in the deaths of three hundred civilians in January 1993 (Kuperman, 2004, p. 74).[24] On their part, the RPF also launched deliberate assaults against Hutu civilians. On 1 December 1991, the rebel group attacked a camp housing 6,000 internally displaced persons (IDPs) in Rwebare. Nineteen civilians were killed during the onslaught (Africa Watch, 1992, p. 23).[25] The civil war's degenerate quality soon shifted gears towards a much more deadly series of events including the assassination of President Habyarimana (Kuperman, 2004, p. 79).[26]

The 1994 genocide

The plane carrying President Juvénal Habyarimana and Burundian President Cyprien Ntaryamira was shot down by surface-to-air missiles close to Kigali international airport at 8.30pm on 6 April 1994. The two presidents, accompanied by other dignitaries, were returning from peace negotiations in Dar Es Salaam, Tanzania, regarding the implementation of the Arusha Accords. On 28 June 1994, the UN sent a special envoy to investigate the connection between the assassinations and the violence that followed, but did not launch a formal investigation of the missile attack itself, citing a lack of funds as the reason for its failure to commission an inquiry into the deaths (Bruguière, 2006, p. 3). The International Criminal Tribunal for Rwanda (ICTR) also declined to investigate the attack (ibid., p. 4). On 31 August 1997, family members of the French pilot who was also killed filed a complaint to the French Chief of Justice. In October 2006 an order to execute legal process was launched in France (ibid., p. 5).

An investigation led by French Judge Jean-Louis Bruguière was put in place that same year. This report blamed Paul Kagame and the RPF for organising the missile strikes. Bruguière claimed that the RPF wanted to ignite further conflict in order to legitimise its seizure of power (ibid., p. 39). He issued nine international arrest warrants for rebel group members deemed responsible for the attack and requested that President Kagame be tried at the ICTR (ibid.,

24 This attack brought the total of Tutsi civilian deaths to 2,000 from when the invasion began in October 1990 up to January 1993 (Kuperman, 2004, p. 74).

25 See Africa Watch report for details of other alleged RPF attacks against civilians, including the murder of six nurses and patients in a Nyarurema hospital in December 1991 (1992, p. 23).

26 Shaw differentiates between *degenerate war* and *genocide* by arguing that the latter is shaped by the purposeful killing of members of a civilian group or groups because the perpetrators perceive these groups to be *the enemy* rather than supporters of the opposing enemy force. Shaw qualifies that genocide can be understood as an extension of degenerate war (2003, p. 5).

pp. 46–7). The report relied on the testimonies of several former RPF soldiers who had defected, several of whom claimed to hold inside information about the crash, but later retracted their statements. Bruguière's report did not include evidence gathered from the site of the attack or any interviews with the top-ranking RPF officers it accused. President Kagame insisted that the assassinations were ordered and carried out by Hutu extremists who considered Habyarimana too moderate (BBC News, 10 January 2012). Kagame also accused former French President François Mitterand's government of training and arming the Hutu militia members who carried out the attack. The report's release prompted the RPF government to sever diplomatic ties with France in 2006 (*The Guardian*, 10 January 2010).

French Judge Marc Trévidic ordered a second report into the attack with the full cooperation of the RPF government in 2010. It concluded that the missiles were launched from the Kanombe military camp, an area controlled by Rwandan government forces, not the RPF. The report relies on testimony from missile and air accident experts. Although the investigation does not name the assailants, the Rwandan government claims that the report fully exonerates President Kagame and the RPF (BBC News, 10 January 2012). The RPF government agreed to renew diplomatic ties with France in 2009 (Reuters, 29 November 2009).

The downing of the plane killed the Burundian and Rwandan presidents, seven dignitaries and three French crew members, and triggered the 1994 genocide. By 9.18pm on 6 April 1994, roadblocks had been assembled throughout the capital (*The Prosecutor v. Théoneste Bagosora et al.*). That same night, General Roméo Dallaire, the force commander of the UN peacekeeping mission in Rwanda (UNAMIR),[27] ordered an escort to protect Prime Minister Agathe Uwilingiyimana. The ten Belgian peacekeepers who arrived at her residence the next morning were murdered, as was Prime Minister Uwilingiyimana who was also sexually assaulted by her attackers (ibid.). This ambush prompted Belgian officials to evacuate the remaining members of the peacekeeping contingent (Jones, 2006, p. 238). Other Hutu, including opponents to the Habyarimana regime, were killed on 7 April 1994 (*The Prosecutor v. Théoneste Bagosora et al.*).[28] Tutsi civilians whose names had been printed on lists carried by the Interahamwe were also murdered. Two days

27 For background information on UNAMIR see www.un.org/en/peacekeeping/missions/past/unamirFT.htm (accessed 23 March 2015).

28 This reference is taken from the trial case notes of Hutu officials including Théoneste Bagosora at the ICTR. Bagosora was the Ministry of Defence's cabinet director during the 1994 genocide. On 14 December 2011, the ICTR Appeal Chamber confirmed Bagosora's convictions of genocide, crimes against humanity and violations the Geneva Protocol II's Article 3. Bagosora was sentenced to 35 years' imprisonment (Bradfield, 2011).

later, soldiers began to check Tutsi identity cards at checkpoints across the city (ibid.).

On 10 April 1994, the UN sent military observers to Gisenyi near the border between Rwanda and eastern Zaire where tens of thousands of Tutsi had already been massacred. These observers reported their findings to the UN who, along with American, Belgian and French policymakers, were aware that genocide had begun in Rwanda (ibid., 239; Des Forges, 1999, p. 19). The UN forbade UNAMIR soldiers from intervening to prevent the massacres that continued to sweep through the hillside (Jones, 2006, p. 238). Upwards of 45,000 people hiding in and around the parish church in Karama in Butare were killed in under six hours on 20 April 1994 (ibid., p. 239). According to an American military expert, quoted by Alison Des Forges, former senior advisor to the Human Rights Watch Africa Division, had 5,000 international soldiers been deployed in the later weeks of the 1994 genocide, the violence could have been halted (ibid., p. 468).

International dimensions of the 1994 genocide

The UN's failure to send an appropriate number of troops to Rwanda during the 1994 genocide reflects just one of many instances of international inaction during the civil war and 1994 genocide. As early as 1992, evidence emerged that mass violence was about to spread across the country. A speech given by one of Habyarimana's representatives in December of that year incited violence by publicly encouraging Hutu civilians in north-west Rwanda to 'liberate' the area of all Tutsi. This provocation led the Rwandan NGO, Collectif des Ligues et Associations de Défense des Droits de l'Homme au Rwanda (CLADHO), to call for the creation of an international commission to investigate human rights abuses and violations in the country (HRW, 1995, p. 2). The International Commission Investigation on Human Rights Violations in Rwanda included ten international observers from such NGOs as Africa Watch and the Paris-based International Federation of Human Rights. Habyarimana allegedly welcomed the commission's arrival in January 1993. During its three-week stay, the commission collected data from government documents and hundreds of testimonies given by civilians and government officials. Its members also recorded the excavation of two mass graves filled with Tutsi bodies (ibid.).

The UN launched a related investigation following allegations that Rwandan officials had intimidated witnesses who gave evidence to the international commission. Bacre Waly Ndiaye, then Special Rapporteur on Extrajudicial, Summary, or Arbitrary Executions, arrived in Rwanda on 8 April 1993 and spent a week investigating alleged human rights violations (Klinghoffer, 1998, p. 23). Ndiaye claimed to have evidence that members 'at the highest level' of Habyarimana's army, FAR, were actively involved in killing Tutsi civilians (Ndiaye, 11 August 1993, p. 11, as cited by Klinghoffer, p. 23). Ndiaye stated that Tutsi civilians were being killed 'solely because of their membership of a certain ethnic group, and for no other objective reason' (Ndiaye, p. 45, as cited by Klinghoffer, p. 23). Although he did not explicitly use the term 'genocide' to describe the massacres, he did clarify that violating the right to life of Tutsi could fall within Convention on the Prevention and Punishment of Genocide parameters (ibid., p. 24). Ndiaye recommended that the UN take a series of steps in order to prevent further violence, but was 'largely ignored by key actors within the United Nations system' (UN Secretary General, 1999, p. 7).

The letter just cited was sent by former Secretary General Kofi Annan to the president of the Security Council on 16 December 1999. It outlines the 1994 genocide events, as well as UNAMIR's stated mandate, and also summarises the findings of an independent inquiry, launched on 18 March 1999, to look into UN (in)actions during the 1994 genocide. The inquiry identified 18 reasons for the UN's failure to intervene, ranging from weaknesses in UNAMIR's mandate to logistical problems related to the flow of information from the field to the Secretariat. The inquiry also found that Rwanda's membership of the Security Council was problematic, as it had allegedly influenced decisions regarding action during the 1994 genocide (ibid., pp. 30–50). The overriding reasons for the UN's failure to prevent or to end the 1994 genocide were identified as the non-availability of resources and a 'lack of will to take the commitment which would have been necessary to prevent or to stop the genocide' (ibid., p. 30).

International inaction during the 1994 genocide was purportedly rooted in the fact that key Security Council members refused to acknowledge publicly that genocide was taking place in Rwanda. Using the term 'genocide' to describe events in Rwanda would have resulted in an international obligation to intervene (ibid., p. 38).[29] The Clinton administration in the US refused to use the term 'genocide' throughout April, May and June of 1994 (Klinghoffer, 1998, p. 99). It allegedly cited the United States' military interventions in Macedonia and Bosnia as reasons not to intervene in Rwanda. Moreover, the Rwandan crisis followed that of Somalia, during which 18 American soldiers had been brutally killed (ibid., p. 95). On 25 May 1994, President Clinton stated that the US should not intervene, as it did not have a strategic interest in Rwanda (ibid., p. 97).

Former UN Secretary-General Boutros Boutros-Ghali is reported to have said that the Americans were 100 per cent responsible for the 1994 genocide. He allegedly made this statement with regard to the US's repeated attempts to prevent an adequate number of UN troops being deployed to Rwanda (Philpot, 2003, p. 11). Des Forges offered this explanation for the failure of the UN, and in particular the US, to intervene during the 1994 genocide: 'Rwanda

29 See Article 1 of the 1948 Convention on the Prevention and Punishment of the Crime of Genocide and Chapter VII of the 1945 UN Charter.

was simply too remote, too far, too poor, too little, and probably too black to be worthwhile' (Des Forges, 1996, as cited by Jones, 2006, p. 233).

Herman and Peterson posit an alternative interpretation of the United States' efforts to prevent international intervention in Rwanda. They argue that the Clinton administration's actions during this period were guided by an interest in securing the RPF as the government of Rwanda after the 1994 genocide had ended. This interest purportedly related to a quid pro quo agreement between the US and RPF, an arrangement that had significant benefits for both parties as it sought to secure US military presence in Central Africa, increase American influence in former European colonies and garner US access to proxy armies and mineral resources in Zaire. It also gave the RPF freedom to restore a Tutsi minority government, increase its access to weapons and foreign investment, eradicate its enemies, and bolster international prestige (Herman and Peterson, 2010, p. 61).

France played a markedly different role in the violence during the civil war and 1994 genocide in Rwanda, which stemmed primarily from geopolitical interests in the region and the relationship between Habyarimana and Mitterand's government. On 2 October 1990, one day after the RPF launched

Figure 2.1. Placard in Murambi, southern Rwanda, indicating mass graves upon which Opération Turquoise soldiers played volleyball during the final stages of the 1994 genocide (author's photo, 3 February 2009)

its invasion, Habyarimana allegedly telephoned President Mitterand's son Jean-Christophe to seek assistance (Klinghoffer, 1998, p. 16). France provided financial and military support to Habyarimana's MRND during the civil war, including funding used to train the Interahamwe militia, and to purchase weapons from Egypt and South Africa. France also maintained roadblocks and interrogated RPF prisoners (ibid.; Mamdani, 1996, p. 28). Its intervention in Rwandan affairs was allegedly fuelled by the French government's interest in extending its sphere of control over Belgium's former colonies by incorporating Rwanda into its Franco-African community (Klinghoffer, 1998, p. 18).

In mid June 1994, the French authorities launched Opération Turquoise with the stated mandate to establish a humanitarian zone in southwest Rwanda in order to prevent further civilian deaths (Des Forges, 1999, p. 23). The 2,500 Opération Turquoise soldiers saved 15,000 to 17,000 lives during the 1994 genocide. They also permitted and in some cases arranged the evacuation of members of Habyarimana's regime, including his wife Agathe and her family (ibid., p. 24; Klinghoffer, p. 80).

In an interview with *Jeune Afrique* on 5 April 2014, President Kagame accused both France and Belgium of aiding the political preparation of the genocide and the former of participating in the violence. France responded by cancelling its official participation in the event (*Jeune Afrique*, 5 June 2014). President Kagame drew further attention to international action and inaction in his official speech, given on 7 April 2014 at the 20th Commemoration Ceremony at Kigali's Amahoro Stadium,

> The people who planned and carried out the Genocide were Rwandans, but the history and root causes go beyond this country. This is why Rwandans continue to seek the most complete explanation for what happened…
>
> Twenty years is short or long depending on where you stand but there is no justification for false moral equivalence. The passage of time should not obscure the facts, lessen responsibility, or turn victims into villains.
>
> People cannot be bribed or forced into changing their history. And no country is powerful enough, even when they think that they are, to change the facts. After all, les faits sont têtus.[30]

Nearing the end of the genocide

By mid June 1994, the RPF had successfully pushed FAR troops into the country's south-western corner. The genocide officially ended several weeks later on 4 July when the RPF took full control of the capital (Jones, 2006, p. 244).[31] Over 80 per cent of the domestic Tutsi population in Rwanda prior to

30 *Les faits sont têtus* translates to, 'the facts are stubborn'.

31 Other towns, including Butare in southern Rwanda and Ruhengeri in the northwest, were captured within two weeks of the fall of Kigali to the RPF (Anyidoho, 1998, p.

the 1994 genocide had been killed in one hundred days (Kuperman, 2004, p. 79). The genocide was the culmination of a number of different tensions that had bubbled below the surface for many years,[32] the first of which was shaped by the perception of antagonistic identities. The notion that all Tutsi were the enemy, devised many years prior to the 1994 genocide, was broadcast to the masses through anti-Tutsi propaganda in the 1990s. This identity was also fuelled by a second tension related to political control, as Hutu extremists allegedly feared a return to the Tutsi hegemony of the colonial period. The RPF invasion in 1990 created further insecurity during a period of economic decline. International inaction did little to ease this tension or slow the growing conflict. Ultimately, the proliferation of anti-Tutsi violence was devastating, yet it paradoxically resulted in a Tutsi rebel group being installed as political leaders.

The rise of the RPF as a political power

In the words of Timothy Longman, 'In the post-genocide era, Rwanda has made a transition from one type of authoritarian regime to another' (2011a, p. 26). Two overarching forces shaped the immediate post-conflict period: devastation created by the 1994 genocide and political dominance secured and executed by the RPF. The devastation was reflected in a mixture of pressure and constraint on Rwanda's social and economic landscape. These constraints included the near decimation of the country's economy, infrastructure and human capital.[33] On the ground, many of those who remained in Rwanda were affected by trauma, injury and emotional distress. Insecurity abounded during this period as two million Rwandans fled the country in the months following the end of the 1994 genocide (Prunier, 1995, p. 312). Many of these refugees included FAR and Interahamwe members who sought refuge in camps in eastern Zaire (ibid., p. 314). In 1995, Amnesty International (AI) estimated that 25,000 to 30,000 Interahamwe and FAR soldiers regrouped and rearmed during this period with the stated intention to launch attacks on Rwanda (AI, 1995, p. 4). By December 1996, Rwanda faced extreme economic pressure related to the return of over one million refugees from Zaire and Tanzania.

RPF influence in Rwanda

The RPF's seizure of political power took shape amidst growing social and economic difficulties. The rebel invaders turned political leaders established

114). The day the RPF officially ended the genocide, 4 July 1994, is commemorated as 'Liberation Day'.

32 See Fujii (2009) and Straus (2006) for in-depth discussions of why civilians chose to participate in the violence.

33 See Newbury and Baldwin (2000) for detailed discussion of economic pressures and trauma experienced by women during this period.

and displayed their dominance through a series of political and military manoeuvres that on several occasions spilled over the border into neighbouring Zaire. The first major political action took place in the weeks immediately after 4 July 1994. On 19 July the Government of National Unity (GNU) was formed as a coalition government comprising the existing political parties save former President Habyarimana's MRND and the Hutu extremist CDR. Initially, the GNU's composition reflected Arusha Accord terms with regard to power-sharing between the parties involved and the installation of Faustin Twagiramungu as Rwanda's prime minister. The change was short-lived; Twagiramungu resigned and went into exile in August 1995, accusing the RPF of abuses of power, mass human rights violations and discrimination against Hutu and Tutsi survivors (Reyntjens, 2004, p. 180). Interior Minister Seth Sendashonga and Justice Minister Alphonse Nkubito also resigned that August. Sendashonga and many others, including army officers, journalists, diplomats and national football team members, left Rwanda during this period. On departure they accused the RPF of similar transgressions to those Twagiramungu had listed (ibid.). These accusations followed formal changes made by the RPF to the Fundamental Law related to the Arusha Accords, modifications which included establishing an executive presidency and restructuring Parliament, both of which functioned to consolidate RPF power within the GNU (ibid., p. 178). The military also remained under the RPF's political control, as the vast majority of soldiers in the newly formed Rwandan Patriotic Army (RPA) were Tutsi (Vandeginste, 2001, p. 228).

Rwanda received substantial amounts of financial aid from the international community in the years following the 1994 genocide. Many international donors had pulled out of Rwanda early that year before the genocide began, leaving only the Red Cross to manage the humanitarian crisis (Hayman, 2007, p. 9). Canada, Germany and Switzerland implemented reviews of their actions during the genocide and subsequently increased their aid to Rwanda in 1994–5. Belgium, France and Japan also restarted their aid agreements with Rwanda, but continually decreased their donations between 1991 and 2001 (Hayman, 2006, as cited by Hayman, 2007, p. 9). Hayman explains that Belgium and France reduced aid and froze programmes during this period due to concerns about the RPF's management of such issues as democracy, human rights, refugees and justice. Countries that had not previously provided aid to Rwanda, such as Norway, the UK, the Netherlands and Sweden, were allegedly motivated to donate by the magnitude of the tragedy and international community's failure to intervene in 1994 (Hayman, 2007, p. 9). Significant funds began to flow into the wider Great Lakes Region in support of refugees and reconstruction projects (Hayman, 2009, p. 584).

In January 1995, upwards of US$600 million of foreign aid was promised to Rwanda. Filip Reyntjens[34] contends that the aid was offered and accepted without considering the 'rapidly deteriorating human rights situation' in the country at the time (2004, p. 179). This deterioration refers not only to the narrowing of the RPF's power base, but to the harassment and imprisonment of Hutu officials. During this period, the RPA allegedly killed provincial governors, mayors, head teachers and judges thought to be Hutu (ibid., p. 180). Donors' willingness to overlook human rights abuses committed by the RPA shortly after the 1994 genocide may be explained by donor naivety regarding political dynamics in Rwanda. It may also stem from guilt purportedly related to the failure of the UN and individual nation states to intervene in the 1994 genocide (Hayman, 2011, p. 127; Hayman, 2007, p. 19).[35]

Violence escalated during the post-conflict period as the RPA killed civilians during the Kibeho tragedy of April 1995. The Kibeho camp was one of eight camps for IDPs still in operation at that time. The GNU had been negotiating with the UN the closure of these camps. The transitional government accused the camps of sheltering civilians and militia members who had participated in the 1994 genocide. On 17 April 1995, the GNU closed the Kibeho camp leaving 80,000 IDPs trapped inside without adequate shelter, food, or sanitation. Five days later, as civilians attempted to flee the camp, the RPA opened fire. According to a UN Security Council (UNSC) report published two months later, '[a] large number of deaths occurred from firing by government forces, trampling and crushing during the stampede and machete attacks by hard-liners in the camp, who assaulted and intimidated those who wished to leave' (1995, p. 3). Amnesty International estimates that the RPA killed upwards of several thousand IDPs at Kibeho (1996, p. 18).

The GNU publicly justified closing the Kibeho camp as an attempt to prevent future violence by flushing out ex-FAR soldiers and ex-Interahamwe militia members who were hiding among the refugees (ibid.). The perceived threat of violence was also used to legitimise an RPA attack in Zaire during the same period. In October 1996, the RPF received details of a planned attack against Zairian Tutsi by Hutu militants in Zaire. The RPA, in cooperation with Zairian rebels who opposed President Mobutu, launched an invasion with the stated mandate to 'dismantle the camps' (Kagame, as quoted by Pomfret,

34 Filip Reyntjens is a professor of African law and politics at the University of Antwerp. In 1978, during his time as a professor of law at the National University of Rwanda (NUR), he and two councillors from the Ministry of Justice drafted the 1978 Constitution of Rwanda under the presidency of Juvénal Habyarimana (Reyntjens, 1998, p. 1). Reyntjens has since provided expert testimony at the ICTR and accused the RPF of committing crimes against humanity in Rwanda and DRC (ibid., p. 5).

35 Chapter 6 examines the relationship between international donors and the RPF more closely.

1997, p. A01). The attack's second stated objective was to forcibly scatter and repatriate the militia members in order to destabilise their organisational structure. The third goal was to overthrow Sese Seko Mobutu, the Zairian president. The invasion resulted in the return of 500,000 Hutu refugees to Rwanda and the deaths of thousands more, many of whom were unarmed civilians (ibid.; Reyntjens, 2011, p. 135).

RPF influence in Zaire/DRC

The RPA's stated objective to topple Mobutu's regime was realised in 1997 when the Alliance des Forces Démocratiques pour la Libération du Congo (AFDL), the Congolese rebel force supported by the RPA, seized Kinshasa (Lemarchand, 2009, p. 17). Laurent Désiré Kabila, the AFDL leader, became president of the newly renamed Democratic Republic of Congo (DRC).

> There are not many people who thought that Mobutu was very weak. They thought of Mobutu as a big monster who wouldn't be defeated, with his big hat and his big stick. They thought little Rwanda and big Zaire. Only when we started did they look at the map and see the possibilities (Kagame, as quoted by Pomfret, 1997, p. A01).

The RPF's political and military endeavour received financial and tactical support from the Clinton administration (Renton et al., 1997, p. 178).[36] In 1996, the US government sent American soldiers and spies to Rwanda and provided intelligence to the AFDL in eastern Zaire (ibid., p. 179). President Clinton allegedly used the RPA to secure American interests in the region. These interests included undermining the Sudanese government in order to restrict the growth of Islamist militancy in Sudan. The US sought to weaken Islamist power in Sudan by providing military assistance to nearby countries including Eritrea, Ethiopia and Uganda (*Le Monde*, February 1997, as cited by Renton et al., p. 183). Providing support to the Rwandan government was deemed to be an essential element in maintaining stability in Uganda (Renton et al., 2007, p. 183). The other major American interest in the area was securing access to DRC's rich mineral reserves (ibid., p. 181).

The Second Congo War was initiated in part when President Laurent Kabila pushed for the RPA to leave the country. This request was poorly received and violence erupted with leaders in both Kigali and Kampala launching new rebel initiatives in DRC (Stearns and Bordello, 2011, p. 157). The RPA maintained

36 American support for the RPF's incursions in DRC during this period reflects the quid pro quo between the US and Rwanda described by Herman and Peterson. The authors argue that this arrangement ensured Rwandan access to weapons and military support and provided the US with access to rich mineral reserves in Zaire/DRC (2010, p. 61).

its military and political presence in DRC throughout the war.[37] This ongoing warfare formalised strong anti-Tutsi sentiment inside DRC, an anger that was particularly acute in the North and South Kivu provinces, which share a border with Rwanda. Lemarchand argues that this 'visceral hatred of all Tutsi, whether of Rwandan or Congolese origin', by non-Tutsi in DRC was caused by political exclusion, the violence created by occupying forces, and the RPA's economic exploitation (ibid., p. 34).

Both Ugandan and Rwandan forces were heavily involved in plundering minerals throughout the Second Congo War (Renton et al., 2007, p. 194). Rwanda's trade of coltan, mined in DRC in 1999 and 2000, allegedly funded the RPA's entire military intervention during the war (ibid., p. 193). Sénat de Belgique estimates that the revenue the RPA collected from coltan reached US$80–100 million in 2000 (2003, p. 72, as cited by Reyntjens, 2011, p. 139). The RPF justified Rwandan presence in DRC as integral to flushing out Hutu militants who had participated in the 1994 genocide (ibid., p. 196). The RPA officially withdrew from DRC in 2002, but allegedly maintained a clandestine presence in the country until the war ended in 2003 (Reyntjens, 2004, p. 206).

The RPF demonstrated its political and military might in DRC while advancing its political agenda under the guise of the GNU inside Rwanda.[38] One of the earliest objectives was to arrest and jail as many suspected genocide perpetrators as possible. In April 1995, Human Rights Watch (HRW) published a report examining the implications of mass arrests across Rwanda. The NGO estimated that within the first nine months of being established, the GNU jailed upwards of 30,000 suspected perpetrators (HRW, 1995, p. 3). The judicial system had nearly been destroyed by the 1994 genocide and the rate at which these arrests took place only added pressure to the system (ibid., p. 4).

The sweeping arrest of Hutu civilians and the fear it created demonstrated the RPF's domestic political dominance. By the late 1990s, the RPF had established a firm hold on power inside Rwanda and greatly influenced the political landscape in neighbouring DRC. Both of these endeavours were informed by the violence of the past including that which took place during: the 1959 Social Revolution; the 1990 RPF invasion; the civil war; and the 1994 genocide. On many occasions, the movement of refugees away from Rwanda sparked or exacerbated social and political conflicts inside host countries. The RPF was faced with the additional social, political and economic pressure created by the return of refugees from Burundi, Zaire/DRC,

37 See Prunier (2002) and Nabudere (2004) for more detailed discussions of the Second Congo War.

38 Although the RPF governed Rwanda as a part of the coalition GNU, I refer to the government as the RPF during this period to demonstrate the group's political dominance within the GNU.

Tanzania and Uganda. In DRC, the movement of Hutu refugees across its borders after the 1994 genocide had a devastating impact on peace and security in the area. The violence of the 1994 genocide and the RPF's attempts to 'flush out' Hutu militants contributed to the Second Congo War and ongoing conflict in the Kivu provinces. As the Second Congo War raged on, the RPF stated a commitment to promoting 'national reconciliation' inside Rwanda. The National Unity and Reconciliation Programme demonstrated the RPF's response to mass violence, the perceived need for justice and threats to the RPF's political hegemony from inside Rwanda and neighbouring DRC.

Unity and 'national reconciliation' after genocide

The transitional government did not publicly endorse an official reconciliation initiative during the first few years after the 1994 genocide concluded. Government silence on the matter contrasted starkly with UN actions aimed at promoting the creation of a national reconciliation programme in Rwanda. A United Nations Refugee Agency (UNHCR) memorandum from 23–24 June 1995 stated that:

> Owing to the sheer magnitude of the tragedy and the extent of violence and atrocities during the conflict, Rwanda highlights more than any other crisis that achieving credibility of the government and national reconciliation are key for all other reconstruction activities, including the return of refugees and internally displaced persons (p. 12).

The desire to create an official national reconciliation programme inside Rwanda lagged behind that expressed at the international level for several reasons. Prioritising justice resulted in the pursuit of a largely retributive approach in the post-conflict period as demonstrated by the mass arrest of predominantly Hutu citizens suspected of crimes related to the 1994 genocide. This endeavour swept through the capital and hillside and led to the arrest of more than 120,000 suspects between 1994 and 2000 (Uvin, 2000, p. 3).

The GNU's reluctance to pursue an official reconciliation programme was also due in part to increasing pressure from survivor groups. Reyntjens and Vandeginste contend that survivor advocacy groups equated the promotion of reconciliation between survivors and perpetrators with unpalatable outcomes of forgiveness, amnesty and impunity. The influence of these organisations on government policy began to wane towards the end of the 1990s (Reyntjens and Vandeginste, 2005, p. 102). However, tension mounted between the government and several of these organisations in 1999 when the GNU released 3,365 prisoners against whom little or no evidence was available (*Le Verdict*, July 1999, as cited by Reyntjens and Vandeginste, 2005, p. 102).

As discussed in the previous chapter, the GNU understood national reconciliation to be synonymous with power-sharing and Hutu majority rule. By 1999, the organisation of a powerful Hutu opposition was perceived as no longer posing a credible threat to the government. Banning political parties and the fact that opposition leaders had emigrated to avoid incarceration reduced this threat. The risk of attack from Hutu military groups in eastern DRC had been diminished by the RPF invasion across the border in August 1998 (Reyntjens and Vandeginste, 2005, p. 102). Both events created what Reyntjens and Vandeginste call a 'comfortable' environment for the transitional government to pursue a policy of national reconciliation (ibid., p. 103).

Earlier in this post-conflict period, the GNU reached out to the UN for support in creating an international criminal tribunal to prosecute individuals suspected of having organised or committed crimes of genocide. This request was informed by the devastation of Rwanda's domestic legal system following the deaths and exile of many lawyers and judges during the 1994 genocide as well as the destruction of related infrastructure (Sosnov, 2008, p. 128). Security Council Resolution 995 established the ICTR on 8 November 1994:

> The International Criminal Tribunal for Rwanda shall have the power to prosecute persons responsible for serious violations of international humanitarian law committed in the territory of Rwanda and Rwandan citizens responsible for such violations committed in the territory of neighbouring States, between 1 January 1994 and 31 December 1994, in accordance with the provisions of the present Statute (UNSC, 1994, p. 3).

Two overarching interests purportedly shaped resolution 955: halting and addressing violations that threaten international peace and security, and promoting peace and reconciliation in Rwanda (Des Forges and Longman, 2004, p. 3).

After seeking help from the UN, Rwanda was the only UNSC member to vote against the tribunal's formation (Sosnov, 2008, p. 129; Dubois, 1997, p. 1). The GNU objected to the ICTR for several reasons including the ICTR's focus on crimes committed in 1994. The government denounced this narrow time frame as it precluded convictions related to earlier massacres and it failed to take account of the planning period before the 1994 genocide (Dubois, 1997, p. 1). The government also took issue with the shared Appeals Chamber and Prosecutor at the ICTR and the International Criminal Tribunal for the former Yugoslavia (ICTY). Other objections included the nomination of judges for the tribunal by countries that had supported Habyarimana's regime during the 1994 genocide and the incarceration of convicted perpetrators outside Rwanda (ibid., p. 2). The government also objected to the non-existence of capital punishment. This omission created a major discrepancy between maximum levels of punishment in domestic courts and the ICTR, as perpetrators found guilty of lesser crimes in Rwanda could be given the death sentence.[39] Lastly,

39 Capital punishment was abolished in Rwanda in 2007, although the final death sentence was imposed in 2003. The use of capital punishment prevented the

the GNU opposed the tribunal's location in Arusha Tanzania, insisting that it ought to operate inside Rwanda (ibid.). The ICTR's location was decided by the UNSC 'with regard to considerations of justice and fairness', as stated in resolution 955, indicating the Security Council's perception of due process in Rwanda (UNSC, 1994, p. 2).

Because this book focuses on the National Unity and Reconciliation Programme in Rwanda, it does not engage deeply with the ICTR's work as the tribunal operates outside Rwanda and includes a stated mandate devised by the UN, not the RPF. The four pillars of global legal order shape this mandate: international human rights law; international humanitarian law; international criminal law; and international refugee law (Scharf, 2008, p. 1). Chapter VII of the 1945 UN Charter also guides it: 'Action with respect to threats to peace, breaches of the peace, and acts of aggression'. Its Article 42 could have been, but was not applied during the 1994 genocide. It sanctions the use of demonstrations, blockades and military action by forces of UN member countries to restore international peace and security. The ICTR's mandate was purportedly also informed by the assumption that justice is an essential element for the maintenance of peace. According to this understanding, peace could not be restored after the 1994 genocide without international intervention, as Rwanda did not have the institutional capacity to prosecute crimes related to the genocide.

UN Security Council Resolution 995 includes an objective to 'contribute to the process of national reconciliation and the restoration and maintenance of peace in Rwanda' (1994, p. 1). The ICTR is not discussed, however, in major government policies or documents, nor does it feature in official reconciliation discourse inside Rwanda. Of particular relevance, however, are the RPF government's successful attempts to block former Chief Prosecutor Carla Del Ponte's investigation of crimes allegedly perpetrated by the RPF against Hutu civilians in 1994 (Peskin, 2008). The ICTR has yet to indict any RPF members for crimes committed in 1994 (ibid. p. 225).

Despite the government's stated objections to the ICTR, justice remained a major priority in the first years after the 1994 genocide. The GNU began to pursue justice at the domestic level in the mid 1990s through the Military Tribunal of Rwanda and later through restoring community-level gacaca courts.[40] The Military Tribunal was mandated to try cases of genocide and crimes against humanity committed by military personnel between 1 October

extradition of genocide perpetrators living abroad and on trial at the ICTR to Rwanda (see AI, 2 August 2007).

40 Gacaca was a historical conflict resolution mechanism purportedly used in the pre-colonial era to resolve disputes related to land and relationships. It was restored in the post-conflict period to try cases of genocide and crimes against humanity. The reinvention of gacaca and the courts' mandate to promote reconciliation will be discussed in detail in the next chapter.

1990 and 31 December 1994 (Sosnov, 2008, p. 133). Members of the RPF were retroactively considered to be members of a military organisation, yet only 20 cases of 'vengeance killings' by RPF soldiers were tried between 1994 and 2002 (Strain and Keyes, 2003, as cited by Sosnov, 2008, p. 133). This number pales in comparison with the reported killings of 25,000 to 45,000 Hutu civilians by RPF rebels as described in the Gersony Report (Des Forges, 1999, p. 18).[41]

Gacaca courts reflected the GNU's pursuit of justice on a much larger scale. Like the Military Tribunal, gacaca was mandated to try cases of genocide and crimes against humanity committed inside Rwanda between 1 October 1990 and 31 December 1994. Gacaca was designed to speed up the trials of the 120,000 suspects initially arrested after the genocide but would eventually hear more than 1.2 million cases by 2010 (Bikesha interview, 20 July 2010).[42] Gacaca received significant funding from international donors including Belgium, Switzerland, the UK and Sweden. Oomen states that the vast majority of international donors provided some level of support to the gacaca process by 2002 (2005a, p. 902).

The influence of international donors and foreign investors is also reflected in the government's creation of the National Unity and Reconciliation Commission (NURC) in 1999. Reyntjens and Vandeginste contend that the NURC was established to please donors and funding agencies (2005, p. 103). Oomen argues that the GNU settled for a 'watered-down' NURC to prevent the creation of an independent reconciliation commission with the power to grant amnesty (2005a, p. 897). The 'watered-down' nature of the commission refers to its lack of legal power and its mandate to advise the government, conduct research and educate the population about unity and 'national reconciliation'.[43]

The commission's stated mandate to promote 'national reconciliation' features heavily in pertinent government documents including the 2003 Constitution and the 2007 Reconciliation Policy. Since its inception in 1999, the NURC has been charged with the task of promoting unity and 'national

41 The Gersony Report describes the United Nations Refugee Agency (UNHCR) mission led by Robert Gersony to investigate ways of speeding up refugee repatriation after the 1994 genocide. The team gathered data about RPF/RPA-led attacks against civilians in Rwanda. Gersony estimated that the RPF had killed between 25,000 and 45,000 civilians between April and the end of August 1994. The UN directed him to never discuss the report or share the data, an order he has largely followed (Des Forges, 1999).

42 Klaas de Jonge clarifies that this estimate does not necessarily reflect the true number of genocide perpetrators in Rwanda as individual defendants could appear in multiple cases. He also explains that over 50% of these cases were related to crimes against property (2010, p. 3).

43 See Article 178 of the 2003 Constitution of the Republic of Rwanda for a full list of the NURC's responsibilities.

reconciliation' and ridding Rwanda of the effects of past 'bad governance' (NURC, 2006, p. 277).

> Against the past of Rwanda, characterized by a type of governance based on criminality, political uniqueness (divisionism, extremism, nepotism, and paternalism) and genocide ideology, the NURC has been assigned to overcome all the barriers and face the unimaginable challenges to wash all the past dirtiness down and to re-invent a 'new social intelligence' through which the people of Rwanda supported by his development partners proceeded to a fundamental change and rebuilt a holistically unified, pacified, hatred-free [country], and committed to forge hand-in-hand a new country armed with a new mind-set and values (ibid.).

The NURC's efforts to wipe away 'past dirtiness' created by 'divisionism' and 'genocide ideology' are supported by several criminal statutes (ibid.). These laws include the 2001 Law on Prevention, Suppression and Punishment of the Crime of Discrimination and Sectarianism. Civilians found guilty of 'sectarianism' face prison sentences of three months to two years and/or fines between 50,000 and 300,000 Rwandan francs (RwF).[44] Current and former government officials, members of political parties and domestic NGOs face much harsher sentences if found guilty. Punishment includes sentences of one to five years in jail and fines between 500,000 and two million RwF (Parliament, 2001, Art. 5).[45] Consequently, any actions perceived to divide the population or promote genocide in some way may be seen as crimes of 'sectarianism' or 'divisionism', and can be harshly punished.

Conclusion

Periods of mass violence in Rwanda have been shaped by outpourings of refugees, economic pressure and political tensions. The pre-colonial era may not have forged wholly antagonistic relationships between Hutu and Tutsi citizens, but it did lay the foundation for an increasingly stratified political and economic system. Colonial rulers played a significant role in manipulating what they presumed to be a 'natural' social order. The exclusion of Hutu civilians from political power had devastating consequences for the Tutsi population in the late 1950s and early 1960s. Violence against Tutsi was legitimised as an attempt to escape the highly inequitable monarchist system of the past.

As independence arrived, it was the Tutsi population who would soon be excluded from political control. This exclusion did not pertain solely to

44 As of May 2015, 50,000 Rwandan Francs (RwF) is roughly equivalent to £45 and 300,000 RwF is approximately £271. See XE Currency Exchange, www.xe.com (accessed 18 May 2015).

45 As of May 2015, 500,000 RwFs is equivalent to £455. Two million RwF is roughly equivalent to £1,820. See ibid.

Rwanda; Tutsi refugees in Uganda who had fled the violence of the Social Revolution faced violent expulsions. Prejudice against Rwandan Tutsi refugees purportedly encouraged the creation of the RPF and motivated the group's invasion of Rwanda in 1990. The RPF's attempt to seize political control from Habyarimana resulted in a 'degenerate' civil war that led to the deaths of thousands of Hutu and Tutsi civilians. The RPF's advances fuelled anti-Tutsi propaganda that spurred many Hutu civilians to commit genocide against Tutsi civilians. The RPF's political and military maneuvers ended the 1994 genocide, facilitated the group's transition from rebel invaders to political leaders and supported the toppling of Mobutu's regime in Zaire.

The RPF's political interests informed not only the October 1990 invasion, but also the group's rise to power in the post-conflict period. Since the 1994 genocide ended, the RPF has maintained political control of the country. As such, it is responsible for rebuilding a nation decimated by genocide. Achieving this was complicated by the mass exodus and repatriation of refugees, social and economic upheaval, and continued violence inside and outside of Rwanda's borders. At first, the government ignored the international community's calls for a formal reconciliation process, but it did eventually establish the National Unity and Reconciliation Programme. As the next chapter will show, the first major theme to emerge from this programme was the pursuit of justice on a massive scale.

Chapter 3

Gacaca: justice and reconciliation at the community genocide courts

Only justice delivered in Rwanda, mainly by Rwandans, according to Rwandan and universal principles, can genuinely contribute to peace, healing and reconciliation (Kagame, 2008, p. xxv).

Two years after the 1994 genocide ended the GNU faced pressure from donors, diplomats and other international community representatives to publish the Organic Law of 30 August 1996. This law relates to the 'organization of prosecutions for offences constituting the crimes of genocide or crimes against humanity since 1 October 1990' (Vandeginste, 1998, p. 2).[1] In addition to defining the parameters of acts of genocide and crimes against humanity, the law codifies the GNU's stated commitment to eradicating impunity in order to promote justice and 'national reconciliation' across the country (TNA, 1996, p. 18). The pursuit of justice was demonstrated by the arrests of more than 120,000 genocide suspects between 1994 and 2000 (Waldorf, 2007, p. 425). By late 1998, the GNU, under Pasteur Bizimungu's presidency, was considering creating what political scientist Peter Uvin later described as an 'unprecedented legal-social experiment' (Uvin, 2000, p. 3).[2] This experiment would involve applying a traditional process of conflict resolution to the criminal trials of those accused of acts of genocide and crimes against humanity (ibid.).

1 This law defines acts of genocide and crimes against humanity according to the Convention on the Prevention and Punishment of the Crime of Genocide of 9 December 1948. It is limited to crimes committed inside Rwanda between 1 October 1990 and 31 December 1994.

2 Pasteur Bizimungu was Rwanda's president, 19 July 1994–23 March 2000. He allegedly resigned 'for personal reasons' but was accused of crimes including tax fraud and preventing parliamentary inquiries into corruption (Reyntjens, 2004, p. 181). Bizimungu, who was publicly critical of the RPF, was arrested in 2001 and sentenced to 15 years in prison. He was released in 2007 following a pardon from President Kagame (Reuters, 6 April 2007). Bizimungu's resignation came shortly after that of Joseph Sebarenzi, the Speaker of the National Assembly and Prime Minister Pierre-Célestin Rwigema. Sebarenzi and Rwigema both fled Rwanda and settled in North America (Reyntjens, 2004, p. 181).

This approach was informed by a dual interest in increasing popular participation in the judicial system and advancing the rate at which cases could be heard and processed (Uvin, 2000, p. 3; Waldorf, 2007, p. 427).[3] The GNU proposed to meet these goals by means of the traditional process called gacaca, a form of mediation during which male elders or heads of households passed judgment on disputes related to land, property and marital relationships. This system takes its name from the grass on which its procedures most commonly took place (Clark, 2010a, p. 52). According to Clark, by the turn of the 20th century, gacaca was the primary means through which 'uncomplicated cases' of inheritance, marriage and livestock disputes were resolved and social order was maintained across the country (ibid., p. 341).[4]

The uncomplicated nature of conflicts resolved at gacaca was a far cry from the responsibilities bestowed upon the system in 2001. The GNU passed a law in January of that year formally establishing gacaca as a criminal court through which cases of genocide and crimes against humanity would be tried (TNA, 2001, p. 1).[5] The retooled gacaca model was shaped by multiple stated objectives including: revealing the truth about 1994 genocide events; speeding along genocide trials; eradicating impunity; promoting unity and reconciliation; and proving that Rwandans can solve their own problems (NSGJ, n.d.(b), p. 1). It was also guided by high expectations from the NURC, 'When every Rwandan, wherever he/she is at any time, will have understood his/her role to play in this process, there is no doubt unity and reconciliation will be achieved. Conflict between Rwandan people, suspicion, divisions, hatred and woes that befell and destroyed this country will have been defeated and Rwandan people will live in prosperity forever' (2001, p. 23). These objectives and expectations reflect the two overarching themes of the GNU's responses to crimes related to the 1994 genocide: maximal justice[6] and reconciliation. As such, this chapter seeks

3 National courts were also trying cases related to genocide and crimes against humanity during this period. They were deemed to be too slow and ineffectual, as only an estimated 9,000 cases were tried between 1996 and 2003 (Waldorf, 2007, p. 425).

4 Waldorf takes a more critical view of traditional gacaca. He draws attention to the dominance of male elders in the gacaca system, as women were not permitted to speak during sessions. Moreover, he contends that gacaca did not hear cases of crimes such as cattle theft. He clarifies that gacaca courts commonly meted out collective punishment as members of the accused's family or clan were commonly obligated to provide reparations to the victim (2010, p. 186).

5 The full title of the law is 'Organic Law no. 40/2000 of 26/01/2001 setting up gacaca jurisdictions and organizing prosecutions for offences constituting the crime of genocide or crimes against humanity committed between October 1, 1990 and December 31, 1994' (TNA, 2001, p. 1).

6 Newbury and Baldwin use the term 'maximal justice' in conjunction with repression to describe the RPF's approach to governance in the post-conflict context (2000, p. 243). My use of the term refers only to gacaca and thus more closely reflects

to compare primary and secondary data about practice at gacaca with state discourse about justice and 'national reconciliation'.

Clark raises this issue when he asks, '[t]o what degree then should Rwanda pursue reconciliation and what degree of reconciliation is possible through gacaca?' (2010a, p. 334). Clark points to the importance of evaluating the concept as the rebuilding of interconnected relationships. This understanding resembles arguments made by other authors including Lederach (1997), Daly and Sarkin (1997) and Villa-Vicencio (2005), who analyse what they deem to be the positive correlation between rebuilding relationships and promoting interpersonal reconciliation. Clark's example is more specific, however, as it refers to reconciliation as rebuilding interconnected relationships between differing groups of people at the 'individual-to-individual' level, 'individual-to-group' level and 'group-to-group' level (2010a, p. 338).

In the post-conflict Rwandan context, 'rebuilding relationships' refers to the restoration of social connections that were damaged or destroyed by the 1994 genocide. Also referred to as 'social cohesion' in government documents, these pre-genocide social relationships were purportedly built upon trust, cooperation and friendship.

> Rwanda is gradually making progress on the road to reconciliation reflected in general high trust in Government action and good marks for newly decentralized political structures. However, it is also struggling to overcome widespread interpersonal distrust and continuing divisions between genocide survivors and those accused of or convicted for crimes of genocide.
>
> Division and exclusion rather than cohesion marked Rwandan society from independence up to the genocide in 1994. Enormous efforts have been undertaken to bridge the deep rifts in society and heal the wounds inflicted by the genocide (NURC, 2008a, p. 1).

Interviews with government officials and NURC documentation have revealed the two broad categories of relationships in need of rebuilding. This process is referred to as 'horizontal' and 'vertical' reconciliation (Bakusi interview, 23 July 2010; NURC, 2010).[7] The former is described as a 'common level

Clark's reference to 'comprehensive justice' or Jones' use of 'maximal accountability' to describe the government's attempts to prosecute all civilians suspected of acts of genocide and crimes against humanity (Clark and Waldorf debate, 3 March 2010, Oxford; Jones, 2010, p. 52).

7 The 'Rwanda reconciliation barometer' was published in October 2010 by the NURC with support from the Department for International Development and the UN Development Programme. It is a national public opinion survey that measures progress towards 'national reconciliation' (2010, p. 23) and uses a mixture of quantitative and qualitative methods to question public opinion on six main topics: human security; political culture and governance; crosscutting relations; historical confrontation; social cohesion; and integration (ibid., p. 31).

of reconciliation' that focuses on rebuilding connections between citizens (Bakusi interview, 23 July 2010). Alphonse Bakusi, then the director of the NURC's Civic Education Department, used the example of rebuilding former relationships between survivors and those who killed their families to describe the government's conception of 'horizontal' reconciliation (ibid.). Other examples could include those between former perpetrators serving sentences in community service camps[8] and survivors living in the surrounding area. This vision is shaped by the assumption that, 'if trust increases between Rwandan citizens, and particularly those on different sides of the genocide, reconciliation is more likely to occur' (NURC, 2010, p. 11). The three relationship levels Clark identifies most closely resemble those the RPF call 'horizontal' relations (2010a).

The RPF's conception of 'vertical' reconciliation refers to the relationship between citizens and the government with particular emphasis on building trust in institutions (ibid.). This association reflects the assumption that if 'citizens view political structures, institutions, values and leadership as legitimate and effective, reconciliation is more likely to occur' (ibid., p. 36). In the context of gacaca, 'vertical' reconciliation includes building trust in the justice system as well as rebuilding the relationship between civilians and the government that restored and monitored court proceedings.

Gacaca in the post-conflict period

Organisation and implementation

A nationwide data collection programme commenced in 2002 during which judges heard testimonies and began compiling potential cases to be tried at gacaca. This process reflected elements of the middle range of Crocker's reconciliation spectrum as it prioritised dialogue between individuals about their experiences of the 1994 genocide as well as their input into how the justice process should proceed (2000, p. 108). Between January and April 2005, a new local administration structure began to help judges collect data at the *inyumbi* level, which was later validated according to testimonies given in the *cells* (Bikesha interview, 9 June 2009).[9] Trials officially started later that year. Two hundred thousand judges, of whom there were nine per bench, heard cases in 100,000 local areas across Rwanda (Waldorf, 2007, p. 422).[10] These judges,

8 These camps are referred to as Travail d'Intérêt Général (TIG). Individuals serving sentences at these camps are called 'tigistes'.

9 Inyumbi level refers to groups of ten houses, whereas cells comprise groups of at least two hundred adults per area.

10 Waldorf contends that the information-gathering phase led to an 'avalanche of accusations' amounting to over one million cases, 450,000 of which included accusations of violent crimes (2010, p. 189).

referred to as *inyangamugayo*, represented a more diverse cross-section of the population than those who had resolved disputes during traditional hearings prior to and during the pre-colonial period.[11] For instance, upwards of one third of inyangamugayo at modern gacaca were women, starkly contrasting with the male dominance of traditional cases (Waldorf, 2010, p. 188). In the post-conflict period, local communities elected inyangamugayo according to their perceived level of integrity. These positions were relatively exclusive as they were restricted to those who were thought to hold no bias or political affiliations and had not participated in the 1994 genocide (Parliament, 2006, p. 4).

Cases heard by modern inyangamugayo were divided into four categories that referred to classifications of acts of genocide and crimes against humanity. These classifications were later reduced to three in the revised version of Organic Law in 2008 to include: 'masterminds' of the genocide who planned and/or supervised acts of genocide and crimes against humanity but did not necessarily commit acts of murder;[12] government officials, religious leaders or military personnel who perpetrated acts of genocide or crimes against humanity or encouraged other to do so; and persons who committed acts of rape or sexual torture in Category 1. Category 2 includes: well-known murderers who used excessive cruelty; persons who carried out acts of torture regardless of whether the act ended in the victim's death; persons who perpetrated acts that 'dehumanised' victims' bodies; persons who killed without the intention

11 The term 'traditional gacaca' refers to hearings that took place prior to the arrival of German colonists in the late 19th century. This distinction is important as later gacaca hearings reflected the colonial period's ethnically stratified political system, as Belgian leaders gave local Tutsi administrators control over judge selection. Hearings also began to take place at regular intervals rather than as they were needed (Karekezi, 2001, p. 32, as cited by Clark, 2010a). See Karekezi (2001)for further details about the historical development of gacaca.

12 As Oomen states, there is significant overlap between the mandates of gacaca and the ICTR to prosecute cases of genocide and crimes against humanity, described as Category 1 above. These mandates differ, however, with regard to timeframe as the ICTR prosecutes crimes committed in 1994, while gacaca prosecuted those perpetrated between 1990–4. The ICTR may also prosecute persons accused of the aforementioned crimes in Rwanda's neighbouring states, whereas gacaca may only try cases allegedly committed inside Rwanda. Oomen outlines the notion of 'complementarity' with regard to the overlap of these mandates. Complementarity, as used in the Rome Statute, defines the jurisdiction of international tribunals over cases that domestic courts are unable or unwilling to investigate or prosecute (2005b, p. 2). A state may be deemed 'unwilling' to prosecute a case if the proceedings are being carried out in order to shield the person of interest from prosecution; there is significant delay in the proceedings with the intention to prevent prosecution; or the proceedings are not or will not be carried out independently or impartially (ICC Statute, as cited by Williamson, 2006, p. 117).

Figure 3.1. Spectators listen to testimonies given by defendants at gacaca in Burema, Kigali Province, Rwanda (author's photo, 5 May 2009)

to commit murder; and those who attempted to kill, but did not succeed. Category 3 includes persons who carried out crimes against property. Category 1 and 2 cases could also be heard in domestic courts and the Military Tribunal, but were most commonly tried at gacaca (Parliament, 2008a, pp. 18–21).

Attendance at gacaca cases was mandatory for all community members living in the hearings' catchment areas. Mass participation was crucial in the first few years of gacaca as witnesses provided the only evidence available to the court. As the 1994 genocide was widespread and left virtually no forensic evidence, gacaca relied on community members telling the court 'what they saw, what they heard, and what they did' (victim interview, 3 May 2009). Judges were apparently able to identify false testimonies through comparison with the detailed records compiled during the data collection period. It was also possible for community members and other spectators to question the accuracy of statements given during the trials, leading to charges of false testimony against the witnesses. Community members were encouraged to pose questions to defendants and victims directly. In this context, 'gacaca doesn't depend on the smartness of lawyers', as spectators often played the roles of both prosecutors and defence lawyers (Bikesha interview, 9 June 2009; Parliament, 2008a, p. 8).[13]

13 Although lawyers were permitted at gacaca, they were rarely present due to cost and availability (Bikesha interview, 9 June 2009). Gacaca has been criticised for

The direct communication between defendants and survivors within the court setting had the potential to yield more than testimonies and corroboration. There was a significant emphasis on confession, apology and forgiveness within the gacaca system. In fact, pleading guilty, confessing, apologising and repenting in front of the Bench of the Gacaca Court, the Judicial Officer, or the Public Prosecution Officer in charge of the case prior to the court hearing could have resulted in a reduced sentence (Parliament, 2007, p. 7). For instance, if successful, defendants charged with Category 2 crimes would spend a third of their sentence in jail; half of their full term would be spent in a community service camp or TIG and a sixth of the sentence would be suspended (ibid.).[14]

Victims, perpetrators and community members attending trials were not the only stakeholders in the gacaca process. International donors began to provide a significant amount of support to the development and day-to-day operation of the courts as early as 2002 (Oomen, 2005a, p. 902). Gacaca received technical and financial assistance from governmental and non-governmental organisations, such as Belgian Technical Cooperation, and multilateral groups including the EU, UNDP and UNICEF. Gacaca also received donor support from America, Canada, the UK, France and Japan among many others (ibid., p. 898). International benefactors assisted more than one hundred projects related to the promotion of justice in Rwanda. This included: the provision of fuel and vehicles; training of lawyers, judges and police; supplementing judges' salaries; and constructing prisons and libraries (Uvin, 2000, p. 2). Oomen argues that while international donors provided financing to other judicial bodies trying cases related to the 1994 genocide, including the ICTR and Rwanda's domestic courts, they were particularly supportive of gacaca (2005a, pp. 895, 898). This may have been due to gacaca's use of participatory justice, which reflected an international interest in democratisation, decentralisation and 'alternative systems of justice' during this period (ibid., p. 903).

Themes of maximal justice and reconciliation

Gacaca was funded in part by international donors, yet it remained a state-sponsored apparatus under the Rwandan government's guidance throughout its development and operation, until its official closure on 18 June 2012.

> The Gacaca Courts system will allow the population of the same Cell, the same Sector to work together in order to judge those who have participated in the genocide, identify the victims and rehabilitate the innocents. The Gacaca Courts system will thus become the basis of

numerous violations of due process including the absence of legal representation at trials (see HRW, 2011a).

14 A suspended sentence allowed the convicted perpetrator to live at home with the obligation to meet periodically with the National Service of Gacaca Jurisdictions (NSGJ) prosecution department.

> collaboration and unity, mainly because when the truth will be known, there will be no more suspicion, the author will be punished, justice will be done to the victim and to the innocent prisoner who will be reintegrated in the Rwandan society (NSGJ, n.d.(b), p. 1).

This quotation illustrates two overarching themes that informed the government's conception of gacaca in the post-conflict context: maximal justice and reconciliation. The former refers to the government's attempt to try the cases of everyone suspected of participation in the 1994 genocide, including those who committed crimes against property (Parliament, 2008a, p. 21). The inclusion of gacaca in the government's approach to 'national reconciliation' contrasts starkly with the amnesty process at the South African Truth and Reconciliation Commission (TRC) during which individual applicants could apply for and be granted amnesty (Wilson, 2001, p. 23).[15]

The pursuit of maximal justice at gacaca was informed not only by the high levels of public participation in crimes of genocide, but also by the government's stated commitment to eradicating impunity in Rwanda. Jones refers to the GNU's rejection of a blanket amnesty in 1995 as an attempt to dismantle the 'entrenched and institutionalized culture of impunity' (2010, p. 51).[16] Moreover, the speed at which gacaca processed cases and the individualised punishments the inyangamugayo meted out added to the gacaca system's retributive nature.

The theme of reconciliation refers to the government's stated commitment to promoting collaboration, truth, rehabilitation and community participation at gacaca, which had both pragmatic and social implications. As previously discussed, community members and witnesses were required to provide evidence and question the accuracy of testimonies at gacaca. This interaction created a forum in which survivors and perpetrators engaged directly with each other, a condition Kiss identifies as central to restorative justice (2000, p. 79). Moreover, this dialogue resulted in a process that included the acknowledgement of past transgressions during the data collection phase (Sarkin, 2001, p. 147). These acknowledgements at gacaca commonly came in the form of confession or repentance. In the broad body of literature, confession and repentance are commonly related to forgiveness, which multiple authors including

15 In the context of amnesty application at the TRC, applicants were obliged to disclose the details of their actions, prove that the violation in question had been informed by a political objective, and that it took place within a particular timeframe (Wilson, 2001, p. 23).

16 Jones refers to an international conference, convened by President Bizimungu in November 1995, during which the option of a blanket amnesty was formally dismissed (Government, 1995, p. 16, as cited by Jones, 2010, p. 51). A specialised chamber for the prosecution of suspected genocide perpetrators was chosen in its place (2010, p. 52).

Villa-Vicencio (2005) and Worthington Jr. (2006) argue is supportive of reconciliation, but not a prerequisite for its taking place.[17]

'Vertical' reconciliation

Individuals and the government

In its broadest form, the relationship between the government and individual Rwandans in the context of modern gacaca was informed by the Rwandan government's role as *reinventors* of the gacaca system.[18] The transition from its 'semi-official and neo-traditional' use after independence in 1962, was instigated, monitored and guided by the government (Reyntjens, 1990, as cited by Waldorf, 2010, p. 186).[19] The state-guided implementation of gacaca was explained to the population through a nationwide Sensitisation Programme. According to Dennis Bikesha, former director of training, mobilisation and sensitisation at gacaca, the system needed to be explained because, 'most Rwandans didn't support it or understand it' (interview, 9 June 2009). The public scepticism alluded to in this quotation is antithetical to the government's emphasis of gacaca's 'home-grown' appeal.[20] A nationwide survey about social cohesion, led by the NURC with funding from the United States Agency for International Development (USAID), found public perception of gacaca between 2005 and 2007 to be mixed. The results showed that, although many survivors were hopeful that gacaca would bring closure, justice and peace, both survivors and prisoners remained concerned about the accuracy and credibility of the process. Moreover, survivors, prisoners, judges and witnesses expressed fears of reprisal related to their participation at gacaca (NURC, 2008b, p. 6).

Purportedly, President Kagame and his 'inner circle' were also sceptical of the gacaca system prior to its adoption (Clark, 2010b, p. 2). Clark claims that Kagame opposed the use of gacaca to try cases of genocide and crimes against humanity fearing that it would mete out sentences too lenient for genocide perpetrators. Clark explains that the courts were established in 2001 following significant pressure from other officials within the RPF, who allegedly highlighted the gacaca system's benefits with reference to collecting

17 Villa-Vicencio describes reconciliation as a political process that includes reparations, acknowledgement and time for mourning (2005). Worthington Jr. conceives it as the process of rebuilding relationships damaged by conflict. He stipulates that although forgiveness may make reconciliation between individuals easier to achieve, it is not a necessary component (2006).

18 Waldorf refers to modern gacaca as a '(re)invented tradition' that shares nothing beyond its name with the traditional conflict resolution mechanism (2010, p. 189).

19 Reyntjens describes the use of gacaca by local authorities shortly after independence as an extra-legal resource for resolving conflicts (1990, as cited by Waldorf, 2010, p. 186).

20 See President Kagame's 'Preface' in Clark and Kaufman (eds.) (2008).

information about the 1994 genocide events and the pursuit of reconciliation (ibid.).

The Sensitisation Programme also focused on bolstering popular participation at gacaca (Bikesha interview, 9 June 2009). The opportunity to participate in administering justice, integral to the promotion of 'truth-telling' and 'truth-hearing', as described by Clark (2010a), was thrust upon the population by the government (African Rights, 2003, p. 2). As we have seen, community members' participation at gacaca was shaped by both theoretical and practical imperatives. At the theoretical level it was guided by the assumption that the gacaca process would uncover the truth, and that truth promotes justice. From a more pragmatic perspective, participation at gacaca formed the primary method for gathering data, corroborating and contradicting testimonies. This participation was often coerced, however, as witnesses risked jail time if they failed to appear in court, or if the inyangamugayo found their testimonies to be false or incomplete (gacaca trial, Butare, 13 May 2009). In May 2009, the inyangamugayo threatened a witness at the trial of 15 suspected perpetrators of Category 1 crimes with six months' jail time following several accusations from spectators that she was withholding information (ibid.).

The mandatory nature of participation at gacaca was not restricted to witnesses. Waldorf highlights the forced closure of shops on days of weekly hearings as well as the threat of fines for truancy as evidence that the local population was being pressured to attend gacaca (Avocats sans Frontières, 2004, p. 4, as cited by Waldorf, 2010, p. 190). Coercion was apparent when a hearing was postponed on 11 February 2009 to facilitate a meeting between several judges and the police. The meeting resulted in the rescindment of an inyangamugayo's resignation after he was purportedly 'strong-armed' by the police and other judges into the decision to return to the bench (gacaca trial, Butare, 11 February 2009).

Although spectators were encouraged to engage with victims and defendants, they were rarely given opportunities to speak directly with government members during trials. State representatives did occasionally attend hearings in order to monitor proceedings. For instance, members of the Peace Building and Conflict Management (PBCM) department at the NURC occasionally monitored cases and produced reports on their findings. The PBCM attempted to 'correct injustice' by making recommendations to either the National Service of Gacaca Jurisdictions (NSGJ), the TIG office, or the Ministry of Justice (Minijust) (Mukajiranga interview, 9 June 2009). Representatives from the NSGJ also monitored cases from time to time (Bikesha interview, 9 June 2009). Although government representatives were infrequently in attendance at gacaca, the GNU stated a commitment which had the potential to foster trust between individuals and the state: that reparations would be provided to survivors for material losses suffered during the 1994 genocide (Waldorf, 2010, p. 191).

These losses were officially recorded during the data collection period in 2001 with the stated intention of communicating this information to the Compensation Fund for remuneration. Waldorf states that, as of 2009, this fund had not been created (Waldorf, 2010). On 15 June 2012, the Survivors Fund (SURF), an advocacy group for genocide survivors, wrote of its concerns about how thousands of compensation and restitution awards granted by gacaca would be enforced after the courts' official closure on 18 June 2012. The group called for a Task Force for Reparations to be created to identify compensation cases that have not yet been fulfilled (SURF, 2012). As of May 2014, the government had not yet enforced compensation awards made through the courts including gacaca (SURF, 2014b, p. 4). An official Minijust statement explained that the government has committed 132 billion RwF to date to support survivors' basic healthcare and education needs, but compensation, reparation and support for their social protection are not priorities at this time (Minijust, 2014).

Article 95 of Organic Law no. 16/2004 refers to the compensation that ought to be provided to those survivors whose property was looted or otherwise damaged between 1 October 1990 and 31 December 1994. It stipulates that suspects found guilty of crimes against property must pay for or repair the damage caused whenever possible (Parliament, 2004, p. 26). This was often not feasible, however, as most perpetrators were too poor to repay the full value of the goods they stole or damaged (Waldorf, 2010, p. 191). That there was no indemnification law to ensure compensation regardless of perpetrators' ability to pay may have created tension in the relationship between individual survivors and the government (PRI, 2010, p. 46). It may also have damaged victims' trust in the gacaca institution. The lack of legislative support is compounded by inadequate compensation through government-led initiatives including the Fund for the Support of Genocide Survivors (FARG) and the *imidugudu* resettlement scheme for the rural population that led to houses being destroyed without remuneration in 2001 (HRW, 2001, p. 2).[21]

Survivors who had their property damaged or destroyed were not the only individuals who did not receive reparations from the government. Those who were wrongly imprisoned following the 1994 genocide and the families of innocent people who died in prison have not been compensated. In December 2003, an NURC meeting resulted in a formal recommendation to create a separate compensation fund for these individuals. As of June 2014, there was no evidence that such a fund had been created. The government's failure to compensate those wrongly accused or to adequately subsidise the reparations that perpetrators could not pay may have had devastating consequences for relationships between individuals and the state:

21 The consequences of inadequate support from organisations including FARG and projects like imidugudu for survivors will be discussed in more detail in chapter 6.

> In many contexts, reparations have been shown to be a key element of the reconciliation process. Whatever their form, reparations hold a particular significance, representing a form of 'symbolic healing', for losses suffered, as well as social acknowledgement for the suffering of survivors. Far from being a separate issue, reparations are part and parcel of transitional justice mechanisms, alongside truth-seeking and justice …
>
> The delays in addressing the compensation issue and the continued absence of a clear decision by the Rwandan authorities led to the bitter disillusionment of survivors, many of whom lost all hope of being officially compensated. Some survivors turned their backs on the *Gacaca* process as a result, resorting to individual agreements with released detainees, who effectively bought their silence (ibid., pp. 45–6).

Groups and the government

The state-led de facto ban of Hutu, Tutsi and Twa identities led to the creation of new group identities derived from events during and after the 1994 genocide[22] including refugees, victims, survivors and perpetrators (Mamdani, 2001, p. 266). Mamdani clarifies that the term 'refugees' is composed of two smaller groups including 'old' and 'new caseload' refugees and indicates the ethnic nature of these terms. 'Old caseload' refers to Tutsi who fled systematic violence before the 1994 genocide began, whereas 'new caseload' refugees are exclusively Hutu who left Rwanda after the 1994 genocide ended (ibid.).

In the context of gacaca, group identities included victims, defendants, convicted perpetrators and those attending TIG (tigistes). Unlike the groups of refugees listed above, these identities did not relate exclusively to ethnicity. The labels of defendants, perpetrators and tigistes were assigned according to accusations and judgments at gacaca and were primarily assigned to Hutu, although some Tutsi were sentenced for crimes against humanity and acts of genocide (Bikesha interview, 9 June 2009).[23] In contrast, membership of the

22 The de facto ban of ethnicity in public discourse is identifiable in Article 9 of the 2003 Constitution. It states, 'The State of Rwanda commits itself to conform to the following principles and to promote and enforce the respect thereof: 1) fighting the ideology of genocide and all its manifestations; 2) eradication of ethnic, regional and other divisions and promotion of national unity' (MOD, 2003, p. 4). I use the term 'de facto' with reference to the ban because no law has been written explicitly banning the use of ethnic labels in government documents or public discourse. Instead, the use of these identifiers is discouraged by laws against 'sectarianism' and 'genocide ideology' as well as government rhetoric about the unity of all Rwandans.

23 Statistics about the ethnicity of defendants at gacaca were not requested or provided during this interview. Instead, Bikesha observed that 'most [defendants] identified as Hutu' in response to a question about the promotion of collective guilt at gacaca (interview, 9 June 2009).

victim group belonged exclusively to Tutsi. The label 'victim' at gacaca, like that of 'survivor' more generally, referred to Tutsi who remained in Rwanda during the 1994 genocide. Excluding Hutu and Twa from this group may have created tension between multiple groups and the government.

The exclusive nature of membership in the survivor group is dictated in part by the 'victor's narrative' of the events leading up to and during the 1994 genocide. For instance, although the government maintains that upwards of 60,000 'moderate Hutu' were killed during that time, these murders are considered to be crimes against humanity rather than acts of genocide (Hintjens, 2008, p. 84). For Helen Hintjens this is a 'drastic underestimate', who contends that a more accurate figure lies somewhere between the RPF's estimate of 60,000 and the 500,000 gauged by Christian Davenport, a sociologist who conducts research about genocide and political conflict (ibid., 2008, pp. 84–5).

The limited parameters of these post-conflict identities are demonstrated by the fact that 'moderate Hutu' – targeted for extermination immediately after the genocide began – were excluded from the survivor and victim groups. As discussed in the introduction, the definition of genocide outlined in the 1948 Convention on the Prevention and Punishment of the Crime of Genocide does not include acts committed with the intention to destroy political groups (UN, 1948, Article II). As such, it is the term 'moderate' that transforms the intentional mass murder of this group into crimes against humanity rather than acts of genocide. Even if the term 'genocide' is not used to describe the systematic murders of 'Hutu moderates', the terms 'survivor' and 'victim' would capture the trauma and violence associated with their massacre. This exclusion further separates Hutu and Tutsi experiences during the 1994 genocide and for some may devalue the trauma and violence suffered by the former group. Membership of the victim and survivor groups was made all the more restrictive in 2009 when the term 'Genocide against the Tutsi' was introduced.

Lemarchand points to the murders of former Prime Minister Agathe Uwilingiyimana, the leaders of the opposition Parti Social Démocratique, 49 journalists who criticised the 1994 genocide, and tens of thousands of Hutu opposition party members, among others, to highlight the danger of forgetting those Hutu who were targeted during the genocide those who had refused to join in the killing, and those who actively protected Tutsi friends and neighbours from attack (2008, p. 50). In the context of gacaca, failure to officially acknowledge many Hutus' resistance to the violence may also have impeded the building of trust between the government and Hutu civilians who did not participate in the 1994 genocide. Although President Kagame contends that the RPF government recognises the heroism of Hutu civilians who opposed the genocide, authors including Hintjens (2008), Waldorf (2007) and Lemarchand (2008) discuss the dangers of the government-level assumption that *all Hutu* in Rwanda are either guilty of genocide acts or have

Figure 3.2. Sign commemorating the 'Jenoside Yakorewe Abatutsi' (Genocide against the Tutsi) at former Ecole Technique Officielle, Kicukiro, Kigali Province (author's photo, 7 April 2009)

directly benefited from the crimes committed by others. The collective guilt of Hutu that these authors touch upon stems from the notion of victor's justice in which the RPF, in its joint role as political party and rebel group which ended the 1994 genocide, decided who may or may not be considered a survivor and receive justice at gacaca (Waldorf, 2010, p. 191).

Victor's justice also relates to the exclusion of crimes perpetrated by the RPF from prosecution at gacaca. This omission was supported by the government's vehement denials that RPF/RPA members carried out acts of genocide or crimes against humanity during or after the 1994 genocide. President Kagame does contend, however, that appropriate judicial bodies have punished individual RPF members found guilty of 'vengeance' crimes between 1990–4. He also identifies any accusations of genocide or crimes against humanity made against the RPF as incorrect and a clear propagation of 'genocide ideology'. 'To try to construct a case of moral equivalency between genocide crimes and isolated crimes committed by rogue RPF members is morally bankrupt and an insult to all Rwandans, especially survivors of the genocide' (Kagame, 2008, p. xxii).

The RPF's impunity at gacaca, like that at the ICTR, demonstrates a political interest in preventing official acknowledgement and criminal responsibility for human rights abuses and violations perpetrated by RPF members during the civil war and 1994 genocide, or the RPA after the latter concluded. At gacaca, this strategy may have impeded the successful rebuilding of relationships between the RPF and civilians directly affected by these crimes as well as the Hutu population more generally. Legally dismissing testimonies against the RPF prevented accountability on both sides of the conflict and expunged from 'official' memory those whose rights were abused by the RPF rebels (Lemarchand, 2008, p. 69). More broadly, it directly contradicted the RPF's stated commitment to eradicating the 'entrenched and institutionalized culture of impunity', as described by Jones (2010, p. 51). This result was accentuated by RPF crimes being referred to as acts of 'vengeance' committed by rogue RPF members, a description which added moral legitimacy to these murders and prevented these acts being associated with cases of genocide or crimes against humanity.

The political interests that guided the omission of RPF crimes from gacaca and excluded Hutu from survivor and victim groups had the potential to not only frustrate the building of trust between groups and the state, but also to actively damage the relationship. Damage may have been caused by the perception that gacaca was a political instrument used solely to punish Hutu civilians collectively, one that may not have been entirely accurate, as punishment at gacaca was individualised and Tutsi were sometimes, albeit rarely, prosecuted for crimes related to the 1994 genocide. And yet, as Vandeginste argues, the mere existence of this negative perception may have diminished gacaca's ability to promote truth (1999, p. 12). Moreover, the RPF's impunity at gacaca and failure to recognise the heroism and suffering of many Hutu civilians may have damaged groups' trust in the gacaca process. It may also have decreased the likelihood of 'vertical reconciliation' since it limited trust in the government as the purveyor of justice and reconciliation in the post-conflict context.

'Horizontal' reconciliation

Groups with other groups

Phil Clark describes the different relationships between groups and individuals at gacaca, which he names as 'group-to-group', 'individual-to-group' and 'individual-to-individual' reconciliation (2010a, p. 333). As the gacaca process was shaped by the popular participation of those living in the areas surrounding the courts, group-to-group interactions may have included victims, defendants, tigistes and community members. Arguably, the most pertinent relationship to be rebuilt at gacaca was that of victims and defendants or survivors and perpetrators more broadly. As previously discussed, dialogue between these two groups at gacaca was primarily shaped by testimonies, confessions and apologies given during court proceedings. 'Gacaca Courts function on the principle of dialogue and speech which must circulate, liberate, accuse and testify. Testimony is thus the cornerstone of the Gacaca process' (Avocats sans Frontières, 2008, p. 40). Testimony given by both groups, as well as by witnesses, was presumed to uncover the truth about 1994 genocide events (NSGJ n.d.(b), p. 1).[24]

Jeremy Sarkin defines the concept of truth in the gacaca context as relating to the official acknowledgement of past human rights abuses. He argues that recognising these abuses can create dialogue between groups and individuals in society (2001, p. 147). In the context of gacaca hearings, acknowledging past wrongdoings may have been limited by the trial's focus. For instance, the details uncovered may have related to the acts of a small number of defendants or may have been limited by the amount of participation from defendants, judges, witnesses and community members on a particular day (Daly and Sarkin, 2007, p. 28).[25] Moreover, the truth uncovered at gacaca may have been mostly 'forensic' in nature since it was revealed through public denunciations and pertained mostly to the details of who, where, how and against whom crimes were committed (Ingelaere, 2007, p. 36). Ingelaere refers to truth at gacaca as forensic at best, arguing that the reasons for genocide crimes having been perpetrated were commonly omitted from testimonies (ibid., p. 36). He clarifies that these details do not fit the 'logic of criminal trials' as the goal of gacaca was to establish whether evidence was provided for specific charges to be given, rather than to understand perpetrators' motives (ibid.). Ingelaere's analysis refers to the data-collection phase of the gacaca process that began in 2002.

In some cases, these details may have been enough to encourage survivors and perpetrators to engage in further dialogue. 'Survivors are trying to understand what happened to them; if perpetrators talk to them, help them and listen to them, it will help' (victim interview, 17 July 2010). In other cases, testimonies and confessions may have failed to give survivors any pertinent information, as they may not have been entirely truthful. Waldorf questions the quality of truth-telling during gacaca proceedings as all participants had many incentives to lie, such as fear of reprisal upon testifying or passing the blame in an attempt to evade conviction (2007, p. 428). In some cases, passing the blame took place when defendants accused those who were not present of criminal responsibility or claimed that superiors in the militia or government

24 The 'objectives' of gacaca describe the relationship between testimony and truth as, 'the way in which the Gacaca Institution has been conceived will allow [them] to discover the truth because: the citizens who have been the eyewitnesses of the facts that occurred mainly in their cells will give evidence' (NSGJ, n.d.(b), p. 1).

25 The quality of participation may have been affected by logistical problems associated with local trials. Longman argues that the decentralised nature of gacaca proceedings made it challenging to try cases when violence was not contained to the local area. For instance, many perpetrators committed acts of genocide or crimes against humanity in communities other than their own but commonly faced accusations only in their local region (2006, p. 220).

forced them to commit crimes (gacaca trial, Burema, 12 February 2009; PRI, 2010, p. 45). The defendants at a trial in Burema, a Kigali suburb, repeatedly blamed the murder of four civilians on a man who had died before the trial began. Nine out of the 11 defendants accused were later given sentences ranging from two to 15 years (gacaca trial, Burema, 12 February 2009). Avocats sans Frontières (ASF) found most defendants in the cases it monitored between October 2006 and April 2007 accepted only partial responsibility for crimes they had committed. Instead, defendants attempted to make the crime appear collective in order to reduce their own individual culpability (2008, p. 49).

This appeal to collective responsibility may have damaged relationships between Hutu and Tutsi more generally as it emphasised the perceived guilt of all Hutu for acts of genocide (ibid., p. 44). The sense of collective responsibility would have been particularly detrimental in light of the RPF's impunity at gacaca for crimes against Hutu civilians. It also presented a contradiction between the emphasis on ethnicity, whether directly or indirectly at gacaca, and the construction of a singular national identity devoid of ethnic labels in the post-conflict period. Although ethnicity could have been discussed at gacaca, the perception of Hutu civilians' collective guilt stands in stark contrast to the government message of national unity in official reconciliation discourse, government documents and public events (Waldorf, 2009, p. 104).

Individuals and groups

The relationship between individuals and groups at gacaca was primarily shaped by direct communication related to apology, sentencing and reintegration. Although these interactions may have been informed by differing moral and pragmatic incentives, all were impacted by the participatory nature of gacaca. This communal character, with regard to community participation and the fact that many courts were set in communities where the violence had taken place, may have created a number of different dynamics between individuals and groups. The first of these was influenced by the act of public shaming. Daly and Sarkin argue that the shaming of individual defendants by groups of community members at gacaca, which include victims and witnesses, may have promoted social cohesion in the community (2007, p. 84). Moreover, they contend that the public's participation and commitment to the trial may have legitimised the entire process by demonstrating popular support for the sentence meted out to the defendant. This sense of legitimacy, they argue, could in turn have supported the subsequent reintegration of the defendant into the community after the sentence was completed (ibid.).

It is plausible that public shaming resulted in confession, apology and/or repentance from the defendant at gacaca, who could choose to apologise to a single victim, the community, or even the nation. A defendant being tried for Category 2 crimes in Burema repeatedly apologised to community members present and the nation of Rwanda, but refused to apologise directly to the victim during the trial (gacaca trial, Burema, 12 February 2009). Villa-Vicencio highlights the importance of apology in promoting reconciliation. He contends that apologies may restore dignity to the victim or support the development of a relationship between the wrongdoer and those who have been wronged (2005, p. 59). Confession, apology and repentance also had pragmatic value for defendants at gacaca as they could have resulted in drastically reduced sentences when made in conjunction with guilty pleas (Parliament, 2007).

In order to receive a reduced sentence, these convicted perpetrators were required to complete community service at TIG, a programme which represents a shift towards the reeducation and reintegration of perpetrators into society, particularly their own communities.[26] At TIG camps in Rebero and Nyanza, tigistes wake up at 4am to breakfast and a prayer session, begin working at 6am and finish at 2pm (Ndoli interview, 19 June 2009). They spend their working hours constructing terraces, building roads, breaking stones for paving and building houses for survivors. Although the principal activity in the camps is community service, the stated goal of the programme is to 'change their [the tigistes] minds' with regard to violence, 'divisionism', 'genocide ideology' and the promotion of 'national reconciliation' (Kabayiza interview, 19 June 2009).

Secondary stated goals of the TIG programme include punishing perpetrators and supporting the country's reconstruction and development. In addition to the skills tigistes learn from their community service activities, they are given lessons in reading, writing, craft-making and hygiene. Tigistes are also given lectures about the National Unity and Reconciliation Programme and peaceful coexistence in a purported effort to 'turn these bad guys into good guys' (ibid.).[27] In some cases, they interact directly and regularly with survivors living near the camps, interactions which revolve around services to the community such as bringing water to vulnerable survivors or building and repairing survivors' houses that may have been damaged during the 1994 genocide (Ndoli interview, 19 June 2009). As individual perpetrators are normally sent to camps near their home communities, it is possible they will interact with survivors who have been directly affected by the crimes they committed. This interaction is particularly poignant as tigistes are most commonly perpetrators convicted of Category 2 crimes including murder and assault. When asked about the risk of tension or violence between survivors and tigistes living in the same area, Kabayiza responded that he '[had] never seen peasants throwing rocks at tigistes or tigistes using machetes to kill people on the outside' (interview, 19 June 2009).

26 Although the gacaca courts officially closed in June 2012, the TIG programme continues to operate.

27 See PRI (2004), p. 17 for a detailed outline of lectures given to detainees attending TIG.

The TIG programme represents much of the reparative aspect of what can be described as restorative justice in Rwanda (Melvin, 2010, p. 943). Perpetrators found guilty at gacaca were required to compensate victims to the best of their ability and to donate to the FARG (Kabayiza interview, 19 June 2009). As many perpetrators were not able to compensate victims financially, TIG provides the framework through which they perform acts that aid survivors. Clark suggests that these reparative acts may in some cases demonstrate tigistes' remorse, sincerity, or intention to rebuild relationships with those they have harmed, elements Lederach describes as integral to post-conflict reconciliation (Clark, 2008, p. 351; Lederach, 1997, p. 26).

Although this may be true in some cases, exchanging repentance and apology for a reduced sentence may have weakened the sincerity of a tigiste's desire to rebuild damaged relationships. Waldorf highlights the differences between Rwandans' perceptions of gacaca's reduced punishment, arguing that many Hutu perceived gacaca as a means through which wrongly imprisoned family members could have been released from prison. This perception opposes that of many Tutsi survivors who viewed gacaca as a form of 'disguised amnesty' (2007, p. 428).

The latter description closely resembles that of Jean Baptiste Kayigamba, a journalist and genocide survivor, who fears that the RPF's official reconciliation programme fosters impunity. Kayigamba argues that the failure to bring about justice for crimes of genocide, in an attempt to promote the government's vision of 'national reconciliation' or reintegration, may produce the opposite effect. Shortcuts to justice, such as plea-bargaining at gacaca, may have released perpetrators and those who planned the 1994 genocide from guilt and reduced their accountability for the crimes they committed (2008, p. 41). This fear, purportedly shared by many survivors, may have been exacerbated by the risk of reprisal attacks and murders of survivors by defendants and released perpetrators; a risk Dennis Bikesha argues was the genocide court's greatest obstacle (ibid.; Bikesha interview, 9 June 2009).

Individuals with other individuals

Phil Clark argues that gacaca provided participants with an opportunity to share their thoughts about what they had witnessed and experienced during the genocide (2010a, p. 330). As previously discussed, dialogue between individuals during trials, like that between groups may have been restricted by the case parameters. As such, it may have symbolised the beginning of longer-term discussion between individuals and groups, rather than have brought about a deeper sense of connection between individuals. A 2010 Penal Reform International (PRI) report touches on gacaca's potential to facilitate dialogue between survivors and perpetrators. It discusses gacaca's importance as a forum for such discussion but, like Clark, points to the need for dialogue to continue between both parties after the trial concludes (2010, p. 66).

This form of engagement was in some cases paired with an expectation of forgiveness at gacaca, which in this context could have been sought by the defendant and granted by the victim. The pressure felt by some survivors to absolve perpetrators during the gacaca process likely resulted from the 'state-sponsored "requirement" to seek and grant forgiveness' (ibid., p. 51).[28] This expectation resembles the thicker end of Crocker's reconciliation spectrum. Crocker warns that forgiveness is unlikely to occur following the relatively short proceedings of transitional justice mechanisms. Moreover, he contends that it is 'morally objectionable' to force people to agree about the past and forgive following conflict (2000, p. 108).

The perception of a requirement to forgive at gacaca is antithetical to Martha Minow's argument that the power to do so belongs to victims and cannot be claimed by others as a right (1998, p. 17). This perceived pressure resembles the emphasis on forgiveness at Human Rights Violations Hearings and during the application process for amnesty at the South African TRC (Wilson, 2001, p. 119). As with the TRC, forgiveness at gacaca was influenced by political and religious overtones. The perceived pressure to forgive may have created further tension between victims and defendants at gacaca. For instance, it may have created an unrealistic expectation of being forgiven, diminished the sincerity of the sentiment, or caused offence or resentment if an individual survivor was not ready to forgive (PRI, 2010, p. 51). While attending the trial of those accused of murdering five members of his family, the victim explained that forgiveness 'c'est un long chemin' (is a long road) (interview, 17 July 2010).

Interactions at gacaca may also have been accompanied by expectations of a moral transformation on the part of the defendant at the trial, at TIG, or in prison. The hope for moral conversion was in some cases related to confession: 'Those who are cured, I think they are the majority, they are doing it from their heart. That is the best' (Bikesha interview, 20 July 2010). This expectation, like that of forgiveness, could have put undue pressure on the relationship between individual survivors and perpetrators. It could have created unrealistic expectations of change in a relatively short period, or it may have fostered complacency with regard to further dialogue about the actions taken and decisions made by perpetrators during the 1994 genocide.

Conclusion

Gacaca's stated objectives reiterate the RPF's stated commitments to truth, justice and reconciliation. In practice, the relationship between the gacaca courts and the government's vision of 'horizontal' and 'vertical' reconciliation is

28 The PRI report, 'Eight years on ... a record of gacaca monitoring in Rwanda', discusses the perceived requirement to forgive with reference to 'numerous cases' in which survivors felt pressured by the government or the Church (2010, p. 51).

more tenuous, a tension created by contradictions between these commitments and the ways in which gacaca functioned in social and political practice. For instance, the stated commitment to eradicating impunity was made less meaningful when RPF crimes were excluded from prosecution. This restriction effectively denied justice to Hutu civilians targeted during the genocide and damaged the potential for building trust between this group and the state. That damage was made potentially more severe by the term 'Genocide against the Tutsi' being introduced and by the contradiction between gacaca's emphasis on ethnic identities and the government's construction of a singular national identity that supersedes ethnic labels.

In a more general sense, the way in which gacaca functioned was shaped by its reinventors' political interests. State influence was particularly evident with regard to 'vertical' reconciliation at gacaca. The government's failure to provide adequate compensation, accept responsibility for crimes committed by the RPF or RPA, and officially acknowledge Hutu victims of the civil war and 1994 genocide may have damaged connections between individuals/groups and the government. The influence of the RPF was also detectable with regard to 'horizontal' reconciliation. Like all relationships at gacaca, these connections were informed by the assumption that truth promotes justice and justice leads to reconciliation. In some documented cases the impetus to lay blame on others promoted collective guilt and obscured or manipulated the truth about events during the 1994 genocide. Moreover, the incentive to confess in order to receive a reduced sentence may not have yielded accurate testimonies or the sincerity sought by some victims. The perceived pressure to forgive or make a moral transformation may have also hindered relationship rebuilding between victims and defendants. If we apply Lederach's conception of reconciliation here, there is hope that continued dialogue between individuals after gacaca concludes might support the rebuilding of both trust and relationships more generally as it creates the opportunity to share experiences of the past and thoughts of the future.

Chapter 4

Nation-building and a return to unity

The RPF's stated commitment to promoting its vision of 'national reconciliation' is outlined in official documents including Vision 2020 and the 2003 Constitution. It was not until 2007, however, that the National Unity and Reconciliation Programme's objectives were officially stated, with the publication of the National Policy of Unity and Reconciliation. These objectives include 'building a new nation that promotes the national pride and equal rights to all citizens' (NURC, 2007, p. 15). This stated commitment to building a new nation is echoed in presidential speeches, government documents and official reconciliation discourse.

Nation-building can be understood as '*a political objective as well as a strategy*, for reaching specific political objectives', as described by political scientist Jochen Hippler (2005, p. 2).[1] Hippler contends that this particular understanding includes the creation or solidification of a political system by internal or external leaders who are seeking to promote their own interests or to increase their own political control (ibid.). He continues by outlining what he deems to be the three central components of successful nation-building programmes. The first component, '*integrative ideology*', legitimises political restructuring and encourages public support by including the population in a shared national identity (ibid., p. 8).[2] The second refers to the integration of loosely connected groups into the single society. The final component includes creating a strong central state apparatus that can effectively govern the entire nation (ibid., p. 9).

In the Rwandan context, the main driver of nation-building is the RPF government. This agenda was formally articulated in Vision 2020, published in 2000, which focuses primarily on the government's plan to support the nation's economic development. Vision 2020 also poses pertinent questions

1 Text italicised here and below as in original. Hippler offers a second definition of nation-building as a '*process of sociopolitical development*', which includes integrating loosely connected communities into a single nation-state over a long period (2005, p. 6). He contends that these overlapping definitions frequently suffer from inconsistent and unclear application (ibid.).

2 Text italicised as in original.

related to how the nation will be rebuilt following the 1994 genocide. 'How do Rwandans envisage their future? What kind of society do they want to become? How can they construct a united and inclusive Rwandan identity? What are the transformations needed to emerge from a deeply unsatisfactory social and economic situation?' (Minecofin, 2000, p. 1). The RPF's nation-building agenda reflects several elements highlighted by Hippler, including constructing and disseminating an inclusive national ideology, and creating a strong central state apparatus that tolerates little opposition or criticism. This agenda also functions to secure the RPF's political dominance and advance the government's economic objectives.

Vision 2020 opens with a preface by President Kagame in which he describes the aspirations of *all* Rwandans to transform the nation into a middle-income country by the year 2020 (Minecofin, 2000, p. 2). This purportedly communal ambition to foster prosperity provides insight into not only the RPF's vision for development, but also its vision of unity and nation-building more broadly. Stepping away from the RPF's plans to promote economic development, a point to which I will return in chapter 6, we are left with a description of the government's aspirations for the future: 'Vision 2020 aspires for Rwanda to become a modern, strong and united nation, proud of its fundamental values, politically stable and without discrimination amongst its citizens' (ibid., p. 4).

This quotation sheds light on government priorities within the Vision 2020 development programme as well as the National Unity and Reconciliation Programme more generally. Although 'unity' and 'reconciliation' are commonly linked as 'national unity and reconciliation' in government documents and official discourse, the terms relate to separate concepts and priorities within National Unity and Reconciliation Programme parameters. For instance if the quotation above is analysed in conjunction with the RPF's stated commitments to unity and nation-building, the aspiration for Rwanda 'to become a modern, strong and united nation', can be understood as a major goal of the official programme (ibid.). And, as we shall see, the promotion of Rwandan values, political stability and eradication of discrimination can be interpreted as the steps the government deemed necessary to achieve this goal. This particular arrangement has significant implications for the promotion of the RPF's vision of 'national reconciliation' after the 1994 genocide.

Overlapping agendas

The path to national unity

The government's stated commitment to promoting national unity and to building the nation imbues 'national reconciliation' with both forward-

and backward-looking gazes, structures and presuppositions.[3] Unity is most commonly depicted in official discourse and documents as 'national unity'. According to the 2003 Constitution's preamble, national unity and reconciliation were 'seriously shaken by the genocide and its consequences' (MOD, 2003, p. 1). It can be inferred from this quotation as well as from numerous other examples of official reconciliation discourse and documents that the government perceives national unity to have existed prior to 1994.[4]

> There are people who can ascertain that it is not necessary to prove that there was the unity of Rwandans before the Colonialists' arrival. However it is necessary, because there are many people who are currently writing that killings during the genocide and massacres which took place in Rwanda from 1959 until the culminating war of 1994 took root in bad relations between Hutus and Tutsis before the White People's arrival. This was written by some of the White People and Rwandans.
>
> The truth from history is that before the Colonial period, i.e. before the year 1900, that Catholic Missionaries began to live in our country, in which there was strong unity, between Rwandans: no ethnical war took place between them before that year...
>
> That unity was for all Rwandans: Hutus, Tutsis and Twas. They were making up all together what our ancestors called 'The King's People'. All of them also knew they were Rwandans, that Rwanda was their country, that nobody could say that he had the right to it more than the others. Even though they said that Rwanda was belonging to the King (Rwanda's Owner, the Country's Owner), they ascertained that 'the King was supported by the warriors' (Office of the President, 1999, p. 6).

Although this document and official discourse more generally emphasise the role of German and Belgian colonists in propagating ethnic tension in Rwanda,

3 Zorbas describes the backward- and forward-looking pillars of what she refers to as the 'RPF Healing Truth' (2009, p. 128). This narrative blames the 1994 genocide violence upon the 'divisionism' and 'genocide ideology' of the past. It also looks to the future to prevent the recurrence of genocide by seeking to build a 'prosperous, peaceful future for the country' (ibid., p. 136). The backward- and forward-looking gazes discussed in this book extend beyond the 1994 genocide to include the social cohesion and national unity that allegedly existed during the pre-colonial era. They also refer to the RPF's stated commitment to foster this form of social cohesion in the future.

4 These examples include: 'The unity of the Rwandans before the colonial period' (Office of the President, 1999), from which the above quotation is taken; Aggée Shyaka Mugabe's report, 'Community conflicts in Rwanda' (NURC, 2007); and 'Report on the evaluation of national unity and reconciliation' (NURC, 2001).

neither colonial power is included in the official reconciliation programme. This absence may relate to priorities that shape the RPF's nation-building agenda and development programme. For instance, as Belgium and Germany are both bilateral donors, the RPF may fear potential damage to the positive relationship between Rwanda and these former colonial rulers should they be included in the programme.[5] Holding these nations to account for alleged wrongdoing during the colonial period may also be perceived to detract from the goals of the nation-building agenda. Rather than rebuilding relationships with former colonising countries, this agenda prioritises the *restoration* of the unity that was purportedly destroyed by colonial leaders' segregationist policies (ibid., p. 52). This metaphorical *return* to the unity that existed between 'The King's People' prior to the arrival of German and Belgian colonists, serves multiple functions with regard to promoting the government's conception of national unity (ibid., p. 7),[6] the first of which is to promote the image of a pre-colonial utopia. The utopian qualities of harmonious coexistence are most prominently illustrated by the government's essentialist rendering of social relations between ethnic groups in Rwanda during this period.

The 'victor's narrative' describes these relations as having been highly flexible. Ethnic labels allegedly reflected social status rather than immutable racial qualities as institutionalised by colonial leaders (NURC, 2007, p. 4; ingando lecture, 3 July 2009).[7] Johan Pottier, a sociologist specialising in the Great Lakes Region, accuses the government of over-simplifying the nation's pre-colonial history. He argues that the historical narrative the RPF government disseminated glosses over the origins of ethnicity in Rwanda. Pottier contends that the RPF emphasises pre-colonial ethnic unity in order to make ethnicity appear irrelevant within the ruling party, which he argues is dominated by a Tutsi minority (2002, p. 111).

5 In 2011, Belgium and Rwanda agreed upon an Indicative Development Programme that includes €160 million in bilateral aid to be donated by Belgium during the period 2011–14 (see the Kingdom of Belgium Foreign Affairs website at: http://diplomatie.belgium.be/en/policy/development_cooperation/where_we_work/partner_countries/rwanda/ (accessed 12 March 2015)). In that same year, Germany pledged an annual aid donation of €20 million to Rwanda over three years (AFP, 29 July 2012).

6 'The King's People' refers to all Hutu, Tutsi and Twa living in Rwanda during the pre-colonial period (Office of the President, 1999, p. 6). Reference to 'The King' appears elsewhere in the document as a unity symbol based on his supposed transcendence of ethnicity: 'After he was enthroned, people said that, "he was not umututsi any more", but the King for the people' (ibid., p. 8).

7 Eltringham refers to the introduction of mandatory identity cards for all Rwandan citizens as the culmination of the 'process of racialization' during the colonial era. Belgian leaders issued these cards, which listed the carrier's ethnic identity, during the 1933–4 census (2004, p. 18).

More broadly, the RPF's depiction of ethnic relations in Rwandan history may restrict the ways in which unity and 'national reconciliation' are promoted in the present. As political theorist Andrew Schaap argues, a focus on the *return* to a form of social unity that allegedly existed in a country's past may have detrimental consequences for current reconciliation processes. Schaap locates the rhetorical invocation of such collective terms as 'we' and 'the people' within the religious dimensions of reconciliation as a peacemaking paradigm (2006, p. 616). He warns that applying a religious metaphor of redemption to an entire nation may presuppose the existence of an 'original unity' that did not exist as well an 'ultimate unity' that has yet to be attained (ibid.). The assumption that social unity existed and that the nation ought to return to it may restrict the ways in which the conflict in question is represented and render the concept of reconciliation purely ideological (ibid., p. 618).

Schaap points to the 're' in 'reconciliation' as the impetus to return to or restore the harmony and relationships that were destroyed during the conflict or wrongdoing. He argues that this restorative dimension may be unsuitable for addressing legacies of colonialism, state violence and oppression committed by one group against another (ibid., p. 622). The Rwandan example differs slightly from this arrangement, as the goal of restoring unity is not to recognise the complexities of systematic violence, ethnic relations or the effects of colonialism. Instead, it functions to legitimise the RPF's conception of unity and render it more understandable to the population. As Schaap argues, social conflict is best understood when it is contrasted with the notion of social unity (ibid.). The 'victor's narrative' states that social conflict began during the colonial period. As such, the pre-colonial era provides the background of national unity against which the conflict is contrasted. Moreover, the presupposition that unity existed in the past constructs a prescriptive path on which unity may be attained in the future. The RPF designs and maintains this path and promotes social and cultural values chosen by the government to best represent its vision of Rwanda's past and future.

In an interview, Alphonse Bakusi, then the director of the NURC's Civic Education Department, discussed the importance of promoting Rwandan social values in government documents and specific projects within the official reconciliation programme including itorero ry'igihugu civic education camps. He explained that 'we are revising moral values to promote social cohesion and development' (interview, 23 July 2010). These values are identified in government documents, including the 2003 Constitution, as having belonged to 'our ancestors' and as being vital to the 'flourishing of our nation' (MOD, 2003, p. 1). As Bakusi's statement indicates, the retrospective identification and subsequent promotion of purportedly historical values is a strictly top-down operation. His use of the word 'we' to describe who is revising moral values, refers to the NURC and RPF more broadly. This action reinforces the RPF's 'monopoly over knowledge production', as outlined by Pottier (2002,

p. 19). The government has the capacity to restore values which may never have existed and/or promote those which represent its own political interests. The most blatant example is the stated commitment to restoring pre-colonial Rwandan values that discourage misusing public funds for private gain. Other examples include *ibigyie*, a Kinyarwanda term that reflects hard work and pride. Bakusi argued that it is the RPF's intention to promote development as a means of uniting citizens in Rwanda (interview, 23 July 2010).

Building the 'Rwandan nation'

Nation-building in the Rwandan context represents the process through which the RPF's interpretation of the nation's history is applied to its vision of the future. President Kagame compared this undertaking in a post-conflict Rwanda to that of building a house in a speech he gave to the International Institute for Strategic Studies on 16 September 2010:

> You start with the foundation before you build the structure. The foundation comprises security, peace, and stability. But let me also reiterate that, while acknowledging the value of external support and partnership, nation building cannot be dictated from outside. It should reflect and be informed by the history and particular circumstances of a country (p. 9).

The image of erecting a 'Rwandan house' illustrates two key features of the RPF's nation-building agenda; the first of which is structure. Once the foundation of security, peace and stability was suitably laid, the government set forth to 'transform our society' through a formal top-down approach to structural and political change (ibid.). These stated changes included: effective problem solving; establishing a formal decentralisation programme; and creating Vision 2020 as a framework for socio-economic development (Kagame speech, March 2009, p. 3). The RPF's stated commitment to building the nation is repeated in official discourse, policy and projects related to the promotion of national unity and 'national reconciliation'.[8]

The second feature ensures that the nation-building process is a wholly Rwandan project. The RPF maintains ownership of the programme by rejecting interference from the international community and incorporating Rwandan social values as articulated by the government. Kagame's assertion that nation-building ought to be dictated from the inside legitimises the government's agenda by devaluing international criticism of the project. For instance, during his opening address at the 9th National Dialogue Council meeting in Kigali on 15 December 2011, Kagame expressed his frustration with international

8 See NURC (2008b), NURC (2007), NURC (2001), as well as Vision 2020 (Minecofin, 2000), the 2003 Constitution (MOD, 2003) and the 2007 Reconciliation Policy (NURC, 2007).

human rights NGOs and journalists who had criticised the regime's approach to free speech and ethnic identities in Rwanda.

> Who is a minority? I am not from the minority. I am from the RPF and it's the majority. I am from these Rwandans and they are not minority in their own country. Imagine these are the people who want to give lessons to Rwandans about governance and freedoms.

The nation-building agenda's structured top-down nature is made all the more inflexible by the legal consequences associated with thoughts and actions perceived to threaten political stability or promote discrimination. These two acts could be detrimental to building the 'modern, strong and united nation' envisaged in the Vision 2020 quotation near the beginning of this chapter. Both acts relate to accusations of 'genocide ideology' and 'divisionism'. The risk of being accused and convicted of either of these 'negative ideologies' may deter interference, disagreement with or criticism of the nation-building project by Rwandans living inside the country.

Commonality, identity and ethnicity

The definition of 'national unity and reconciliation' outlined in the 2007 Reconciliation Policy provides insight into concepts that inform the RPF's notion of national unity and the nation-building process. The definition states:

> The unity and reconciliation of Rwanda are instinctive to people who accept that they share nationality, culture and equal rights, characterized by credibility, humanity, respect, equality. Complementarity, truth, healing one another's moral wounds, inflicted on them during the appalling events of the past [are essential] in order to be able to progress peacefully. It requires every citizen to change their mind completely; hence unity will spread all over the nation – Rwandans will be free, and so too will the country which is always eager to ensure a better future for every Rwandan (NURC, 2007, p. 2).

Although somewhat convoluted, the official definition highlights the concepts of commonality, equality and civic education, among others, as elements of the RPF's official reconciliation programme that will purportedly enable the country to 'progress peacefully' (ibid.). Commonality is the most ubiquitous concept in this regard. The definition above provides a relatively short list of attributes allegedly shared by all Rwandans including nationality, culture and equal rights. Shared history and language are included in other government documents such as the 2003 Constitution preamble (MOD, 2003, p. 1). Unlike the 2003 Constitution, however, the 2007 Reconciliation Policy outlines Rwandans' specific common interests including 'building the country' (NURC, 2007, p. 4). It also stipulates that these interests, along with citizenship, hold more value than 'ethnics, family, relationships, religious belongings, regions, sex and so forth' (ibid.).

The concept of commonality, as depicted in official reconciliation discourse and government documents, is posited in opposition to the 'divisionism' that allegedly shaped the 'bad history' of not only the 1994 genocide, but also the Social Revolution, civil war and colonial era (ibid., p. 2).[9] According to a group of 15 students at ingando solidarity camp,[10] 'divisionism can divide people by skin, ethnic origins. Colonial masters tried to divide Rwanda by ethnic groups like schools for Hutu and others for Tutsi. Rwandans started believing they were different' (ingando lecture, 15 June 2009). They were responding to the question '[w]hat can be done to eliminate divisionism in order to abort divisionism encouraged by colonialists and missionaries?' (ibid.). The quotation and the discussion from which it is taken are examples of the stated requirement in the official definition described on the previous page for all Rwandans to 'change their minds' about national unity and reconciliation. The stated commitment to reeducating the population is put into practice at the live-in itorero ry'igihugu and ingando civic education camps as well as in the new history book published by the NURC (Bawaya interview, 30 May 2009). This commitment will be discussed in the next chapter.

The RPF government's repetition of the purportedly collective interest of *all Rwandans* in building the nation legitimises the RPF's nation-building agenda (NURC, 2007, p. 3; Minecofin, 2000, p. 1). The process, in this particular context, more closely resembles the formal act of redefining 'nationhood'. Nationhood can be understood as an exercise that develops the relationship between citizens and the state (Boyce, 1999, p. 236). Boyce argues that nationhood is fully developed when citizens experience a sense of belonging to a particular territory, identify with state institutions, and share a sense of common values and identity with others (ibid.). At the conceptual level, nation-building in Rwanda may be better understood as a process of nationhood-building as the RPF's agenda includes a stated commitment to building a strong relationship between the state and citizens through 'good governance' as well as an emphasis on the shared values, culture, history and identity of all Rwandans as outlined in Vision 2020 (Minecofin, 2000, pp. 2, 4). This depiction of nationhood-building resembles the RPF's definition of 'vertical' reconciliation, which is guided by the stated mandate to foster belonging and build trust in state institutions.

9 See Waldorf for a detailed discussion of the development of the RPF's 'prohibition on divisionism' (2009, p. 108). Waldorf argues that although Rwanda needs laws to protect its citizens from genocide denial and ideology, current laws against 'divisionism' and 'genocide ideology' promote a culture of accusation, legitimise the silencing of NGOs and political opponents, and promote the collective guilt of all Hutu (ibid., p. 118). This argument will be reexamined in chapter 6.

10 Solidarity camps are a form of mandatory live-in education camp. This one was organised for students entering university.

The top-down nature of the nationhood-building process not only seeks to create a bond between citizens and the state, but also to unite the people of the nation. The emphasis on common attributes and the shared experience of 'bad history' provides the rhetorical basis upon which citizens' bond of 'horizontal comradeship' is built (Anderson, 2006, p. 7).[11] The 'bond' between citizens as members of a nation reflects elements of what is commonly described as interpersonal reconciliation in the broader body of the literature. In particular, the nation-building agenda emphasises the rebuilding of relationships between individuals, as it seeks to transform these individuals into a single 'people'.

Etienne Balibar, a Marxist philosopher, argues that modern nations are not naturally occupied by any given group of people. Instead, the country's people continually 'produce themselves' as a community belonging to 'the nation'. He contends that the concept of unity will make group members appear to everyone in the nation 'as a people' and will provide the origin of and basis upon which political power is consolidated (1996, p. 138). Balibar uses the example of ethnic groups to support his argument about the construction of a people, one which is also applicable to promoting nation-building and national unity in Rwanda. In this particular context, the group being made to continually produce itself is the national community as a whole, bound together not only by the shared attributes of language, culture and experience, but also by a singular national identity referred to as the Banyarwanda.

David Kiwuwa, a political scientist who focuses on the politics of ethnic identity and democratisation, argues that a collective identity, such as that promoted by the RPF, is the result of homogenising multiple identities within a nation. He contends that this project may be mandated to prevent fracturing of the state in the post-conflict period (2007, p. 9). It may also serve a more shrewd political purpose. As Powell suggests, '[t]hrough nationhood or through race, the nation and myself become one, which means that I have nothing to fear from state power and must approve its judgments, for they are my own' (2011, p. 250). Kagame's assertion, 'I am from the RPF and it's the majority', quoted earlier in this chapter, universalises the appeal of the current regime (speech, 15 December 2011). In so doing, it appears that the government is

11 Anderson has investigated the development and subsequent spread of nationalism in the 19th century, defining nations as social constructs or 'imagined communities' (1983). In the revised edition of his seminal text Anderson uses the term 'horizontal comradeship' to describe the nation's deep sense of fraternity (2006). In that edition, he uses the willingness of millions of people to die for their nation in times of war to exemplify the commitment to what he determines to be 'limited imaginings' (ibid., p. 7). I use the term to demonstrate the conception of unity constructed and implemented by the RPF, a unity that joins all Rwandans together as members of a single community: the nation.

controlled by and serves the interests of the Banyarwanda rather than what can arguably be described as a minority of Tutsi officials.[12]

This national identity and the RPF's emphasis on commonality represent a nationalist ideology in the post-conflict context:

> An ideology replaces another: Rwandans should choose between a nationalist ideology (Ubumwe bw' Abanyarwanda) and Parmehutu's (*Rubanda nyamwinshi/Bene Sebahinzi*) … The main strategy to fight it consists in exposing Rwandans to its divisive and sectarian intentions, and showing them the advantages of national unity – ubunyarwanda (NURC, 2008c, p. 19).

The Kinyarwanda words *Ubumwe bw' Abanyarwanda* translate to 'the unity of Rwandans', reflecting the Banyarwanda's singular national identity and illustrating the RPF regime's stated commitment to promoting unity for all Rwandans. The statement *Rubanda nyamwinshi/Bene Sebahinzi* loosely translates to 'the mass population', a reference to the colonial period during which the population was purportedly 'divided' into two groups. It depicts the colonial rulers' reference to Hutu as cultivators of the land and to Tutsi as those who owned cattle. The term *Rubanda nyamwhinshi* was also used to describe the Hutu majority in anti-Tutsi propaganda prior to and during the 1994 genocide.

The RPF constructs its 'nationalist ideology' as the antithesis of 'genocide ideology'. Authors including Waldorf (2009) and Simon (2012) argue that 'negative ideologies' do continue to exist in Rwandan society. Simon points to the acute overcrowding of Rwandan prisons between 1997 and 2005 as a major facilitator of anti-Tutsi sentiment in the post-conflict era. He argues that 'genocide ideology' continued unabated in prisons among many convicted genocide perpetrators, contending that it was repeated in private settings, as perpetrators were not required to demonstrate remorse upon their release. Instead, ex-prisoners who continued to subscribe to 'genocide ideology' shared it with their families (2012, p. 262).

The concepts of 'divisionism' and 'genocide ideology' play important discursive roles within the RPF's conception of national unity and its nation-building agenda. The RPF uses both concepts to legitimise the construction of the singular national identity by illuminating the 'perils' of ethnic identities:

> There is a lot one can say about the origins and social relationships between Batutsi, Hutus and Twas. Let us just take the following idea: Banyarwanda must understand that maintaining themselves prisoners of their belonging to ethnic Hutu, Tutsi and Twa groups is one of the

12 I use the term 'arguably' here because I am referring back to Pottier's assertion that the RPF government is dominated by a small group of Tutsi members (2002). I did not enquire as to the ethnic identities of research participants and do not assume to know the identities of those I interviewed apart from the few individuals who openly discussed their own ethnicity.

> big obstacles standing in their way to development. In fact, to remain prisoner of one's ethnic group without having anything positive in mind, is like locking oneself up in a cave so that one cannot look outside. What matters is to live together peacefully, work together for the development of their country, so that Banyarwanda can tackle and solve their common problems, and break their narcissism and wake up to the progress the world has achieved (Office of the President, 1999, p. 58).

The shared national identity of the Banyarwanda is posited as the 'solution' to problems purportedly created by ethnic identities having been propagated in post-conflict Rwanda. The challenges include impediments to development, 'divisionism' and 'genocide ideology'. Murray Edelman, a political scientist, argues that leaders manipulate depictions of problems in society in order to construct 'facts' that undermine particular courses of action and perpetuate government-sponsored ideologies (1988, pp. 10–11). The 'fact' advanced by the RPF government states that ethnicity is intricately connected to the 'divisionism' and 'genocide ideology' that allegedly led to the 1994 genocide. It informs the assumption that the continued existence of ethnic identities in society promotes these negative ideologies. The proposed 'solution' to these problems, a singular national identity that supersedes ethnicity, is imbued with RPF ideology: this shared identity will promote national unity and 'national reconciliation' and help to build a 'modern, strong and united nation' (Minecofin, 2000, p. 4).

The RPF has promoted the de facto banning of ethnic labels from public discourse and government documents in an attempt to eradicate 'genocide ideology' and 'divisions' in society more generally. The banning has been achieved in part by eliminating ethnicity from identity cards and regional quotas for schools, as well as by manipulating the moral debate about identity in Rwanda (NURC, 2008c, p. 13; Ranger, 1999, p. 23).[13] As Ranger argues, the concepts of nationalism and ethnicity are neither inherently good nor bad. The perceived consequences of these constructions are defined by the prevailing voice in the moral debate on the issue (1999, p. 23). The RPF, as 'moral guardians', has depreciated the moral value of ethnic terms by equating their use with the promotion of 'divisionism' and 'genocide ideology' (Pottier, 2002, p. 207).

The government's stated commitment to eradicating 'genocide ideology' adds significant moral value to the singular national identity of the Banyarwanda. The NURC describes it as 'any ideology that would see the extermination of the other group – considered as the enemy – as the (final) solution to problems

13 Although using ethnic labels has been banned from public discourse, such as radio broadcasts and public speeches, they continue to be employed in more private settings between friends and family members (interview with son of returnee, 8 April 2009).

of its society' (NURC, 2008c, p. 7). This definition suggests that should the ideology spread, a return to genocide would be imminent (Waldorf, 2009, p. 109). As such, the depiction of the singular national identity of all Rwandans as a safeguard against a return to genocide supports its construction. As the 2003 Constitution's preamble makes clear, 'We, the People of Rwanda … resolved to fight the ideology of genocide and all its manifestations and to eradicate ethnic, regional, and any other form of divisions' (MOD, 2003, p. 1).

The singular national identity is also promoted through fostering 'nationalist enthusiasm' (Anderson, 2006, p. 163). Anderson describes this sense of excitement as taking place in the context of the nation-building policies of new states. He argues that it takes two forms simultaneously: a genuine and popular expression of the people, and a nationalist ideology systematically promoted to citizens in a top-down manner through media, civic education and government policies (ibid.). The Rwandan government has put the latter method of fostering nationalist enthusiasm into practice through introducing a new national flag in 2001 and a national anthem in 2002 (Fawcett, 2003, as cited by Kiwuwa, 2007, p. 19). This sense of enthusiasm is also promoted at ingando and itorero ry'igihugu camps, which emphasise the importance of unity, national pride and the benefits of a singular national identity (NURC, 2009a, pp. 12–13).[14]

The implications of unity and nation-building for 'national reconciliation'

The RPF as arbiter

President Kagame reminded the population of its shared ownership of the nation during an RPF rally in Kirehe district days before winning a 93 per cent majority in the August 2010 presidential election (Rwanda News Agency, 4 August 2010; Reuters, 11 August 2010). Kagame reiterated the message of a singular Rwandan identity when he asked, '[w]hich majority are they talking about because the majority is you people and Rwanda doesn't belong to Hutu, Tutsi or Twa – it belongs to Rwandans' (ibid.). Kagame was responding to suggestions that FDU-Inkingi leader Victoire Ingabire was fighting for

14 Although the syllabi of both ingando and itorero ry'igihugu engage heavily with the Rwandan national identity, there are several features that distinguish the mandates of each camp. According to the NURC, the stated mandate of ingando is to 'promote reflection and discussion on post-conflict national reconciliation and reconstruction challenges with a view to mapping out solutions to address them' (NURC, 2009a, p. 9). The stated goals of itorero are, however, 'to promote values of unity, truth, culture and of hard work and avoiding attitudes and mindsets that deter development all aimed at speeding up the attainment of Vision 2020' (ibid., p. 12).

Hutu people's rights and thus represented the interests of the majority of Rwandan citizens (ibid.). FDU-Inkingi was barred from running in the 2010 presidential elections and Ingabire faced numerous accusations related to her alleged promotion of 'genocide ideology' (BBC News, 25 October 2010).[15] This quotation demonstrates the political value of the Banyarwanda's singular national identity in two ways. Firstly, Kagame's appeal to unity discredits political support for Ingabire and FDU-Inkingi by equating it to 'divisionism', as it allegedly singles out one ethnic group for representation. Secondly, as discussed earlier, the inclusive nature of the identity of the Banyarwanda serves as a rallying point which fosters support for the RPF.

The top-down manner in which the RPF promotes its conceptions of unity, nation-building and national identity presents multiple challenges for achieving the National Unity and Reconciliation Programme's stated goals. The first challenge relates to the RPF's forceful approach to institutionalising a singular national identity for all Rwandans. As Simon states, harsh punishments for public expressions of ethnic identity are counterproductive. Accusations of 'genocide ideology' and 'divisionism' are unlikely to rid the nation of associations with the ethnic identities they held prior to and during the genocide, he argues. Instead, this attack on ethnicity may prevent free expression and foster further animosity between groups, thus preventing the promotion of unity and reconciliation (2012, p. 262).

The second of these challenges relates to the risk that promoting unity, nation-building and national identity could be an entirely elite undertaking. As Kiwuwa asserts, the state is far from a 'neutral arbiter' in the construction of national identity (2007, p. 22). Indeed, the RPF is an active participant in the process as it attempts to eradicate allegiances to ethnic groups. Boyce contends that a nation-building initiative ought to be derived from the national constitution rather than appeal solely to the interests of political elites (1999, p. 238). The 2003 Constitution states that the government is committed to such fundamental principles as eradicating 'genocide ideology' and 'divisionism' as well as promoting unity, equality, social welfare, consensus and dialogue (MOD, 2003, p. 3). Article 9 of the Constitution states:

> The State of Rwanda commits itself to conform to the following fundamental principles and to promote and enforce the respect thereof:
>
> - Fighting the ideology of genocide and all its manifestations;
> - Eradication of ethnic, regional and other divisions and promotion of national unity;
> - Equitable sharing of power;
> - Building a state governed by the rule of law, a pluralistic government, equality of all Rwandans and between women and

15 The impact of accusations of 'genocide ideology' and 'divisionism' on political space in Rwanda will be explored in detail in chapters 5 and 6.

men reflected by ensuring that women are granted at least thirty per cent of posts in decision-making organs;

- Building a state committed to promoting social welfare and establishing appropriate mechanisms for ensuring social justice;
- The constant quest for solutions through dialogue and consensus (ibid.).

Although the RPF stated a commitment to promoting equality, social welfare and dialogue, the rigid nature of its approach to national unity and nation-building hinders these pledges from being realised.

The absence of equity and equality for survivors and the Twa community

The pursuit of national unity and nation-building, through constructing a singular national identity, conflicts with the promotion of equality, social welfare and free speech. Rwanda's population in the post-conflict context is diverse. Contrary to what Kagame stated in the excerpt above, taken from his speech at the RPF rally in Kirehe District, the population of Rwanda is far more varied than the ethnic labels Hutu, Tutsi or Twa would suggest. These divisions include political identities created by the RPF that relate to experiences of violence prior to and during the 1994 genocide. As discussed in chapter 3, these identities include those of ex-combatants, genocide perpetrators, survivors, returning groups of 'new caseload' refugees who fled during the 1994 genocide, and 'old caseload' refugees who fled during periods of violence in the 1950s and 1960s (Hintjens, 2008, p. 80). The disparity of experiences from which these identities stem runs counter to the shared identity and common experience of 'bad history' emphasised by the RPF (NURC, 2007, p. 2).[16]

This disparity is compounded in the post-conflict context by the absence of equity and equality for some. For instance, survivors continue to be among the most marginalised groups in the country. President Kagame acknowledged the challenges facing many survivors and firmly placed the blame on the poor performance of 'bad politicians' (speech, 7 April 2010). Kagame encouraged all citizens to hold those responsible accountable for their actions so that survivors could join in the communal processes of nation-building and development (ibid.). This appeal to nation-building, unity and national identity fails to get to grips with the issues of equality and social welfare that continue to plague many survivors. According to the Survivors Fund (SURF), these include extreme poverty since 50,000 survivor households were reported to be without income in 2008 (2008, p. 6).[17]

16 See Lemarchand and Niwese for discussion about how differing memories of the genocide affect how groups understand and interact with each other in Rwanda (2007, p. 166). The authors argue that the RPF uses nation-building to restrain what they refer to as 'the public expression of ethnic memories' (ibid., p. 181).

17 Issues affecting many survivors, including poverty, difficulties accessing healthcare and inadequate housing will be examined in more detail in chapter 6.

The fact that many survivors did not receive social welfare is made all the more apparent when compared with the support given to ex-combatants returning from the Great Lakes Region. Upon completing the demobilisation process at Mutobo camp, ex-combatants, including former members of the FDLR,[18] receive 60,000 Rwf from the RPF government and an additional 100,000 RwF three months later for use in investment, trade and developing small businesses (Kanyambo interview, 27 June 2009).[19] Rather than levelling the playing field, the financial support given to ex-combatants may exacerbate tensions in the communities to which they return. Disparity created by this financial aid is pertinent as 60 per cent of the Rwandan population lives in poverty, 42 per cent of them in absolute destitution (UNDP, 2011, p. 1).[20] The demobilisation process also increases inequality with regard to justice. Since 2005, no officially reintegrated ex-combatants have been tried at gacaca for crimes committed between 1990–4 (Waldorf and Clark debate, 3 March 2010). When asked about the conviction rate of ex-combatants at gacaca John Kanyambo, then assistant centre manager at Mutobo Demobilisation and Reintegration Camp, replied 'justice from 1994 is not really our concern' (interview, 27 June 2009).

Widespread impunity for demobilised and reintegrated ex-combatants may be granted for several reasons. The first, as Kanyambo explained, is to encourage ex-soldiers and rebels to return, who would not do so willingly if they were to face conviction at gacaca (ibid.). This point is disputable, however, as none of the six hundred ex-combatants at Mutobo camp at the time of this interview entered Rwanda willingly. They had all been captured by MONUC, now MONUSCO, the United Nations' Peacekeeping mission in DRC. Once captured, they began the demobilisation process in Goma, eastern DRC, and

18 Approximately 90% of ex-combatants at Mutobo camp, when I visited in June 2009, knew each other from their time in the Forces Démocratiques pour la Libération du Rwanda (FDLR) (Kanyambo interview, 27 June 2009). The FDLR is a predominantly Hutu rebel force that has been involved in violent conflict in eastern DRC, including killings, rapes and abductions of thousands of Congolese civilians since 2000 (HRW, 2009, pp. 10, 30). The FDLR, some members of which participated in the 1994 genocide, continue to pose a significant threat to civilians living in DRC's North and South Kivu provinces near the Rwandan border. An arrest warrant was issued for FDLR Commander Sylvestre Mudacumura by the ICC in July 2012 on nine counts of war crimes committed in 2009 and 2010. As of July 2015 he has still not been arrested (HRW, 13 July 2015).

19 In May 2015, 60,000 RwF was equal to approximately £55 and 100,000 RwF was equivalent to £92 (XE Currency Exchange, 14 May 2015).

20 Chapter 2 of the 1995 report on the World Summit on Social Development Programme of Action in Copenhagen defines 'absolute poverty' as a 'condition characterized by severe deprivation of basic human needs, including food, safe drinking water, sanitation facilities, health, shelter, education and information. It depends not only on income but also on access to social services' (UN, 1995, p.1).

then crossed the border into the reintegration programme at Mutobo in north-western Rwanda (ibid.). Secondly, excluding ex-combatants from gacaca trials may have been partially or fully informed by the impetus to finish hearing new genocide cases and complete the gacaca process. Thirdly, this impunity may more closely reflect the same political interests that may inform allotting financial support to ex-combatants once they have completed ingando training at demobilisation camp.[21] Impunity may be used to appease ex-combatants in order to circumvent any political discord or violence from these predominantly Hutu combatants inside Rwanda's borders. Prioritising reintegration and the political interests that inform it may impede the rebuilding of relationships between ex-combatants and those living in the communities to which they return. It may also frustrate many survivors as they continue to struggle with extreme poverty (Melvin, 2010, p. 944).

The Twa minority faces an altogether different struggle of marginalisation and poverty that is magnified by the implementation of a singular national identity. The Twa people are believed to be the first inhabitants of the Great Lakes Region's equatorial forest areas. Twa groups continue to live in Burundi, southern Uganda, Rwanda and eastern areas of DRC (Lewis, 2000, p. 3). Prior to the arrival of European colonists, they shared a common hunter-gatherer history (ibid., p. 5). The Twa in Rwanda, who consider themselves to be an indigenous people, have not been granted political identities related to the events of 1994 as they were for the most part not directly involved in the civil war or the genocide. They were, however, affected by the displacement, uncertainty and violence it caused (ibid., p. 23). Minority Rights Group International (MRGI) states that, in 1994, the Twa accounted for up to 0.4 per cent of Rwanda's population. The NGO estimates that 30 per cent of the Twa population died or was killed as a result of the 1994 genocide (ibid.).[22] Many Twa fled during the conflict, while the majority of those who remained were displaced (ibid., p. 24).

In 2007, CAURWA (Community of the Rwandese Autochtons), an NGO which promotes Twa rights, conflicted with the RPF over the official recognition of the Twa as an indigenous group in Rwanda. The government argued that it would promote 'divisionism' (COPORWA, n.d.) and also threatened to suspend aid to Twa communities if they continued to refer to themselves as a distinct people (MRGI, 2012, p. 1). In 2006, the Ministry of

21 Ex-combatants at Mutobo demobilisation camp attend an ingando session that lasts several months. It includes lectures about 'national reconciliation', as well as more practical lessons about hygiene and how to apply for bank loans (Kanyambo interview, 27 June 2009).

22 Dorothy Jackson, who conducted research for MRGI, stated that these deaths were never officially acknowledged (2003). In April 2012, MRGI explained that the suffering of Twa people caused by the 1994 genocide has still 'gone largely unrecognized' (2012, p. 1).

Justice (Minijust) threatened to suspend CAURWA's charities licence unless the organisation agreed to stop referring to Twa as Rwanda's first inhabitants, and removed the terms 'indigenous' or 'autochtons' from the NGO's title (ibid.). CAURWA eventually reached an agreement with the government to refer to the Twa community by the most prominent profession of its members - pottery - and to change its name to COPORWA (Rwandese Community of Potters) (COPORWA, n.d.; Ndahinda, 2011, p. 239).

Although the term 'Twa' has been replaced with 'Potter' in a purported attempt to unite the nation, this group continues to be isolated by discrimination, extreme poverty, rampant unemployment, and reduced access to healthcare, education and traditional land (COPORWA, 2009, p. 1; MRGI, 2012, p. 1). Lewis states that the RPF's de facto banning of ethnic terms has helped to reduce some public discrimination experienced by Twa people (2000, p. 24). The group is still at risk, however, of losing its distinct identity as an indigenous group. Moreover, it appears that little consideration has been given to the plight of many Twa living inside Rwanda, 'Nowadays, the relationship between Hutus, Tutsis and Twas has become a conflict between two ethnic groups: Tutsis and Hutus. As for Twas, they seem to have been completely forgotten' (Office of the President, 1999, p. 2). The loss of a distinct identity and the fact that Twa community members were not granted equity and equality further demonstrate the paucity of commitments made to promoting equal rights, social welfare and dialogue in the 2007 Reconciliation Policy and 2003 Constitution.

Unity and 'national reconciliation': process or end goal?

The RPF's focus on the unity and shared role of all citizens in the nation-building process neglects to deal with issues other than ethnicity that could cause future conflict. As Susanne Buckley-Zistel argues, 'the government fabricates unity without reconciliation' (2006, p. 102). She makes this point with reference to the RPF's focus on citizenship as the basis for both unity and reconciliation (ibid.). Her argument is also relevant to the RPF's rhetorical use of the participation of all Rwandans in the nation-building process to gloss over issues of equality, dialogue and social welfare as articulated in the 2003 Constitution. Moreover, prioritising both unity and nation-building may impede the successful promotion of the RPF's vision of 'national reconciliation', as it jumps to the official reconciliation programme's end goals before they have been achieved.

An earlier section of this chapter discussed the relationship between unity, nation-building and 'national reconciliation', as defined by the 2007 Reconciliation Policy. Although it can be deduced from this document and Vision 2020 that unity and nation-building reflect priorities of the RPF's official reconciliation programme, neither document definitively states whether national unity is conceived of as a process or as an end goal of a process:

> Under normal conditions, however, reconciliation takes place between the oppressor and the oppressed through mediation or not. In any case, prior to reconciliation and restoration of mutual friendly relationships, one who has caused harm to the other should admit and regret his/her wrong doings, apologize for them and if need be, give compensation. For the Rwandan case, none of those prerequisites has been fully met. And this constitutes one of the major obstacles for the process to be successful (Mugabe Shyaka, 2004, p. 35).

Unity is depicted in this study, as well as in the 2007 Reconciliation Policy, as an objective of the official reconciliation programme as a whole (NURC, 2007, p. 3). For instance, unity is referred to as something that ought to be fought for as well as the determining criteria of building a unified country (ibid.). Thus, in the context of the National Unity and Reconciliation Programme, the RPF's stated commitment to building a 'strong, modern and united nation' can logically be understood as an end goal of that process (Minecofin, 2000, p. 4). For instance, Vision 2020 states, 'Rwanda will become a modern, united and prosperous nation founded on the positive values of its culture. The nation will be open to the world, including its own Diaspora. Rwandans will be a people, sharing the same vision for the future and ready to contribute to social cohesion, equity and equality of opportunity' (ibid. p. 11). This shared vision of the future resembles elements of 'thick' reconciliation as described by Crocker (2000).

Nation-building and national unity are predicated on the construction of a single people, the Banyarwanda, one that allegedly recognises it has a shared common history, language and culture. It also purportedly shares a comprehensive vision of the future that is committed to building a prosperous and developed nation. The RPF's emphasis on the shared nature of the vision serves the same rhetorical function as the concepts of commonality, shared values and national identity discussed earlier in this chapter; it legitimises the RPF's chosen path to future prosperity. Like the role of the entire population in building the nation, this shared desire glosses over issues of inequity and inequality that plague the government's nation-building agenda and its vision of 'national reconciliation' more generally.

The top-down structure of the nation-building agenda creates further problems in promoting 'national reconciliation'. This inflexible, top-down structure precludes analysis and open discussion, both of which are necessary for fostering trust between civilians and the state or 'vertical' reconciliation. Buckley-Zistel argues that the RPF's top-down approach to promoting its vision of national unity and reconciliation is weakened by a growing sense of mistrust directed at the state, located in issues surrounding the fact that perpetrators feel no remorse, as well as misleading confessions at gacaca, false imprisonment and disregard for victims of the 1994 genocide (2006, p. 111). Additionally, the RPF's failure to promote equality, social welfare and free speech for all citizens, commitments it made in the 2003 Constitution, frustrates the process of 'vertical' reconciliation, as well as the possibility of successfully promoting its vision of unity and 'horizontal' reconciliation between citizens.

The de facto banning of ethnicity from public discourse prevents open debate about the benefits and disadvantages of the new national identity as well as criticism of the government's approach to unity and nation-building. It also limits discussion about whether or not this sense of identity is in fact uniting Rwandans or is even desired by the population. The risk of being accused of 'genocide ideology' or 'divisionism' further limits free debate of unity, nation-building and 'national reconciliation' among citizens. This not only contravenes the RPF's stated commitment to dialogue in the 2003 Constitution, but also limits bottom-up approaches to reconciliation.

Grassroots reconciliation organisations operating in Rwanda must register with the NURC.[23] In so doing, these groups must follow the 2007 Reconciliation Policy guidelines and laws related to 'genocide ideology' and 'divisionism', all of which limit opposition and public discussion of issues related to ethnicity, identity and experiences of the 1994 genocide that deviate from the 'victor's narrative' (Mukajiranga interview, 9 June 2009; NURC, 2007, p. 9).[24] As a volunteer in a religious youth group focusing on forgiveness and reconciliation stated, 'a [genocide ideology] law is needed, but should be reformed to make it safer for us to do our jobs … even if you have good intentions, one small slip of the tongue can put you in jail' (interview, 21 July 2010). These legal and normative restrictions ensure that the RPF maintains control over the ways in which its vision of 'national reconciliation' is promulgated. This level of authority also ensures the continued promotion of the government's conception of Rwanda's past and its future.

Conclusion

Contradictions, political interests and a top-down structure inform the relationship between unity, nation-building and 'national reconciliation' in the Rwandan context. The RPF's prioritisation of unity and nation-building

23 The term 'grassroots reconciliation organisation' refers to any community-driven club, group or cooperative with the stated mandate to promote unity and reconciliation. These groups often have other stated objectives including encouraging forgiveness, repentance and cooperation between survivors and perpetrators.

24 Although there was no database of NURC volunteers at the time of this interview, Laurence Mukajiranga, then acting director of the NURC's peace-building and conflict management department, estimated that there are approximately 1,000 grassroots unity and reconciliation initiatives across the country, all overseen by the NURC (interview, 9 June 2009).

within the National Unity and Reconciliation Programme is evident in official discourse, government documents and reconciliation projects such as ingando and itorero ry'igihugu. The dual gaze (both backward and forward) of unity and nation-building creates a highly prescriptive path along which both priorities are pursued. Moreover, the presupposition of social and cultural values that promote social cohesion is informed by RPF-sponsored historical narrative. The 'victor's narrative' legitimises the RPF's approach to unity and nation-building. It also provides justification for the de facto banning of ethnicity from public discourse and the condemnation of acts and thoughts deemed to promote 'divisionism' or 'genocide ideology'. The impetus to eradicate these acts, thoughts and ideologies further justifies the RPF's construction of the Banyarwanda's singular national identity, one which although it may create 'a people' at the national level, fails to adequately follow through on the government's own stated commitments to equality, social welfare and dialogue. This may not only impede the realisation of national unity and nation-building, but also the government's vision of 'national reconciliation'.

The RPF's conception of national unity and its nation-building agenda also precludes analysis and restricts active participation in the National Unity and Reconciliation Programme. Fear of accusations of 'genocide ideology' and 'divisionism', coupled with the official reconciliation programme's prescriptive top-down structure, leaves little room for open discussion and criticism of pertinent issues, policies and programmes. Although there are close to 1,000 grassroots unity and reconciliation initiatives in Rwanda, they must all abide by the 2007 Reconciliation Policy and face the same risk of being accused of 'negative ideologies' as do journalists, political opponents and NGOs, should they engage with issues of ethnicity and identity or publicly criticise the RPF. The result of this top-down approach is the achievement of a singular national identity with little regard for several of the stated commitments related to promoting the government's own vision of 'national reconciliation'.

The government's failure to make good on its commitments to promote equal rights, social welfare and dialogue is compounded by its 'fabrication' of unity. As described by Buckley-Zistel (2006), this potentially impedes 'national reconciliation' in several ways. The emphasis on national identity and the shared role of all Rwandans in the endeavour promotes the end goal of 'building a modern, strong and united nation' before it has been achieved (Minecofin, 2000, p. 4). Also, if the RPF defines 'national reconciliation' as the rebuilding of 'horizontal' and 'vertical' relationships, it must allow space and time for these connections to develop rather than attempt to construct a single people united by common attributes and experiences. If Buckley-Zistel is correct and mistrust is developing between the state and citizens, the consequences for 'national reconciliation' could be calamitous. Moreover, the absence of equity, equality and free speech could result in further divisions between the people of the nation.

Chapter 5

Teaching the nation: reconciliation through education

> *Historical clarity is a duty of memory that we cannot escape. Behind the words 'Never Again', there is a story whose truth must be told in full, no matter how uncomfortable (Kagame, 20th Commemoration of Genocide against the Tutsi, 7 April 2014)*

Two hundred students dressed in Rwandan Defense Force (RDF) uniforms sat in attendance at ingando at the Peace and Leadership Centre in north-western Rwanda.[1] The speaker that afternoon was Captain Gerald Nyirimanzi of the RDF, whose lecture focused on national unity and included a presentation called, 'Hutu and Tutsi constructed races or ethnic groups: the root causes of the Rwandan conflict system'. After the presentation was over, Nyirimanzi asked the teenagers to raise their hands if they were Hutu. When no hands were raised, he asked the same question of the Tutsi students and received the same lack of response.

Nyirimanzi then asked the group whether they thought the ethnic terms of Hutu and Tutsi should be officially reinstated in Rwanda. A microphone was passed around the hall to give students the opportunity to share their thoughts about the advantages and disadvantages of ethnic identities in the country. One student suggested that the terms should be reinstated and used to reflect social status as they had in the pre-colonial period.[2] She proposed using the term 'Hutu' to represent those on the lower rungs of society and that of 'Tutsi' to depict members of the upper class. The student reasoned that the class difference would inspire Hutu to work harder and rise 'to the top class like Tutsi' (ingando training, 3 June 2009). After a series of arguments

1 The head of ingando training at the Peace and Leadership Centre reported to me that students wear RDF fatigues to 'demystify the uniform'. Asked about the relationship between the RDF and ingando, he stated, 'We don't intend to make you a soldier' (interview with ingando official, 15 June 2009).

2 The depiction of ethnic terms as relatively flexible social identities in the pre-colonial period featured heavily in Nyirimanzi's presentation. The students attending this particular ingando camp were preparing to begin their university studies shortly after this mandatory six-week course concluded.

for and against the restoration of ethnic terms, Nyirimanzi led the students to the conclusion that ethnic identities were among the root causes of violence in Rwanda and the Great Lakes Region. He ended the session by reminding them of the benefits of the government abolishing ethnic labels and the advantages of being unified by a single national identity (ibid.).

This lecture about history and identity at ingando illustrates specific elements of the National Unity and Reconciliation Programme's education remit. The stated commitment to sensitising the population about the need to fight for unity, their role as patriots, and the customs and values that purportedly promote social cohesion appear in the 2007 Reconciliation Policy's 'specific objectives' (NURC, 2007, p. 3). The stated goals of civic education camps include: teaching citizens about their rights and the importance of Vision 2020; giving lessons about unity and 'national reconciliation' in schools; teaching Rwandan history; and promoting ingando seminars in order to foster a culture of peace and 'good governance' across Rwanda (ibid., p. 4).

The perceived need to reeducate the population about unity and 'national reconciliation' was formally expressed in 1999 in the 'Nation-wide grassroots consultations report: unity and reconciliation initiatives in Rwanda'. The consultation was conducted with the stated goal of giving all Rwandans the opportunity to participate in influencing and designing the path towards national unity and reconciliation. It engaged with issues ranging from the perceived causes of 'disunity' in Rwanda to ways in which 'national reconciliation' should be promoted. Since it was not possible for all Rwandans to participate in the grassroots consultation, they were represented by 200 members from key target groups including community leaders, women's committees, business and religious leaders (NURC, 1999). This consultation, led by the newly formed National Unity and Reconciliation Commission (NURC), promoted the use of civic education to enlighten citizens about such issues as human rights, the importance of truth, and the accurate representation of history and national identity (ibid., p. 15). The consultation highlighted the importance of free discussion about issues that purportedly divide Rwandans, as well as the use of 'solidarity' camps to overcome obstacles hindering the promotion of national unity and 'national reconciliation' (ibid., pp. 15, 17). 'Solidarity' camps had been established three years earlier in 1996 with the stated goal of aiding the repatriation and reintegration of Rwandan refugees who had fled during the 1994 genocide (Mgbako, 2005, p. 209). Towards the end of the 1990s, ingando 'solidarity' camps were expanded to include participants from diverse groups, including convicted genocide perpetrators, ex-combatants and students entering university. These mandatory camps became the sole formal source of Rwandan history after the genocide.

Civic education at ingando

Ingando restored

Ingando was described by former NURC executive secretary Fatuma Ndangiza as 'nothing short of a revisit to culture' during an NURC presentation at the 2003 International Conference on Security and Lasting Peace in the Great Lakes Region (2003, p. 7). Like gacaca, ingando purportedly reflects elements of a traditional Rwandan cultural institution that has been restored from its pre-colonial roots to promote the government's vision of 'national reconciliation'. The term 'ingando' is taken from the verb *kugandika*, which in the Kinyarwanda language is the act of interrupting daily activities to reflect upon and find solutions to challenges facing the nation. These periods of coming together to contemplate and problem-solve allegedly took place in times of war, disaster and national catastrophe during the pre-colonial era (ibid.). Legal scholar Chi Mgbako contradicts the NURC's description of ingando's historical origin. She argues that although there is historical evidence of meetings between elders to address issues of interest to the community, there is none to support the claim that the process was called 'ingando', making it an 'invented tradition' (2005, p. 208). Mgbako contends that it most likely refers to a 'pre-war RPF creation' in which participants were mobilised about pro-RPF ideology (ibid.).

The post-conflict iteration of ingando supported the Government of National Unity's (GNU) efforts to reintegrate repatriated citizens who had fled to neighbouring countries prior to and during the 1994 genocide (ibid., p. 209). Mgbako explains that the first camps established in 1996 were designed to reintegrate Tutsi returnees and foster a sense of nationalism among them (ibid.). Unlike Mgbako, the NURC, which took over leadership of ingando camps in 1999, does not specify the ethnicity of the first participants although it does point to a connection between them and ex-combatants by clarifying that refugees entered the camps, 'when they decided to dissociate themselves from ex-FAR and Interahamwe militia', implying that these refugees were Hutu (NURC, 2007, p. 16).

In the years following refugees' initial participation at ingando, separate camps were established for groups including politicians, women's association members, students and ex-combatants. The duration of these mandatory live-in camps ranged from several days to several months (Mgbako, 2005, p. 209). Although the groups attending these camps were diverse, the overarching mandate of all ingando 'solidarity' camps remained the same:

> By any accepted standards of reckoning, the single most important determinant affecting Rwanda's future is the tragic legacy of the social divisions which have plagued the country since ethnic distinctions were first exacerbated during the colonial era. The legacy culminated in one of the most horrific human tragedies in recorded human history: the genocide of 1994 that left the country with deep psychological, social

> and economic scars … It suffices to mention that the only hopeful response is the emergence, at all levels, of well trained and patriotic leaders, who can facilitate intercultural co-existence and peace building initiatives. At another level, members of the community need to be trained and sensitised in order to improve awareness of their societal values, systems of governance, their fundamental human rights and civic responsibilities. This can only be done through community sensitization (Ndangiza, 2003, pp. 4–5).

The perceived necessity to sensitise citizens and leaders reflects the condition that *all Rwandans* must correct their mindsets and bad behaviour (NURC, 2011b, p. 1). The desire to teach all community members about societal values, governance, human rights and civic responsibilities also speaks to large parts of the population having participated in the 1994 genocide. President Kagame estimated that upwards of one million Hutu civilians and officials in Habyarimana's government took part (Hintjens, 2008, p. 82).[3] The dual emphasis on mass participation and reeducation resonates with the controversial assumption that Rwandans are ignorant or culturally predisposed to obedience and were thus easily manipulated into committing acts of genocide, as analysed by Uvin (2001).[4] Authors such as Straus and Fujii reject this simplistic interpretation of participation and provide more nuanced analyses of the decisions made by civilians to join in the killing (Straus, 2006; Fujii, 2009).

The RPF's stated commitment to eradicating 'genocide ideology' and 'divisionism' resounds throughout the National Unity and Reconciliation Programme, and ingando is no different. The NURC's 2006 report about the 'solidarity' camps' impact on the promotion of unity and 'national reconciliation' describes the commission's task as having to

> overcome all the barriers and face the unimaginable challenges to wash all the past dirtiness down and to re-invent a 'new societal intelligence' through which the people of Rwanda supported by his development partners proceeded to a fundamental change and rebuilt a holistically unified, pacified, hatred-free, and committed to forge hand-in-hand a country armed with a new mind-set and values (p. 11).

Karl Mannheim's conception of 'unmasking the mind' is particularly helpful for analysing the ideology that informs the construction of this new societal

3 Kagame also identified the remaining Hutu population, those who did not kill but also did not attempt to stop the killing, as bystanders to the 1994 genocide and thus also culpable in the devastation it caused. According to Hintjens, the highest estimate academics have calculated in relation to active participation by Hutu in the genocide is 10%, or between 350,000 and 600,000 people (2008, p. 82).

4 Uvin analyses three dominant paradigms used by scholars, human rights activists and journalists to describe why the 1994 genocide happened. They include: perpetrators' social and psychological features that made some civilians more likely to participate in the genocide, discussed above; social tension related to resource scarcity; and elite manipulation (2001).

intelligence (1952, p. 140). According to Mannheim, the act of unmasking does not seek to refute or deny an idea, but rather to uncover the social and psychological function it serves in society (ibid., p. 141).[5] In the context of ingando and itorero, ideology functions to denounce ethnicity, 'genocide ideology' and 'divisionism', and bolster support for government programmes including official reconciliation and development.

Ingando narrative and targets

'Ingando is propaganda. I hate it because I love thinking for myself' (interview with volunteer, 21 July 2010). The ingando system provides a particularly rich example of the top-down dissemination of the RPF's conceptualisations of unity, nation-building and identity. As the previous chapter demonstrates, the official historical narrative of pre-colonial unity informs these conceptions. Rwandan history appears in the curricula of all types of ingando, but its largest audience comprises students about to enter university, as the lectures aimed at them form the most prevalent type of 'solidarity' camp (interview with Lliberwaax, 28 June 2009; PRI, 2004; Mgbako, 2005, p. 217). Susan Thomson highlights the RPF's distinction between 'solidarity' and 'education' camps in Rwanda, specifying that the former include ingandos run for the above-mentioned students, politicians and gacaca judges or inyangamugayo. Education camps, she clarifies, are organised for self-confessed genocide perpetrators, commercial sex workers, street children and ex-combatants (2011, p. 333).[6] In the context of 'solidarity' camps for students entering university, Rwandan history is featured as one of six major topics taught in lectures during the ingando programme (NURC, n.d., p. 1).[7] The second chapter, entitled 'Rwandan history', includes a series of topics:

> After this chapter the trainees shall be able:
>
> To show that unity existed in the Rwandan community and was later destroyed by the bad leadership which has led to conflict and genocide.

5 Mannheim distinguishes between the acts of unmasking an ideology and unmasking a lie. The latter action, he argues, discredits the 'moral personality' of the person who has lied rather than simply determining the function served by the lie (1952, p. 140).

6 Thomson is a Canadian scholar whom the RPF forced to attend ingando lectures with self-confessed genocide perpetrators in 2006. The government allegedly sent her to be 'reeducated' as her research was deemed to go 'against national unity and reconciliation' (2011, p. 331). The chapter just cited, entitled 'Reeducation for reconciliation: participant observations on ingando', gives a detailed account of Thomson's experiences at ingando (2011).

7 The full title of this document is 'A summary of lectures used in solidarity camps and other workshops in six lectures'. The other chapters include such titles as, 'nation and nationality', 'human rights and conflict management', 'good governance', 'man and his environment', and 'economy and social welfare' (NURC, n.d., p. 1).

> To show that Rwandans need to take the lead in providing solutions to problems caused/consequences of/ by the genocide.
>
> **Things to be discussed:**
>
> The summary of the Rwandan history 41
>
> Problems caused by ethnic groups in Rwanda and in the Great Lakes region 50
>
> Rwandan citizenship and the nationality of Rwanda 59
>
> Genocide in Rwanda and elsewhere 65
>
> Trauma and counselling 74
>
> Fighting against discrimination and genocide ideology in Rwanda and the Great Lakes region 81
>
> (ibid., p. 2).

Although these topics illustrate the discursive emphasis on identity, ethnicity and 'genocide ideology', it is the methods used to teach this chapter that most greatly restrict critical thinking and dialogue about issues related to identity, the 1994 genocide and the National Unity and Reconciliation Programme more generally. For instance, each lesson given at ingando is accompanied by a set of goals or targets that all students must meet. After absorbing this chapter on Rwandan history, students should be able 'to show that unity existed in the Rwandan community and was later destroyed by the bad leadership which has led to conflict and genocide' (ibid.). These targets demonstrate ingando's highly restrictive nature as it seeks to create a single set of conclusions about Rwandan history (Melvin, 2010, p. 940).

The singular nature of the 'victor's narrative' of history is reflected in other chapters of the ingando syllabus. This narrative informs the lectures given about ethnicity as they describe 'the real state of ethnicity in Rwanda' as well as clarifying 'the origin of the problems about ethnicity in [the] African Great Lakes Region' (NURC, 2003, pp. 3–4). The FDLR's former Major General, Paul Rwarakabije, delivered a lecture on the latter topic to students at ingando in July 2009. Rwarakabije had surrendered in November 2003 and was at the time of his presentation working with the Rwandan Demobilisation and Reintegration Commission (IRIN News, 22 January 2004). The example of Captain Nyirimanzi's lecture, given at the beginning of this chapter, demonstrates the target-oriented pedagogy as well as the singular nature of the narrative disseminated at ingando. The narrow scope of these targets diminishes students' experience of thinking critically about the political rhetoric that imbues their curriculum; a direct contradiction of the goal to promote objective analysis, as outlined by Fatuma Ndangiza in 2003 (Ndangiza, 2003, p. 9; Mgbako, 2005, p. 217).

The paucity of critical evaluation and target-free discussions about the 'victor's narrative' and government conceptions of 'national reconciliation', 'divisionism' and 'genocide ideology' is made all the more poignant in the context of restricted freedom of speech, expression and media in Rwanda. Independent media organisations faced increasing restrictions in the run-up to the presidential elections in August 2010. Reporters without Borders, the international NGO, stated that some 30 radio stations and news publications had been suspended in the week before the elections for failing to register with the Media High Council.[8] On 5 February 2011, opinion pieces published in *Umurabyo* newspaper prior to the election led to the imprisonment of the paper's editor and deputy editor, Agnes Nkusi Uwimana and Saidati Mukakibibi respectively. Uwimana was found guilty of 'genocide ideology', 'divisionism' and defamation, and sentenced to 17 years in prison, while Mukakibibi received a seven-year prison term for threatening state security (AI, 2011, p. 5).

Ingando has the stated mandate to promote critical discussion and 'inculcate into the youth a healthy liberated mind', yet it misses the opportunity to foster critical analysis of the history it teaches or the 'solidarity' it seeks to promote (Ndangiza, 2003, p. 11). The restrictive target-oriented pedagogy ensures that ingando functions as a government-sponsored indoctrination camp that disseminates a singular narrative to a captive audience.[9] Yet, as McLean Hilker argues, it is not possible to entirely silence 'alternative' narratives of the past (2011, p. 327). The fact that there was no public discussion about the existence of multiple historical narratives may instead bolster the perception of separate Hutu and Tutsi understandings of the past. She argues that this may encourage conflict between the RPF-sponsored narrative and counter-narratives of why the 1994 genocide took place (ibid.).[10]

8 The 2009 Media Law required these stations and publications to submit a request for an operating permit (Reporters without Borders, 2010, as cited by Longman, 2011b, p. 1).

9 Mgbako makes a similar point regarding indoctrination at ingando. She refers to the RPF's attempts 'both to plant the seeds of reconciliation, and to disseminate pro-RPF ideology through political indoctrination' (2005, p. 202). This chapter's analysis differs in that it does not examine whether ingando promotes 'true reconciliation', as described by Mgbako (ibid., p. 223). Instead, it analyses the ways in which ingando teaches the government's particular vision of unity and 'national reconciliation' in order to legitimise state programming and bolster political support for the current RPF regime.

10 McLean Hilker points to Eltringham's dichotomy of 'RPF meta-narrative' and 'counter-narrative' to differentiate between two dominant versions of Rwandan history (2011). Eltringham identifies the two narratives in interviews conducted with government officials, journalists and civil society leaders inside Rwanda, and exiled scholars, former government officials and civil society leaders in Europe between 1997–9 (2004, pp. 163, 177–8).

Itorero and Rwandan values

Itorero, like ingando, is an institution with purportedly historical roots that has been retooled to provide mandatory civic education to Rwandans. According to the NURC, the pre-colonial form of itorero ry'igihugu was a traditional school in which students were educated about integrity, problem solving and national values including patriotism, defence of the nation and 'fondness' for the Rwandan culture (NURC, 2009a, p. 12). It also offered cultural activities such as sport, dancing and singing and was used as a formal training programme for national leaders, during which they came to understand how cultural values could benefit their work, outlook and relationships with others (NURC, 2011b, p. 1). Unlike other 'home-grown' initiatives, itorero was not entirely wiped out during the colonial period. According to the NURC's Itorero Programme Strategy, changing the camp's mission was the first mandate of this period as colonisers sought to weaken Rwandan leadership. The result of this transformation was purportedly catastrophic for Rwanda as it facilitated the spread of genocide ideology and discrimination, ultimately resulting in the 1994 genocide (NURC, 2011c, p. 6).

President Kagame officially launched the post-conflict iteration of itorero on 16 November 2007 (NURC, 2009a, p. 3). Itorero and ingando were restored as part of the RPF's stated commitment to changing the minds of the entire population with regard to unity and 'national reconciliation'.

> Despite many achievements of building the Rwandan society after the **1994 genocide** against the Tutsi, there is still a problem with the mindset of Rwandans. Itorero ry'Igihugu is introduced to contribute to problem solving related to **mindset, bad behaviour, bad practices, through applying Rwandan cultural values** (NURC, 2011b, p. 1; document's emphases).

Perceived mindset and behaviour problems may stem from what the NURC describes as low levels among young people of social cohesion and engagement, education and patriotism, and of awareness about unity and reconciliation. Development is also challenged by high levels of unemployment and high risk of contracting HIV/AIDS, in addition to overpopulation and a high level of dependency on aid (NURC, 2011c, p. 6). Itorero seeks to overcome these challenges in part by fostering a culture of volunteerism for young Rwandans, building on the volunteerism that guides other state-led programmes including gacaca, umuganda and *urugerero* (national service). These emphasise the value of cooperation and volunteering, although participation in these projects, as with itorero, is compulsory for target groups.[11]

11 The target group for compulsory participation in urugerero is young people aged 18–35 who are completing their secondary education. Citizens outside of this age group may join the national service voluntarily (NURC, 2011c, p. 9).

Itorero also seeks to overcome challenges and speed up mindset change by merging cultural values with development objectives. This consolidation is achieved through disseminating specific Rwandan values that support unity, patriotism and development goals, as outlined in Vision 2020, the Economic, Development and Poverty Reduction Strategy (EDPRS) and the Millennium Development Goals (NURC, 2011c, p. 2; NURC, 2009b, p. 13). As Alphonse Bakusi explained, 'this country is trying to see how our cultural values can boost development' (interview, 23 July 2010).

The government's conception of cultural values and development plan are taught at itorero to a large number of participants or *intore* from different age groups, education levels and administrative positions.[12] They include young children, unmarried youth and older adults at the village level as well as students, employers, NGOs and leaders at the sector, district and national level itorero camps (NURC, 2011c).

Itorero camps follow similar schedules to those at ingando. The programme can be divided into four overarching modules. The 'Physical' module comprises such activities as marching, hand-to-hand combat, canoeing and practice missions which include night patrols and first-aid training. Two classroom-based modules, 'Nation' and 'Character Building' are also included. The former is guided by lessons about sovereignty, dignity and national security, while the latter consists of games and activities that build self-confidence and teach good values. The fourth module, 'Community Service', is practice-oriented as groups of intore participate in projects that serve society and the environment (NURC, 2011c, p. 20).

The Itorero Task Force was created in December 2008 to identify and mentor the intore whom teachers have selected as having a particularly strong grasp of the values and cultural taboos taught at itorero (ibid., p. 2). They include unity, patriotism, Rwandan spirit, nobility, heroism and 'standing up for national development' (NURC, 2011b, p. 2). More broadly, itorero is mandated to mentor 'a Rwandan citizen to become a positive change maker. *Itorero ry'Igihugu* is important for all citizens in all sectors of economic, social and political life' (ibid.). Every July, the intore deemed most and least ready to contribute to the promotion of 'good governance', patriotism and heroism are singled out by the district-level intore leaders, the National Electoral Commission, and the committee coordinating the anti-corruption and injustice structures among others (ibid., p. 4). The best intore or *indongozi* from different age groups and their mentors are publicly congratulated for their achievements (ibid.).

12 Between 2007–9, 25,000 community leaders and 43,000 primary and secondary school teachers attended itorero (NURC, 2009a, p. 13). As of July 2010, itorero had been expanded to include the mandatory participation of 30,000 intore recently graduated from high school (Bakusi interview, 23 July 2010).

Promoting the qualities described above not only bolsters the RPF's nation-building agenda, but also functions to build the people within that nation. As Balibar argues,

> *Every social community reproduced by the functioning of institutions is imaginary*, that is to say, it is based on the projection of individual existence into the weft of a collective narrative, on the recognition of a common name and on traditions lives as the trace of an immemorial past (even when they have been fabricated and inculcated in the recent past). But this comes down to accepting that, under certain conditions, *only* imaginary communities are real (1996, p. 138; author's emphases).

Balibar contends that in the context of nation-building, the community or 'people' does not exist naturally and must instead be made to continually reproduce itself as a national community (ibid.). Similarly, itorero's dual focus on common cultural values and working together to promote development makes it a particularly effective tool in the construction of the people of Rwanda. Disseminating the 'victor's narrative' at the camp and throughout the National Unity and Reconciliation Programme further strengthens the construction of the national community by focusing on the commonality of all Banyarwanda discussed in the preceding chapter.

The NURC's 2011 description of itorero outlines its stated commitment to fostering 'analytical re-view [sic] of National **values** and their implication in National development' (emphasis as in original text). It is difficult to conclude, however, that critical or oppositional views about these values may be made freely and publicly during these reviews (NURC, 2011b, p. 5). This doubt stems from concerns about the risk of being accused of 'genocide ideology' and 'divisionism', and derives from the singular nature of the historical narrative from which these cultural values and understanding of national unity originate. Moreover, the public identification of the best and worst performers at itorero, with regard to embodying Rwandan values, may also deter intore from openly criticising or questioning these customs or the narrative that informs them.

Open discussion of varied experiences and divergent conclusions is particularly important in analysing identity in the post-conflict context in Rwanda. In light of the de facto ban of ethnic labels in public discourse and government documents, critical analysis of the conceptions that surround national identity has become all the more pertinent. As Buckley-Zistel argues, '"being Rwandan" means different things to different Rwandans, and this is not per se negative or threatening, but an expression of having experienced one of the most horrendous events in history' (2009, p. 48). Itorero is particularly well suited to promoting discussion and examination of these events as it brings together large groups of peers for extended periods. The opportunity to analyse experiences of the past critically, as well as post-conflict constructions of identity, values and 'national reconciliation', is neglected in order to actively promote the RPF's understanding of Rwandan national identity. This may create a sense of exclusion among those who do not agree with the government's interpretation of unity, identity or Rwandan history.

Histoire du Rwanda: history and 'national reconciliation' in the classroom

'Il n'y a pas de peuple sans histoire comme il n'y a pas d'histoire sans peuple' (There are no people without history just as there is no history without people) (NURC, 2011a, p. v). The history of the Rwandan nation and its people has been described in detail in *Histoire du Rwanda: des origines à la fin du xxe siècle* (NURC 2011a). This textbook, produced in cooperation with the National University of Rwanda (NUR), includes seven chapters by different authors which cover a range of topics from 1000BC to the presidential elections of 2003. Although yet to be officially introduced into the public school curriculum, this textbook is set to become a major element of the official reconciliation programme's education remit as it will be the first history book officially used in Rwandan public schools and government offices since the 1994 genocide came to an end (Bawaya interview, 30 May 2009).

Sarah Bawaya, who was the NURC's acting head of syllabus development and training, explained that prior to the 1994 genocide, history had been taught by means of books written by colonial scholars, texts that propagated a primarily Western view of Rwandan history. The GNU banned them in 1994 as they were thought to promote 'divisionism' and 'genocide ideology' (ibid.). This suspension did little to quash allegations of 'genocide ideology' being taught in public schools. In 2008, Rwandan Parliament members conducted a study into the teaching of 'genocide ideology' and 'divisionism' in schools across the country. It determined that 'ethnic hatred' was still prevalent in most of these schools despite the ban on lessons about Rwandan history (BBC News, 19 February 2008).

The lengthy duration of this ban was compounded by the destruction of materials and human resources during the 1994 genocide, and affected by disagreement among citizens, academics and government officials on how to teach students about the events of the civil war and 1994 genocide (Institute of Research and Dialogue for Peace, as cited by Schweisfurth, 2006, p. 701; Freedman et al., 2004, p. 248). Part of this disagreement stemmed from concerns about the significance of different events leading up to and during the 1994 genocide and about teachers' promotion of 'divisionism'. Schweisfurth argues that the curriculum taught by teachers prior to and during 1994 perpetuated tension and violence (Institute of Research and Dialogue for Peace, 2003, as cited by Schweisfurth, 2006, p. 699) and that, for many, the participation of some teachers in the 1994 genocide, as well as the fact that massacres took place in schools, led to 'the total erosion of faith in the education system' (Obura, 2003, cited by Schweisfurth, 2006, p. 700).

The NURC seemingly sought to tackle these concerns by commissioning a new history book for use in public offices and schools following the resumption in 2010 of history teaching in the classroom, at which time classes were guided by a teaching manual rather than a textbook (McLean Hilker, 2010, p. 2). The book's final draft had not been completed at the time this interview was conducted in 2009, but Bawaya explained that the text would criticise the 'bad elements' of history that encourage 'divisionism', and celebrate the positive social factors that promote unity in the country (Bawaya interview, 30 May 2009).[13] *Histoire du Rwanda* was written with the stated mandate to promote 'national reconciliation' and rebuild the nation (NURC, 2011a, p. v). The book is purportedly designed to reach this goal by promoting critical thinking and the *truth* about the events of Rwanda's history (ibid., p. vi). More broadly, it states a commitment to educating the youth about the past:

> Young people need to know the origins and causes of the deep divisions that have shaped recent relations between Rwandans. Otherwise, future generations will have a partial vision of the past, fueled by emotional or popular stories gleaned from parents, friends, newspapers, and other writing or simply from the street (ibid., p. 11).[14]

The 'official version' of the truth may not reflect the views of all Rwandans, but it will be taught to them in public schools when *Histoire du Rwanda* is introduced into the education system.

The 'bad elements' of history

Histoire du Rwanda describes the NURC's understanding of the nation's origins in great detail. The pre-colonial era is particularly relevant to the promotion of unity and 'national reconciliation,' as it is depicted as a time of solidarity and social cohesion, an image that appears throughout the book and the Rwandan government texts it analyses. Peaceful coexistence between the nation's earliest clans is traced back as far as the 14th century at which time Rwanda was a 'small territorial entity' in the area now known as Gasabo district in Kigali Province (NURC, 2011a, p. 85). Even in this early period, the chapter's author, Gamaliel Mbonimana, contends that clans of Gasabo and neighbouring areas lived together peacefully and functioned as a type of 'confederation' (ibid., p. 86).

Themes of cooperation and coexistence are echoed throughout the next chapter covering the later pre-colonial period, which outlines how the era was shaped by the monarchic power of King Kigeri Rwabugiri in the 19th century. Patriotism and the desire to expand Rwanda's borders are identified as common interests of the population at this time. Mbonimana contends that

13 As of June 2015, this history book had still not been introduced into classrooms or government offices.

14 Translation from French, 8 March 2012.

the highly centralised nature of political control was expressed through literary and historical texts espousing the power of the king and queen. It was also exercised through institutions including the *ubuhake* cattle clientelist system, which features heavily in the 'victor's narrative' (ibid., p. 109). Mbonimana defines ubuhake as a voluntary contract between the cattle owner and the individual seeking work and *ubuletwa* as an arrangement whereby the poorest civilians spent two days a week working the fields of wealthier landowners (ibid., pp. 127, 129).

Mbonimana's view of these systems conflicts with those of Eltringham and Prunier who see ubuhake – and ubuletwa, in particular – as examples of the growing power of a minority of individuals who had elite Tutsi status (Eltringham, 2004, p. 13; Prunier, 1995, p. 21).[15] Conversely, the RPF's version of history, as depicted in *Histoire du Rwanda*, rejects the notion of antagonistic identities during this period. Instead, these groups are shown to have been deeply intertwined through intermarriage and cooperation, '[i]n effect, neither Hutu nor Tutsi has the characteristics necessary to constitute two distinct ethnicities. They spoke the same language, shared the same religious beliefs, and lived together. Relationships between these groups were not sources of confrontation' (NURC, 2011a, p. 172).

In *Histoire du Rwanda*, the colonial period of 1884 to 1962 contrasts starkly with the pre-colonial era of peace, cooperation and social cohesion. Elements of the 'victor's narrative' are repeated and expanded upon in this section of the textbook, including colonial leaders' manipulation of the existing political structures and the stratification of ethnic identities, resulting in the growing tension within the Hutu population shortly before independence. *Histoire du Rwanda* places particular emphasis on the role of Belgian leaders and Catholic missionaries in the growing anti-Tutsi sentiment during this period.

Colonial leaders identified Tutsi according to their physical features and perceived aptitude for leadership, purportedly considering the Hutu majority to be nothing more than servants, and the Twa as 'devoid of any humanity' (ibid., p. 249). This particular understanding of ethnic identities was exemplified by Hutu and Twa civilians being barred from administrative positions, which instead were occupied by five per cent of the Tutsi population (ibid., p. 267). As instituted by the Belgian authorities, this system is blamed for 'accentuating sentiments of ethnic identity' (ibid.). Paul Rutayisire, author of the chapter entitled 'Rwanda under German and Belgian colonial rule', contends that colonial leaders misunderstood the ubuhake and ubuletwa systems, using them to exploit Hutu civilians towards the end of the colonial period (ibid., p. 298). Rutayisire refutes Mamdani's descriptions of Belgian and Tutsi pastoralist rule as 'double domination' of Hutu civilians (1996, p. 8). Instead, he firmly places

15 See chapter 2 for further detail about Eltringham and Prunier's interpretations of these systems.

the blame for growing anti-Tutsi sentiment upon colonial officials who sought to achieve the contradictory goals of protecting society's weakest members while increasing the political control of the most powerful group in Rwanda, the Tutsi elite (NURC, 2011a, p. 298).

Rutayisire's chapter shows that as Rwanda neared independence the tide of political control was beginning to turn. Increased public participation had been a stated goal of the trusteeship system established by the UN in 1946 (ibid., p. 328), and Rutayisire argues that the failure of this stated mandate did little to calm the desire for change inside Rwanda (ibid., p. 329). Lemarchand describes the 'Bahutu Manifesto' of 1957 as having outlined the concerns of its Hutu authors about the social, political and economic injustice experienced by the Hutu majority. The manifesto's authors recommended the active promotion of Hutu individuals to public office and increased access to education for the Hutu population (Lemarchand, 1970, p. 149). Rutayisire criticises the manifesto for misunderstanding the relationship between the Hutu majority and Tutsi minority. He contends that the document exacerbated ethnic tension by focusing too narrowly on the exploitation of Hutu masses, while ignoring the social, political and economic injustices experienced by *all* Rwandans at the hands of colonial leaders and Catholic missionaries (NURC, 2011a, p. 368).

Unlike many authors including Mamdani (1996), Lemarchand (1970) and Pottier (2002), Rutayisire does not use the term 'Social Revolution' to describe the violent events of 1959. It only appears in *Histoire du Rwanda* to condemn the rhetoric used by supporters of Kayibanda's Parmehutu to describe the 'cohesive ideology' of all Hutu. Although acknowledging that some Hutu intellectuals shared a sense of common ethnic identity, Rutayisire rejects the notion presented by other authors that the violence of this period was planned or that all Hutu felt oppressed (NURC, 2011a, p. 417). This interpretation differs from that discussed earlier in chapter 2 because it does not depict the 'Bahutu Manifesto' authors as having represented the views of other Hutu, nor does it highlight the growing anti-Tutsi sentiment associated with the monarchic system (Mamdani, 1996, p. 5).

The second 'bad element' of history described in *Histoire du Rwanda* is that of 'bad governance' in the run-up to the 1994 genocide. The regimes of the First and Second Republics, led by Grégoire Kayibanda and Juvénal Habyarimana respectively, are identified by Joseph Jyoni Wa Karega, author of chapter 5, as having promoted the anti-Tutsi propaganda and 'divisionism' that fuelled the 1994 genocide (ibid., p. 427). Jyoni Wa Karega outlines a number of conflicts between civilians who became refugees after the 1963 'inyenzi invasion'.[16] Kayibanda's regime is blamed for having orchestrated one such attack in Gikongoro against Tutsi civilians which resulted in 8,000 to

16 See chapter 2 for an examination of this particular invasion and its effect on the refugee population.

10,000 deaths (ibid., p. 431). The overall death toll from 1961–8 is estimated to be between 25,000 and 35,000. Jyoni Wa Karega highlights the fact that no justice was meted out for Tutsi deaths that occurred during this period and in 1973 (ibid., p. 453). Repression, violence and impunity are highlighted as examples of the 'bad governance' of Kayibanda's regime that killed opposition politicians, both Hutu and Tutsi, concentrated political power into a small 'mono-ethnic' group, and put the 1994 genocide's first acts into practice (ibid., p. 451).

A description of how the monopolistic power of the state prospered throughout the Second Republic of Juvénal Habyarimana then follows. Jyoni Wa Karega depicts Habyarimana's party, the Mouvement Révolutionnaire National pour le Développement (MRND) as 'the centre of all power, centralism took precedence over democracy … It soon became an extraordinary machine of propaganda of the will of its founder into the corners of the most remote areas of the country' (ibid., p. 459). He highlights discrimination against Tutsi as well as Hutu from areas other than Gisenyi in the west and Ruhengeri in the northwest of the country during this period. Hutu civilians and officials in those two regions were purportedly given preferential treatment as they were home to high-powered MRND members (ibid., p. 460). The 'victor's narrative' emphasises the 'bad governance' and 'extremist propaganda' of Habyarimana's inner circle. As stated in the NURC's 2007 Reconciliation Policy:

> During different periods of history, Rwanda has been characterized by the bad governance bound to divisionism, ethnical, regional and religious segregation, regionalization and oligarchy which have negative impacts on the Rwandan society.
>
> Some of those impacts are division of all kinds, exclusion from [the] homeland, killings, refugees, war and 1994 genocide. After genocide, its ideology and mentality related to any segregation that are still being perpetuated by some Rwandans, are the significant hindrance to the process of unity and reconciliation of Rwandans (p. 2).

Jyoni Wa Karega identifies many other examples of 'bad governance' throughout the Second Republic under Habyarimana's leadership. He points to issues of racketeering by members of Habyarimana's government, the monopolisation of land by the rich, economic strife created by the early 1990s Structural Adjustment Programme (SAP), and the increasing isolation of poor civilians who faced significant social disparity (NURC, 2011a, pp. 468–70). The inclusion of the SAP in this 'bad governance' list transforms a much larger international issue into a process belonging exclusively to the Habyarimana regime. Jyoni Wa Karega blames Habyarimana's government for all social, political and economic hardships experienced by Rwandans in the run-up to the 1994 genocide. He also describes Habyarimana's failure to repatriate Rwandan refugees who had fled during earlier periods of violence (ibid., p. 472), arguing that,

> Until 1990, the political class no longer considered refugees as Rwandan. The government prevented them from returning and destabilized them where they had sought refuge, Kigali wanted them to die in extreme poverty and disappear completely. It is the protocol on refugees signed in 1993 under the Arusha negotiations that will reintegrate all the refugees and their rights (ibid., p. 473).

Jyoni Wa Karega's assertion that the Habyarimana regime actively prevented repatriation, and wanted all Tutsi refugees to die in poverty, contradicts the historical interpretations of multiple authors including Kuperman (2004) and Sibomana (1999). These authors argue that Habyarimana actively attempted to repatriate Tutsi refugees living in Uganda in order to prevent the impending RPF invasion in 1990. Jyoni Wa Karega's interpretation of events justifies the RPF's stated motivations for the invasion on 1 October 1990: eradicate anti-Tutsi racism; end the 'bad governance' of Habyarimana's regime; and fix the 'refugee problem' that Habyarimana's regime had allegedly ignored (ibid., p. 477).

These 'bad elements' of the past reached an apex during the 1994 genocide. Faustin Rutembesa, author of chapter 6 in *Histoire du Rwanda*, depicts the 1994 genocide as a highly organised pre-planned massacre of the Tutsi population. He describes how representatives of Habyarimana's government distributed arms to Hutu civilians under the pretense of 'civil self-defense' (ibid., p. 531). Rutembesa also explains the role of elite manipulation, particularly by MRND and CDR party members and military officials, in mobilising civilians to participate in the massacres, as well as the role of anti-Tutsi propaganda and 'genocide ideology':

> Ideology had produced such a demonization of the Tutsi that when the RPF took control of most of the country, those who had conceived and coordinated the genocide became intertwined with those who had no specific role in the violence. This diluted the consciences of those responsible for the genocide and allowed for the continuation of the genocidal dynamic (ibid., p. 532).

He also discusses the UN's refusal to use the term 'genocide' in relation to the 1994 massacres and highlights the role of France and Opération Turquoise in the continued warfare (ibid., pp. 546–8). Rutembesa describes the extreme violence of that time and repeatedly defines the roles of ethnicity, propaganda, 'genocide ideology' and 'bad governance' in this devastating period of Rwanda's history. He does not however, place any blame on the RPF for civilian deaths or retaliative acts during the 1994 genocide, as discussed by authors including Kuperman (2004) and Des Forges (1999).

The 'positive elements' of unity and 'national reconciliation'

The 'bad elements' outlined in *Histoire du Rwanda*: 'divisionism' institutionalised during the colonial period, anti-Tutsi ideology and 'bad governance' serve to highlight the disparity between Habyarimana's regime and the RPF's political interests in the run-up to, during and after the 1994 genocide. The most immediately identifiable difference between the RPF and Habyarimana's regime is anti-Tutsi sentiment. Others identified by Jyoni Wa Karega include the RPF's alleged interest in 'real power-sharing' (ibid., p. 487).[17] This stated goal is repeated in the 'victor's narrative' as an apparent attempt to legitimise the RPF's invasion in 1990, but is contested by authors including Kuperman, who points instead to the RPF's interest in securing 'significant' political control during the civil war and the 1994 genocide (2004, p. 69). This interpretation is consistent with the RPF creating an executive presidency within the GNU in 1995. The RPF's activities during this period are explained multiple times in *Histoire du Rwanda*. For instance, Jyoni Wa Karega justifies its decision to break the ceasefire agreement with the MRND in February 1993, 'The RPF took up arms to force the government to respect the right to life. The renewed fighting is not the cause but the consequence of the violation of the agreements of ceasefire [by government forces]' (2011a, pp. 503–4).

Rutembesa applies the same logic to his explanation and justification of the RPF's political and military manoeuvres during the 1994 genocide. In particular, he highlights the success of RPF military tactics in ending the violence, restoring order and saving the lives of tens of thousands of Tutsi civilians (ibid., p. 570). Rutembesa contends that the RPF began to battle against the negative forces of 'negationism' and 'revisionism' after it had secured the capital and ended the 1994 genocide. He contrasts the RPF's 'positive' steps towards peace with 'negative' acts of denial by those who supported the 1994 genocide. These 'genocide deniers' evaded responsibility by referring to the events of that year not as genocide but as unplanned violence resulting from the RPF invasion in 1990, and describing the brutality as a 'double genocide' against Tutsi *and* Hutu civilians (ibid., pp. 575–80). Rutembesa states, 'The negationist propaganda is based on multiple strategies and techniques: the denial of facts, changing the pattern and circumstances, blurring the details, mixing truth and lies, camouflaging, and misinterpreting and generalizing. Doing this creates false truths and is anti-historical' (ibid., p. 576).

In spite of these challenges, Charles Kabwete Mulinda, author of chapter 7 in the textbook, highlights and expands upon the purportedly 'positive elements' of unity and 'national reconciliation' after the 1994 genocide, depicting these achievements as belonging to the programming the GNU had

17 'Real power-sharing' is used here in reference to the 1993 Arusha Accords. Jyoni Wa Karega stipulates that the RPF rebels sought a power-sharing agreement that would restrict the MRND's political power by preventing the president from maintaining 'excessive power' (ibid., p. 487). This political control would instead be spread among all parties except the CDR.

created and implemented. The GNU stated its commitment to rebuilding the country by outlining an eight-point plan in July 1994 including:

> Restoring a climate of security and peace;
>
> Organizing the Central Government, the prefectures of Commons, Sectors and Cells;
>
> Restoring and consolidating national unity;
>
> Reintegrating refugees and returning property to displaced people;
>
> Improving the living conditions of the population and solving social problems resulting from the war and genocide;
>
> Revitalizing the national economy;
>
> Redefining foreign policy;
>
> Consolidating democracy (ibid., p. 589).

Mulinda describes the GNU's approach to restoring national unity as having been shaped by the desire to teach the people of Rwanda how to live together peacefully (ibid., p. 597).

One of the first 'positive steps' towards 'national reconciliation' highlighted by Mulinda is the GNU's removal of ethnic identities from identification cards (ibid., p. 600). This represents an early move towards the de facto banning of ethnic identities from public discourse. Mulinda highlights the NURC's creation in 1999 as a great benefit to the official reconciliation process. He also extols the virtues of the GNU's approach to unity and 'national reconciliation', one example being the pursuit of maximal justice. Mulinda justifies the arrests of 120,000 civilians in the years after the 1994 genocide as vital to prevent further injustice. He recognises the dearth of judicial support after the deaths and exile of magistrates during the 1994 genocide, yet condemns criticism of the justice system by academics and human rights activists as 'malevolent and irresponsible' (ibid., p. 603). He makes no reference to the 'life-threatening overcrowding and appalling treatment' of Rwandan prisoners after the 1994 genocide (HRW, 1995, p. 1).

Mulinda describes gacaca as a step towards restorative justice that includes the participation of the entire population. Gacaca courts, he argues, were expected to produce positive results including 'truth about the genocide', speedy trials, popular participation, an end to impunity and a stronger sense of national unity (ibid., pp. 605–6). These anticipated results closely resemble the objectives stated by the National Service of Gacaca Jurisdictions (NSGJ).[18] Mulinda quashes further criticism of the system, including that of victor's justice employed by such authors as Waldorf (2010), Tiemessen (2004) and Sarkin (2001) to criticise the RPF's approach to justice at gacaca. He contends that this perspective errs in its assumption that RPF members ought to be tried

18 See chapter 3 for a detailed discussion of the objectives of gacaca as stated by the NSGJ.

for crimes of vengeance, arguing, instead, that acts of genocide committed by Hutu civilians cannot be compared with crimes against humanity allegedly perpetrated by individual RPF members (NURC, 2011a, p. 604).[19]

Other achievements in unity and 'national reconciliation' include the repatriation of 23,658 Rwandan citizens in 2000 and 2001 and the resettlement of refugees who returned to find their homes occupied or destroyed (ibid., p. 646). Mulinda describes the formation of FARG and its positive impact on increased access to primary, secondary and university education for survivors. He also outlines the benefits of healthcare, the imidugudu resettlement programme, and of offering support towards repairing survivors' homes. He does add, however, that many survivors continue to complain about housing problems and the lack of adequate aid and access to scholarships (ibid., p. 648). Mulinda's depiction of survivors' opinions pales in comparison with concerns expressed by Mary Kayitesi-Blewett, founder of the Survivors Fund (SURF), who outlines the many challenges survivors faced such as trauma, extreme poverty and chronic housing shortages (2006, p. 320).

Histoire du Rwanda provides a comprehensive description of the detrimental effects of 'bad governance' and the GNU's stated commitment to unity and 'national reconciliation' following the 1994 genocide. Although rich in detail, this historical rendering fails to touch on some important issues discussed by other authors. The first is the growth of a highly inequitable economic system during the pre-colonial period. As previously discussed in chapter 2, Prunier makes a connection between the development of cattle clientage and political stratification in pre-colonial Rwanda. He describes 'a centre versus periphery affair' with reference to the disproportionate amount of political power held by a small minority of civilians with elite Tutsi status (1995, p. 21). Conversely, the pre-colonial cattle clientage systems are depicted in *Histoire du Rwanda* as voluntary contracts that benefited both the land-owners and those who worked the fields, supporting the assertion that unity existed between all Rwandans during the pre-colonial era, as described in the 'victor's narrative'.

Multiple *Histoire du Rwanda* contributors provide extensive information concerning the RPF's supposed intentions in the lead-up to the October 1990 invasion, as well as during and after the 1994 genocide. They also discuss RPF actions during these periods and the outcomes of conflicts between the rebels and government forces between 1990–4. Although it is briefly indicated that some individual RPF members may have perpetrated crimes against humanity during the 1994 genocide, no details or numbers related to these attacks are provided and there is no indication that punishment was meted out in such cases (NURC, 2011a, p. 574).

19 This document is the first to refer to RPF crimes committed in 1994 as crimes against humanity. They are more commonly referred to as individual crimes of vengeance.

Similarly, the accounts of the Kibeho tragedy and conflict in eastern Zaire/DRC do not discuss the crimes committed by RPA members against civilians. Mulinda, author of chapter 7, justifies the RPA's entry into the Kibeho camp for internally displaced persons (IDPs) in 1995 as a concerted effort to close what had allegedly become 'the sanctuary of criminals' (ibid., p. 597). He clarifies that although the RPF laments the 300 civilian deaths that it recognises, the much higher calculations of 4,000 to 8,000 deaths are grossly overestimated by 'critics of the Kigali regime and the RPF in particular' (ibid.). Amnesty International (AI) gauged in 1996 that upwards of 'several thousand' IDPs were killed by the RPF's military wing, the RPA, during this tragedy (1996, p. 18).

Interestingly, neither Mulinda, nor AI (1996), nor the UN (1995) uses the term 'Hutu' to describe the victims of the 1995 Kibeho massacre. If the RPF considered the IDP camps to be a 'sanctuary of criminals', as Mulinda contends, it is likely that most if not all IDPs at Kibeho were Hutu (NURC, 2011a, p. 597). The lack of ethnic identifiers in these reports may serve to legitimise the RPA's attack by making it appear to be an attempt to prevent genocide rather than the systematic massacre of Hutu civilians. Mulinda states that the Independent Commission of Inquiry into the Kibeho tragedy rejected the accusation that the massacre was a planned attempt to exterminate Hutu civilians (ibid.). Launched by the GNU, the commission included members of the Rwandan government, the UN, the African Union and representatives from countries such as Canada, France and the UK (UN, 1995, p. 6). Amnesty International criticised this commission for its failure to comply with international standards of investigation, and to determine the number of victims. Amnesty also found fault with the investigation's conclusion that the deaths had been caused by the actions of both RPA soldiers and armed militants inside the camp (1996, p. 18).

Mulinda justifies the RPF's role in the Second Congo War as one of 'vital interest to safety and survival, more obvious and intense than in neighbouring DRC. This justifies the role of Rwanda in this war, and by extension, the actual weight of other actors whose roles were often exaggerated' (NURC, 2011a, p. 630). Although Mulinda does discuss the RPF's role in toppling Mobutu, he does not provide evidence of it having committed any wrongdoing – there is no reference, for example, to the RPA having extracted or plundered natural resources from Zaire/DRC. Similarly, he justifies the RPF's actions and commends the group's military achievements in increasing safety and security as well as facilitating the repatriation of 1.5 million Rwandans. 'If we had not attacked Zaire, the refugee issue would have remained insoluble forever' (RPA chief of staff, as quoted in NURC, 2011a, p. 635). Unlike the 'Report of the mapping exercise', published by the UN in 2010, which documents human rights abuses perpetrated in Zaire/DRC between 1993–2003, Mulinda does not mention any crimes against humanity committed by the RPA during the war (UNHRC, 2010).

The similarity between Mulinda's depiction of the RPF/RPA's actions in DRC and the 'victor's narrative' demonstrates the singular nature of the history curriculum described in *Histoire du Rwanda.* Freedman et al. discuss the difficulties of encouraging critical thinking with regard to the RPF's official historical narrative in Rwanda's public school system. In their assessment of the intervention project on teaching history in Rwanda, led by the University of California Berkeley Human Rights Centre, they discuss the tension between the RPF's education policy and the implementation of democratic teaching styles that promote critical thinking and debate (Freedman et al., 2008, pp. 664–5):[20]

> In this study, we saw how the victory of one political side – a group that represents a minority population in the wake of the genocide – created a set of tensions that inhibited curricular reform. The inability to discuss issues of ethnic identity, the distortions of a history that the government wishes to tell, the constraints against teaching students how to be critical thinkers, and above all, the fear of productive conflict have profound implications for the establishment of a progressive history curriculum and a healthy democracy (Freedman et al., 2011, p. 309).[21]

This conflict originates in the education policy's stipulation that only the official historical narrative may be taught in schools. This restriction precludes analysis and impedes discussion about the government's rendering of events. For instance, it fails to address the continued use of ethnic labels in Rwandan society as well as persistent fear of ethnic violence (ibid.; Mgbako, 2005, p. 220; interview with son of returnee, 7 April 2009).

The NURC's foray into public school history lessons includes many of the major elements repeated in government-sponsored reconciliation discourse:

20 The intervention project on teaching history in Rwanda arose from an expression of interest made by the Rwandan Ministry of Education (Mineduc) for help with creating secondary-level teaching materials on Rwandan history (Freedman et al., 2008, p. 664). The project involved collaboration between the University of California's Berkeley Human Rights Centre, the National University of Rwanda (NUR), and the Rwandan National Curriculum Development Centre (NCDC) of Mineduc, with support from the American NGO Facing History and Ourselves (FHAO) (ibid.).

21 Bianchini found that students training to become secondary history teachers at the Kigali Institute of Education were divided about whether they ought to employ more democratic teaching styles. Of the 165 students who completed questionnaires, 44% favoured a democratic approach to teaching that facilitated the discussion of identity and divergent narratives of history. A marginally lower percentage (40%) of respondents would prefer to 'restore accurate history with a new course'. 'Accurate history' refers to the RPF-sponsored narrative of Rwandan history, the 'victor's narrative' (2012, pp. 230–1).

the detrimental effects of 'bad governance' and 'genocide ideology' and the beneficial ones of RPF leadership, gacaca and restoration of social cohesion that allegedly thrived during the pre-colonial era. The RPF's assertion that there is only one 'accurate' version of events creates difficulties in encouraging critical thinking and debate about national history in Rwanda's public schools. Once *Histoire du Rwanda* is officially launched, the curriculum in public schools will be dominated by the only official version of history available, that of the RPF.

Conclusion

The restoration of ingando and itorero camps is rife with contradictions in relation to promoting 'national reconciliation' after the 1994 genocide. The size and structure of these camps facilitates the coming together of large peer groups to engage with matters related to social and cultural values, identity and development. Protrais Musoni, the former Minister of Local Government, stated with reference to itorero, 'the programme was initiated to facilitate the healing of broken hearts of many people through promoting culture, fighting genocide ideology and fostering the reconciliation process' (*New Times*, 13 January 2008). Both of these camps are guided by an overarching education remit that seeks to promote unity and 'national reconciliation', while restricting critical analysis, free discussion and divergent conclusions about identity, ethnicity and the nation's history.

The contradictions inherent in this remit may begin with the very notion that all Rwandans must change their minds with regard to unity and reconciliation. Ingando and itorero, guided by NURC-designed syllabi, teach the population about the government's vision of unity and 'national reconciliation'. As such, the stated commitment to reeducating the nation facilitates the top-down dissemination of government-sponsored historical narrative, one that bolsters support for the National Unity and Reconciliation Programme and the current RPF regime more generally. The sense of the population's 'mass ignorance', in conjunction with the lack of critical analysis and multiple historical narratives transforms both camps into powerful indoctrination tools.

Itorero ry'igihugu is in a particularly influential position with regard to facilitating discussion and critical analysis of national unity, 'national reconciliation' and identity. It brings together far larger and more varied groups of participants than the ingando camps do, allowing them to live among their peers and learn about the culture and values that supposedly come from Rwandan history. This focus on values and cultural taboos gives the intore insight into the government's historical narrative and conceptions of unity and national identity. Itorero, like ingando, fails to provide a forum in which participants may openly question and criticise these notions. Free discussion and divergent conclusions about identity and unity are particularly important in light of the government's de facto banning of ethnic terms from public discourse and government documents. Significantly, itorero's focus on the singular nature of identity in Rwanda precludes analysis of the reality that ethnic terms and identities still exist in Rwandan society. The public identification of the best and worst performers at itorero further discourages intore from disagreeing with the 'victor's narrative' and values taught at itorero.

The textbook, *Histoire du Rwanda: des origins à la fin du xxe siècle*, published by the NURC in cooperation with the National University of Rwanda, provides a detailed description of the country's history from the early pre-colonial era up to the presidential elections of 2003. Shaped by a stated commitment to promote unity and 'national reconciliation' through teaching the youth about their nation's history for the first time since 1994, it misses the opportunity to foster critical debate about such important events as colonisation, the 1959 Social Revolution, the RPF invasion, the civil war and the 1994 genocide. In fact, it deliberately limits critical understandings of Rwandan history and RPF actions. Once it is officially adopted, *Histoire du Rwanda* will do little more than disseminate the 'victor's narrative' to an extensive audience. As such, ingando, itorero and *Histoire du Rwanda* meet the broadest goal of the National Unity and Reconciliation Programme's education remit: to change the minds of all Rwandans by teaching the population about the government's vision of unity and 'national reconciliation'. However, they fail to promote more nuanced elements of 'national reconciliation' including critical analysis and open discussion, both camps' stated commitments, and relationship rebuilding, the cornerstone of the government's conception of 'horizontal reconciliation'. Instead, both camps and *Histoire du Rwanda* actively silence opposition, legitimise state programming including Vision 2020, and bolster support for the current RPF regime.

Chapter 6

The functions of 'national reconciliation': political images of Rwanda

Figure 6.1. President Kagame's name spelled out by supporters at an RPF election rally, Amahoro Stadium, Kigali (author's photo, 18 July 2010)

On 9 August 2010, Paul Kagame secured a second consecutive term as the President of Rwanda. Approximately 97.5 per cent of the population voted in the election that won the incumbent president a majority of 93 per cent (BBC News, 11 August 2010). In the preceding weeks, pro-RPF slogans, songs and chants rang through the streets of Kigali. On 18 July 2010, I joined the 40,000 supporters packed into Rwanda's national Amahoro stadium, wearing RPF t-shirts and cheering in excitement for Kagame and the RPF. As millions of Rwandans visited the polls, the RPF faced heated criticism from journalists, political opponents and international NGOs accusing the current regime of consolidating its power by undermining democracy (BBC News, 9 August 2010).[1]

The RPF has dominated the Rwandan political arena since it seized control of the capital in July 1994. This power was initially exerted under the guise of the GNU and subsequently expanded through the 2003 and 2008 parliamentary elections, and the 2003 and 2010 presidential elections.[2] Throughout this period, the RPF has bolstered its political control inside the country and secured its position in the international community through positive relations with foreign donors and membership in the East Africa Community (EAC) and the Commonwealth.[3]

Successfully establishing a strong central state apparatus has shaped the RPF's leadership of Rwanda. The government initially sought to legitimise itself at both the domestic and international levels by agreeing to follow the Arusha Accords guidelines (Hayman, 2007, p. 16). In the years following the establishment of the Government of National Unity (GNU), the RPF has continued to promote its own priorities, programmes and agendas at both the national and international level. The National Unity and Reconciliation Programme plays an important role in maintaining political control and fostering the party's nation-building and development goals.

The government's official reconciliation programme functions as a normative and legal framework through which the RPF successfully constructs and projects two interrelated political images of Rwanda to the domestic population and the international community of donors, investors and NGOs. The term 'political image' refers to the image of the nation projected by both the RPF and the government's own leadership. Both of these images reflect the RPF's successes and its vision of Rwanda, guided by stated commitments to 'good governance', nation-building, 'national reconciliation' and development. This definition builds on Edelman's description of the construction of images as essential to maintaining public and private power relations. Murray Edelman, a political scientist, argues that powerful images stem from established political

1 See HRW (2010) for a chronological summary of the RPF's alleged attempts to silence political opponents, restrict political space and inhibit democratic participation in the elections.

2 This understanding of political dominance is influenced by Lukes' conception of the three-dimensional view of power. Lukes' examination uncovers the ways in which power constrains the interests of those who are dominated by others. For instance, his understanding includes the notion of 'latent conflict', which describes the opposition between the interests of those exercising power and those whose interests are excluded. This inequitable distribution takes place regardless of whether the excluded group is aware of or able to express these interests (2005, p. 28).

3 Rwanda joined the EAC in 2007 and the Commonwealth in 2009.

and economic relationships (2001, p. 13). As such, these images bolster the interests of groups seeking to gain or maintain political control (ibid., p. 15).

The normative and legal aspects of the RPF's official reconciliation programme give shape to these political images. Normative elements include the 'victor's narrative', which, as discussed in chapter 4, legitimises RPF leadership and programming by creating a prescriptive path upon which national unity may be achieved. Other key normative concepts include 'divisionism' and 'genocide ideology', which restrict political space and criticism of the current government. They are particularly prominent due to having been defined and institutionalised by legislation. The 2001 Law, 'Prevention, suppression and punishment of the crime of discrimination and sectarianism', is applied to the criminalisation of 'divisionism' acts. The 2008 and amended 2013 Law, 'Punishment of the crime of genocide ideology', define the parameters of, and punishment for, acts of 'genocide ideology'. Other pertinent forms of legislation include strict registration processes for political parties and candidates as well as for journalists and newspapers. The actions of political parties, journalists and even domestic and international NGOs are further limited by the fact that police approval is required for gatherings of more than five people (Longman, 2011b, p. 1). Such restrictions protect the political images of Rwanda and its leadership from criticism by silencing individual voices and preventing groups who oppose the current government from gathering. As such, the National Unity and Reconciliation Programme is a highly effective framework through which positive images of the nation and its government are projected at home and abroad, despite the political reality inside the country.

Political image: national audience

State-legitimacy and nation-building

At the national level, the RPF's official reconciliation effort functions as an umbrella programme under which a wide variety of policies and projects are grouped together and are administered in a strictly top-down manner. As we have seen, these projects include civic education, gacaca, repatriation and reintegration of refugees and ex-combatants, and development. The Rwandan government has used the programme's stated achievements in all of these areas to solidify political support, legitimise state programming, and construct a nation built upon government-mandated values and a singular national identity (Melvin, 2012, p. 3). According to a 2009 NURC evaluation of official reconciliation work in Rwanda, the programme's stated achievements are both plentiful and pertinent. They include: growth of harmony and trust among the population; the successful release and reeducation of 70,000 convicted genocide perpetrators at ingando civic education camps; and the coordination of various official reconciliation projects at both the district and national level

(NURC, 2009b). The RPF's successes have purportedly coalesced into a single sense of hope, dignity and pride for all Rwandans, as described by President Kagame at a reception hosted by Pierre Prosper, the former Ambassador-At-Large in the Bush administration for war crimes, in Los Angeles (speech, 28 April 2014).

These stated achievements are transformed into powerful political rhetoric when combined with the RPF's assertions of its own commitment to 'good governance'. The latter term has different meanings with reference to the RPF's projection of its leadership to the Rwandan people and the international community of donors and investors. It appears throughout the 2003 Constitution, as well as presidential speeches and evaluations conducted by the NURC. 'Good governance' is not explicitly defined in the NURC's 2007 Reconciliation Policy; its definition can instead be deduced as the antithesis of 'bad governance' described below:

> During different periods of history, Rwanda has been characterized by the bad governance bound to divisionism, ethnical, regional and religious segregation, regionalization and oligarchy which have negative impacts on the Rwandan society. Some of those impacts are division of all kinds, exclusion from homeland, killings, refugees, war and 1994 genocide. After genocide, its ideology and mentality related to any segregation that are still being perpetuated by some Rwandans, are the significant hindrance to [the] process of unity and reconciliation of Rwandans (p. 2).

This account of the 'poor governance' of past regimes serves several political functions. Firstly, it supports the current government's denunciation of what it defines as 'divisionism' and 'genocide ideology'. Secondly, the RPF adds significant moral value to its own leadership by reducing the causes of the 1994 genocide to relatively obtuse concepts and connecting these negative acts to previous regimes and colonial leaders. Thirdly, the RPF leadership's moral value exonerates its members of wrongful acts they may have committed during the civil war, and during and after the 1994 genocide in both Rwanda and DRC. This sense of 'moral value' is accentuated by the RPF's emphasis on its dual role in seizing the capital in July 1994 and founding the official reconciliation programme. As discussed in chapter 4, Pottier uses the term 'moral guardians' to describe the RPF's singular narrative of their role as 'victors' in July 1994 (2002, p. 207). Pottier employs this term to illustrate the ways in which the RPF manipulates the historical narrative to its own advantage with reference to the international community, a point that will be discussed in more detail later in this chapter.

The official reconciliation programme's top-down structure safeguards the 'victor's narrative' and protects the rebel group-turned political party from prosecution at gacaca. As chapter 3 discussed, the restoration of gacaca is the most substantial manifestation of the government pledge to pursue justice for crimes committed during the civil war and 1994 genocide. Gacaca courts across the country made approximately 1.2 million judgments between 2005–12. The court parameters were limited, however, to offences constituting the act of genocide and crimes against humanity perpetrated between 1990–4. As the RPF vehemently denies having carried out any crimes of either type, its members were impervious to conviction at gacaca. Should Rwandan citizens wish to accuse RPF members of any crimes committed inside the country, they must pursue the accusations at the Military Tribunal at their own expense (Bikesha interview, 20 July 2010). Moreover, violations of international humanitarian law allegedly perpetrated by the RPF could not be tried at the International Criminal Tribunal for Rwanda (ICTR). In fact, the RPF actively obstructed ICTR investigations into crimes it may have committed (Waldorf, 2007, p. 431).[4]

The fact that the RPF is not held culpable for any of its crimes not only promotes impunity at gacaca and the ICTR, but also legitimises the violence inflicted upon civilians by this rebel group. For instance, the RPF's invasion in October 1990, which led to nearly four years of civil war prior to the 1994 genocide, has been used in presidential speeches and campaign websites to bolster political support for the current regime:

> The liberation was about rescuing ourselves from a pre- and post-independence leadership that fostered and promoted hatred, sectarianism and genocidal ideologies – culminating in the decision to exterminate its own citizens.
>
> This created a legacy of bad politics, poor governance, disastrous social development philosophies and practices, and an economic system that entrenched a vicious cycle of poverty and dependency.
>
> These pre-liberation governments largely ignored the country's most precious resource – its people – through substandard education and health policies, and sidelined productive enterprise in favour of a system of cronyism within subsistence agriculture that failed to benefit the ordinary Rwandan.
>
> It was these circumstances that inspired us to liberate our country and begin the journey of building a nation worthy of our people (Kagame speech, 4 July 2009).

This quotation conflates the 'liberation invasion' of 1 October 1990 with the 'Liberation Day' of 4 July 1994, considered to be the 1994 genocide's final day. This relatively narrow review of the four bloodiest years in Rwanda's history constructs the RPF's political image as not only victors but also liberators, rather than an invading rebel group. The RPF's rhetorical use of the term 'liberator' thus transforms the current government into a symbol of valour, morality and peace (Edelman, 1998, p. 2). Furthermore, reframing the October 1990 invasion and the ensuing civil war as a 'liberation struggle' absolves the RPF of

4 See chapter 2 for further discussion about the RPF's interference in the ICTR.

any responsibility for violence inflicted by the rebels during this period, and of provoking the 1994 genocide as suggested by Alan J. Kuperman (2004, p. 62).[5]

'Genocide ideology' and restricted political space

The National Unity and Reconciliation Programme functions to legitimise the current leadership's policies, programmes and political images as well as to restrict perceived criticism of these programmes and the RPF. As discussed in previous chapters, journalists face intimidation, harassment and threats of violence if they publish work that is critical of the government or perceived to be 'divisionist'. The RPF further restricts independent media through imposing rigorous regulatory procedures overseen by the Media High Council.

Politically motivated accusations of 'genocide ideology' and 'divisionism' impede democracy by intimidating potential political opposition and silencing dissenting viewpoints of civilians and domestic NGOs.[6] Accusations of 'divisionism' need not pertain to acts that appeal to the perceived divisions between the ethnic groups. Instead, the term may refer to acts the accuser perceives as simply 'dividing' the nation in some way. For instance, Bernard Ntaganda, the PS-Imberakuri party president, was found guilty of 'divisionism' and threatening state security in 2011. Amnesty International alleges that these convictions relate to speeches he gave in 2010 criticising RPF policies (2012, p. 2). The term's vague nature facilitates the RPF's use of 'divisionism' to justify arresting political leaders, editors and journalists who are critical of the government and its programming. Indeed, when asked about the 2010 presidential elections, a Rwandan respondent who had worked in various projects related to the official reconciliation programme stated that 'divisionism and genocide ideology are his weapons. He [Kagame] doesn't want discussion or democracy. He wants to stay in power' (interview, 19 July 2010).

5 Kuperman proposes an alternative narrative for the RPF rebel group's role during the civil war that begins with its invasion of Rwanda from across the Ugandan border in October 1990. He argues that current literature about the 1994 genocide fails to take into account RPF actions beyond the initial invasion, and that the 1994 genocide was foreseeable and could have been prevented if the RPF had agreed to a ceasefire and compromised its political goals. He argues that the rebels' failure to do so created a genocidal backlash against Tutsi civilians (2004).

6 The Commonwealth Human Rights Initiative (CHRI) highlighted these human rights violations along with legal issues related to gacaca in its 2009 assessment of Rwanda's application to join the Commonwealth. The Initiative argued that the 'monopolistic role of the state' in constructing and disseminating Rwandan history and restricting the rights of free speech, expression and media impeded democracy. As such, CHRI recommended that Rwanda not be admitted to the Commonwealth (2009). Rwanda was officially granted membership of the Commonwealth on 29 November 2009 (*The Telegraph*, 2009).

Rwandan NGOs face pressure to promote official reconciliation discourse and government policy. Political scientist Timothy Longman maintains that the RPF achieves this goal by ensuring that NGOs fill their leadership positions with government supporters (2011b, p. 1). He explains that NGOs must also register with the Ministry of Local Government (Minaloc). The Law on Non-Profit Making Organisations, published in 2000, gives Minaloc legal power to interfere in the internal processes of domestic NGOs (Tengera, 2010, as cited by Longman, 2011b, p. 1). Longman also contends that these organisations face threats of violence, intimidation and assassinations from the government made in order to force compliance (ibid.). Human Rights Watch (HRW) also collected reports of intimidation involving human rights defenders in Rwanda (2012, p. 3).

Members of NGOs and domestic media outlets face threats of jail time if they are found guilty of promoting 'divisionism' or are perceived to be harbouring 'genocide ideology'. At the centre of this series of constraints is Law no. 18/2008 of 23/07/2008 Relating to the Punishment of the Crime of Genocide Ideology, which seeks to stamp out the spread of 'dangerous ideology' and 'divisionism' in order to prevent a recurrence of genocide (Parliament, 2008b). The concept of 'genocide ideology' that informs the law is particularly convoluted. It is defined in the NURC's 2008 'Training manual on genocide ideology' as:

> Ideally, a 'genocide ideology' is hardly conceivable since no group of people (party) would claim solving the problems of its society by exterminating another group of the same society. But, shit happens, as they say! Some parties, when not properly checked, may envision that 'final solution' as they euphonically and cynically call genocide. CDR in Rwanda, for instance, pretty much hinted to that when it used to sing that '*its sole enemy is the Tutsi*' (2008c, p. 7).[7]

Being found guilty of propagating 'genocide ideology' can lead to a hefty punishment including fines and/or life imprisonment if the accused has previously been convicted of the crime (Parliament, 2008b). The vague parameters of this law provide a framework through which politically motivated accusations may be made as it targets not only actions, but also thoughts perceived by the accuser(s) to support 'genocide ideology'.

An amended version of the 'genocide ideology' law was officially adopted in October 2013, which includes a more precise definition of the crime and requires evidence of the intention to promote this form of ideology. The maximum sentence has also been reduced from 25 years to nine (HRW, 2014, p. 158). The Assistant Attorney General stated that, 'The new law is clear, spells

7 Coalition pour la Défence de la République (CDR), a Hutu extremist party, was allied with the Mouvement Révolutionaire National pour le Développement (MRND), led by Juvénal Habyarimana.

out elements of the crime and their punishment, so no one should claim that they are being victimized if they are charged with the crime' (*Rwanda Focus*, 5 August 2013). As HRW has warned, the amended law still contains language that could be used to limit free speech (ibid.).

Several high-profile accusations of 'genocide ideology' were made prior to the 2008 law being adopted in 2003 against domestic NGO, the Ligue Rwandaise pour la Promotion et la Défense des Droits de l'Homme (LIPRODHOR), and against AI in 2004 (2010b, p. 27).[8] Similar accusations have also been made against opposition party members such as Victoire Ingabire, the FDU-Inkingi leader, who was prevented from registering for the 2010 Rwandan presidential election.[9] Ingabire was charged with 'genocide ideology', minimising the genocide, and collaborating with a terrorist group in 2010 (ibid., p. 21). These accusations stem primarily from the speech she gave at the Gisozi Genocide Memorial in April 2010 during which she called for investigations into war crimes allegedly committed by the RPF (ibid.). Ingabire was arrested in October 2010 on charges of forming a terrorist organisation (*The Telegraph*, 14 October 2010). This arrest relates to accusations that Ingabire met with FDLR officials in DRC intending to create 'her own militia group' (AI, 2010a, p. 2). Rwanda's Supreme Court upheld Ingabire's conviction in December 2013 and raised her sentence to 15 years (BBC News, 13 December 2013).

Peter Erlinder, an American ICTR defence lawyer who was representing Victoire Ingabire, was arrested in Rwanda in May 2010 on charges of genocide denial, 'genocide ideology' and threatening state security (*The Guardian*, 3 July 2010). He was released from prison in Rwanda on 18 June 2010, following significant international pressure from the ICTR, the UN and US government (*The Guardian*, 30 June 2010). Erlinder was officially removed from his position at the ICTR in April 2011 for failing to appear in court on several occasions, citing threats to his life as the reason. The ICTR has denied such threats existed (*The New York Times*, 27 April 2011).

Accusations of various crimes against the state other than 'genocide ideology' have been made against a number of former government officials who have publicly criticised the RPF. They include the senior government officers and former RPF members, Faustin Nyamwasa, Patrick Karegeya, Gerald Gahima and Théogène Rudasingwa, who were tried in absentia by the Rwandan military

8 A parliamentary commission also accused LIPRODHOR of 'divisionism' and collaborating with the Mouvement Démocratique Républicain opposition party. The commission recommended that the organisation be dissolved and its members arrested. Nine members of the group fled Rwanda in 2004. LIPRODHOR still operates in Rwanda with a new board of directors (International Federation for Human Rights, 14 April 2005)

9 The FDU-Inkingi and Democratic Green Party were not able to acquire the security clearance necessary to organise the public meetings required for official registration in the 2010 presidential election (AI, 2012, p. 2).

court in January 2011 and are all now in exile. The men were found guilty of endangering state security, destabilising public order, 'divisionism', defamation and forming a criminal enterprise. Karegeya and Gahima received 20-year jail terms while Nyamwasa and Rudasingwa were given 24-year sentences (BBC News, 4 March 2011).

The RPF alleges that Lieutenant-General Nyamwasa was connected to the grenade attack in Kigali in January 2011 that killed two people and left 28 more injured (ibid.; Reuters, 29 January 2011).[10] In June 2010, Nyamwasa was shot in the stomach in Johannesburg, South Africa, in an attack his wife said had been orchestrated by President Kagame. Nyamwasa survived (BBC News, 19 June 2010). Three Rwandan citizens and three Tanzanians pleaded guilty to their role in the failed assassination attempt (Rwanda News Agency, 19 March 2012). The RPF has denied any involvement in the shooting (BBC News, 19 June 2010). In May 2011, the Metropolitan Police Service warned two Rwandan exiles living in London that they were in danger of being assassinated by a hit man allegedly hired by the RPF government. Both men, who have publicly criticised President Kagame, belong to political groups opposed to the current regime (BBC News, 21 May 2011). The Metropolitan Police warned a third man of a similar threat in August 2011. The Rwandan government has denied the allegations (BBC News, 2 August 2011).

Nation-building through development

Vision 2020's stated goal is to transform Rwanda into a middle-income country by raising the per capita income from approximately US$220 in 2000 to US$900 by the year 2020 (Minecofin, 2000, p. 3).[11] The programme is structured around six interwoven pillars deemed to promote the development envisioned by the government. They include: 'skilled human capital'; 'vibrant private sector'; 'world-class physical infrastructure and modern agriculture and livestock'; and 'good governance and efficient state', all of which are focused on increasing Rwanda's activities in regional and global markets (ibid., p. 2).

'Good governance' in this context refers to the RPF's stated obligation to be accountable to the Rwandan people and behave transparently and efficiently, particularly in relation to the country's natural resources.[12] It also refers to a

10 Rwanda (Kigali, in particular) has seen a spate of grenade attacks since 2010. These blasts are commonly blamed on FDLR members or supporters.

11 The per capita income was US$638.70 in 2013 (World Bank, 2015).

12 The 2006 'Environmental profile of Rwanda', financed by the European Commission, warns of 'serious pressure' on Rwanda's natural resources including: soil degradation; overexploitation and inappropriate farming systems; deforestation, migration and uncontrolled charcoal and firewood production; pressure on wetlands related to swamp clearing; and water contamination due to a lack of clean drinking water systems and waste water treatment. The report makes a

stated commitment to promoting democratic structures and processes as well as the rule of law and the protection of human rights (ibid., p. 12). This definition combines elements of two forms of 'good governance' to which the RPF has stated an obligation. The first relates to 'political governance', which is defined in opposition to the 'bad governance' of Habyarimana's regime as outlined in the 2007 Reconciliation Policy discussed earlier in this chapter. This definition, constructed by the RPF government, includes the regime's stated adherence to rule of law, democratic structures and the protection of human rights as declared in the 2003 Constitution.

The second form refers to 'technocratic good governance', a key element of the political image of Rwanda and its leadership disseminated by the RPF to the international community (Marysse et al., 2006, p. 13). This form includes the RPF's stated commitment to transparency and accountability with particular reference to economic resources and public programmes, an approach to leadership that has purportedly played a major role in attracting international aid and foreign investment (Reyntjens, 2010, p. 28). This chapter will pick the issue up again later with reference to implications of conflating these two forms of governance within Vision 2020 for 'national reconciliation', development, and constructing political images of Rwanda.

Vision 2020 outlines challenges facing Rwanda's post-conflict economy and describes short-, medium- and long-term development goals. It also disseminates the RPF's commitment to unity and 'national reconciliation'. For instance, this plan is mandated to reduce aid dependency by encouraging private investment, transforming the agrarian economy into one that is knowledge-based, and unifying the population (Minecofin, 2000, p. 3):

> It is important to emphasize the point that this Vision is not only for government. Vision 2020 is a shared purpose for all Rwandans. We need to constantly remind ourselves how our work – in our individual capacities, communities, business and public institutions – contributes towards realizing this Vision. Like all achieving societies whose success is generally inspired by a shared purpose, our Vision 2020 constitutes a bond that holds Rwandans as a people determined to build a better future (ibid., p. 2).

According to Leonard Rugwabiza, then director general of national development, planning and research at the Ministry of Finance and Economic Planning (Minecofin), development programming such as Vision 2020 promotes unity in two ways. The first is to provide citizens, once divided by ethnicity or their experiences of the 1994 genocide, with the chance to work together (Rugwabiza interview, 14 July 2010). Such an opportunity may be created through cooperating on private development projects or through

number of recommendations with regard to improved environmental management (Twagiramungu, 2006, pp. 44–5).

government-sponsored programming. The latter set of projects includes development schemes that fall within National Unity and Reconciliation Programme parameters. *Umuganda*, for instance, is a mandatory unpaid one-day community work programme completed once a month by all citizens over the age of 18 living in Rwanda. Its stated goal is to give citizens the opportunity to work together on reconstruction projects that are of individual and national interest such as repairing roads, planting trees and building health centres (Mukajiranga interview, 9 June 2009).[13]

Umuganda reflects the ubiquity of RPF political dominance, a control that is disseminated through the work's mandatory nature as well as through the meetings between government representatives and community members held after each session. They provide a forum for discussing issues related to the community from which the central government can relay messages to citizens across the country (Rugwabiza interview, 14 July 2010).

Government-sponsored development programming is also used to promote the RPF's vision of 'national reconciliation' by stimulating individual and national pride. According to Rugwabiza, rapid development makes citizens proud and brings them together, an experience so powerful that people purportedly 'see development and start to forget the division' (ibid.). This quotation illustrates the projected influence of development on the population and connects it to the RPF's nation-building agenda. Vision 2020 is an integral part of this process as it states the government's commitment to promoting 'national reconciliation' and building a nation that is competitive in regional and global markets (Minecofin, 2000, p. 2). The relationship between development, 'national reconciliation' and nation-building is further demonstrated in the Republic of Rwanda motto, 'unity, work and patriotism', described in the first chapter of the 2003 Constitution (MOD, 2003, p. 2).

Political image at the international level

Development features heavily in the image of Rwanda the RPF projects to the international community of donors, NGOs and foreign investors, one which relays the country's readiness to provide the type of 'pro-business environment' that purportedly appeals to foreign financiers (Kagame speech, 2 November 2009). This readiness is illustrated by the RPF's portrayal of Rwanda as stable and secure with strong political leadership that does not tolerate corruption and is committed to technocratic 'good governance' (Claver Gatete, Growth Week Conference, 21 September 2010). Official reconciliation's primary function within the construction and dissemination of this image is to portray Rwanda as an attractive place to invest: 'Without successful reconciliation,

13 A 'Global Umuganda' was launched on 29 March 2014 to commemorate the 1994 genocide's 20th anniversary. Events were planned in countries including Canada, Malaysia and India (*New Times*, 28 March 2014).

political stability and security, private investors will not develop confidence in the country' (Minecofin, 2000, p. 8). This assertion fails to demonstrate the complex nature of the relationship between political stability, development and the government's vision of 'national reconciliation'. Instead, 'successful reconciliation' appears as one of a list of boxes that must be ticked in order to please donors and investors.

In reality, donor countries, the UN and many national and international NGOs are far more involved in the RPF's pursuit of 'national reconciliation' than indicated in the quotation above. Firstly, international governmental, non-governmental and multilateral organisations have played an important role in funding, supporting and monitoring the RPF's official reconciliation programme since its inception in the late 1990s. Secondly, the international community's support of the RPF's official programme follows the highly inadequate international intervention to prevent or end the 1994 genocide. This issue has impacted the power dynamics between the government and the donor community, and features prominently in the 'victor's narrative'. Thirdly, reference to the 1994 genocide and the RPF's role in Rwanda's post-conflict reconstruction has afforded the government 'exceptional status' from donors (Zorbas, 2011, p. 106). This increases the amount and types of aid instruments given to Rwanda, alleviates pressure from donors for fully transparent democracy, and prevents what Zorbas describes as 'critical thinking as to why such an exception should be maintained or for how long' (ibid.).

Relations, roles and power dynamics with regard to aid after 1994

The early post-conflict period starting from 1994 saw a major upsurge in aid sent to Rwanda by international donors. In fact, Rwanda received three times as much aid in 1994 as it had in the early 1990s (Marysse et al., 2006, p. 15).[14] This rise is made all the more significant following a drop of per capita GDP from US$251 in 1990 to US$152 in 1994 (ibid., p. 22; World Bank, 2009). Economic growth was stifled in 1994 by a combination of challenges that predated the genocide and new obstacles caused by the violence including high population growth, land shortages and limited natural resources. The large number of deaths, damage to infrastructure and the creation of vulnerable groups - such as widows, child-headed households and internally displaced persons (IDPs) in that year - compounded these problems (Hayman, 2007, p. 5).

Aid took differing forms in Rwanda during the period immediately following the 1994 genocide. Minimal financial support was given directly to the transitional government in Kigali. Hayman explains that the inadequate support from donors for government-led reconstruction and reintegration

14 Rwanda received approximately US$30 per capita in aid in the early 1990s (Marysse et al., 2006, p. 16).

programmes led to considerable bitterness from the RPF (2009, p. 584). This friction was exacerbated by the support multilateral organisations and NGOs gave to refugee camps in other Great Lakes countries sheltering civilians as well as genocide perpetrators (Kumar et al., 1996, cited in Hayman 2009, p. 584; Baaré et al., 1999, cited in Hayman 2007). For instance, an HRW Africa report, published in December 1994, states:

> The new government of Rwanda inherited little but debts from its predecessor. Clearly unable to mount an effective administration with so few resources, it called upon donor nations for aid in funds and personnel. Although the international community has responded generously to the needs of Rwandans in refugee camps outside the country, with the United States alone contributing approximately half a billion dollars, it has not yet delivered any substantial aid to the new government. According to well-placed sources within the European Union, France initially made clear an intention to block any significant assistance from that body. Other donors hesitated as well, many of them concerned about how representative the new government was and about reports of human rights violations by the RPF (p. 19).

Aid began to flow to GNU, the newly formed government, from countries including the US, the Netherlands and Denmark towards the end of November 1994 (ibid.). In the first few years following the 1994 genocide, a significant proportion of aid was donated to promote programmes related to justice, with donors allotting money for the ICTR, the domestic legal system and gacaca (Oomen, 2005a, p. 895). Gacaca received funding and institutional support from a variety of governmental donors from the US, Canada, France, Norway and Switzerland, as well as from multilateral organisations such as the European Union, the United Nations Development Programme (UNDP) and the United Nations Refugee Agency (UNHCR). Gacaca also received assistance from several international NGOs of which 141 were operating in the country in late 1994 (ibid., p. 896).

International donors' readiness to fund gacaca reflects a larger interest in supporting programmes related to promoting the RPF's vision of 'national reconciliation'. Donor willingness to participate in the coordination and monitoring of gacaca in the late 1990s may have been impacted by several trends related to development, peacebuilding and reconciliation at the time. The first reflects the conflation of development with the promotion of justice in the post-conflict context, possibly due in part to the perception of justice as apolitical and a more affordable investment than military or diplomatic interventions by the international community (ibid., p. 892). The 1997 'OECD guidelines for peace, conflict and development cooperation' and the 1998 UN Secretary General's report on 'Priorities for post-conflict peacebuilding' reflect a further shift towards promoting political and social change through donorship and investment in development. For instance, they place 'good governance', justice, security and reconciliation firmly at the top of the development agenda (UNSG 1998 report, as cited by Uvin, 2001, p. 178). The 1997 OECD guidelines state that:

> Post-conflict reconstruction is much more than just repairing physical infrastructure. When civil authority has broken down, the first priority is to restore a sense of security. This includes restoring legitimate government institutions that are regarded by citizens as serving all groups and that are able to allay persisting tensions, while carrying out the challenges and costly tasks of rebuilding. Efforts by developing countries and international assistance must fit within the context of a sound, even if rudimentary, macroeconomic stabilization plan. Post-conflict situations often provide special opportunities for political, legal, economic and administrative reforms to change past systems and structures which may have contributed to economic and social inequities and conflict. Initiatives for participatory debates and assessment of the role of the military in relation to the state and civil society have been productive in post-conflict settings. In the wake of conflict, donors should seize the opportunities to help promote and maintain the momentum for reconciliation and needed reforms (Development Assistance Committee, 1997, p. 3).

The GNU's stated commitment to promoting justice and 'national reconciliation' would have made Rwanda particularly attractive to donors operating with similar priorities. The transitional government's stated prioritisation of 'good governance', justice and stability provided benefactors with the opportunity to invest in a country in transition. Filip Reyntjens describes two further trends that emerged in the relationship between the GNU (and later RPF) and foreign donors. The first is the donors' sense that significant leeway ought to be given to a government facing the challenge of rebuilding a country decimated by war and genocide. Secondly, Reyntjens points to the donation of aid without conditions regarding state behaviour as proof to the RPF that it could act with impunity (2004, p. 179). Benefactors from the international community may have granted this 'liberty' as a form of compensation for its failure to intervene during the 1994 genocide, an inaction all the more poignant given the UN and donor countries' awareness of systematic massacres as they took place in 1994.

On 21 April 1994, the UN Security Council (UNSC) voted to withdraw all but 270 of the 2,500 UNAMIR troops stationed in Kigali since October 1993 (Jones, 2006, pp. 232–3). This withdrawal took place following numerous warnings of impending genocide in the run-up to April 1994, and despite the vote having been held amidst protest from UNAMIR Commander Major-General Roméo Dallaire following the deaths of Prime Minister Agathe Uwilingiyimana and the ten Belgian peacekeepers protecting her (ibid., pp. 232, 238). Following the decision to extract Belgian troops posted at Ecole

Technique Officielle in Kicukiro, approximately 5,000 Tutsi hiding in the complex were massacred on 7 April 1994 (Augustin interview, 7 April 2009).

As discussed in chapter 2, the US played an integral role in discouraging international intervention in the 1994 genocide. The Clinton administration's refusal to use the term 'genocide' reflected geopolitical interests that outweighed the desire to intervene in another conflict (Klinghoffer, 1998, p. 97). As we have seen, Herman and Peterson offer an alternative interpretation of international inaction during the 1994 genocide and the civil war that preceded it. They point to a neoliberal conspiracy in which Washington actively supported Kagame during the civil war and prevented the deployment of adequate UN forces during the 1994 genocide. If Herman and Peterson are correct, this arrangement could have had significant benefits for both parties, as it would have allowed the Rwandan government freedom to eradicate its political and military enemies without damaging its international reputation. For the Americans, it could have granted them the opportunity to usurp their Western rivals in terms of US influence in former European colonies and access to mineral wealth in Zaire, now DRC (Herman and Peterson, 2010, p. 61).

The UN's decision not to intervene in the 1994 genocide has greatly impacted the relationship between the RPF and the donor community. The damage may have been caused not by the notion that the international community did not do enough, but that its inaction actively exacerbated the situation on the ground (Kagame speech, 22 April 2014). The RPF has allegedly used 'genocide credit', stemming from this failure to act, to manipulate the guilt and humiliation purportedly felt by the international community in several ways (Reyntjens, 2004, p. 199). The first has been to maintain significant control of how donor money is spent in Rwanda.[15] The connection between international inaction in 1994 and RPF dominance in post-conflict Rwanda is evident in this excerpt from President Kagame's speech given at Tufts University on 22 April 2014:

> What we have learned as Rwandans is that people must ultimately be responsible for their own fate; if you wait for help to come, you will just perish.
>
> Similarly, if you wait for outsiders to tell you how to rebuild your country, you may find their instinct is to reconstruct the same flawed structure that just collapsed, because they have no other blueprint.

Genocide credit has also been used to mute criticism or what Johan Pottier refers to as 'awkward questions' from outsiders (2002, p. 156). One of the most pertinent is: what role did the RPF/RPA play in civilian deaths during

15 See Zorbas (2011) and Hayman (2009) for detailed analyses of how the 2005 'Paris declaration on aid effectiveness' has promoted the joint ownership of development strategies by national governments and international donors. Both authors discuss how the RPF has gained more control over the definition of development programmes and how resources have been used since 2005.

the 1994 genocide and in the post-conflict era in eastern Zaire, now DRC? The second has been to reproach international criticism of the current regime. President Kagame went so far as to lay partial blame for the 1994 genocide on the international community. At the 15th Commemoration of the 1994 genocide at the Nyanza Memorial Site on 7 April 2009, he stated, 'well, there are people who are guilty, no question. Those who abandoned people they had come here to protect and left them to be murdered, left them to the dogs … aren't they guilty?'

More recently, the RPF has used the UN's inaction in 1994 to discredit the 2010 UN 'Report of the mapping exercise', which documents abuses of human rights and violations of international humanitarian law in DRC including crimes the RPF/RPA allegedly committed between March 1993 and June 2003 (UNHRC, 2010). It responded to the leaked draft of the 'Report' in these terms:

> It is immoral and unacceptable that the United Nations, an organisation that failed outright to prevent genocide in Rwanda and the subsequent refugee [sic] crisis, a direct cause for so much suffering in Congo and Rwanda, now accuses the army that stopped the genocide of committing atrocities in the Democratic Republic of Congo (Rwanda News Agency, 29 August 2010).

The RPF then rejected the document and threatened to withdraw its troops from peacekeeping duties in Darfur if it was published (BBC News, 29 August 2010). When the report was published later on, however, the RPF agreed to keep its troops in Sudan (BBC News, 27 September 2010). The Ministry of Foreign Affairs and Cooperation (Minaffet) has since criticised the report for 'rewriting history', reigniting conflict between Rwanda and DRC, employing flawed methodology and undermining peace and stability in the Great Lakes Region (Rwanda News Agency, 30 September 2010, p. 3).

International donors have responded to accusations of human rights abuses and violations, perpetrated by the RPF/RPA in Rwanda and DRC, in a variety of ways. Although most donors were not deterred by criticism of the RPF's alleged attempts to undermine democracy in the run-up to the 2010 elections, some did respond to the RPF's various military incursions across the border between 1999–2009 (HRW, 2011b, p. 1).[16] Norway suspended bilateral aid in 1999 until the RPF officially withdrew from DRC in 2002 (Hayman, 2007, p. 16). The UK and Sweden delayed payment of aid in 2004–5 following allegations that Rwandan troops were present in DRC. Norway and Sweden suspended financial support to the RPF in 2009 following renewed tension

16 HRW's 'World Report 2011' states that some donor governments privately expressed concerns about the 'crackdown' on political space and media freedom prior to the 2010 presidential elections, but these did not translate into decisive action from donors (HRW, 2011b, p. 1).

in eastern DRC and allegations of the RPF's support of Congolese Tutsi rebel group Congrès National pour la Défense du Peuple (CNDP) led by Laurent Nkunda (Hayman, 2009, p. 592).

The RPF had been accused of supporting Nkunda and using the CNDP to fight a proxy war against the Hutu FDLR after the RPF's military branch, the RPA, officially pulled out of DRC in 2002 (BBC News, 23 January 2009; BBC News, 19 October 2007). Nkunda was arrested in Rwanda on 22 January 2009 following significant pressure from international donors, particularly the US and the UK (*The Telegraph*, 23 January 2009). He remains under house arrest in Kigali. Attempts to bring his case to court have reportedly been blocked by the RPF (HRW, 2012, p. 4; BBC News, 5 June 2014).

The RPF government faced new allegations of supporting unrest in DRC in 2012. An addendum to a report by a UN Group of Experts accused the RPF of violating the arms embargo and sanctions against its neighbour by actions such as providing weapons, military supplies and Rwandan recruits to the Congolese rebel group M23 (UNSC, 2012, p. 2). The M23 rebel group comprised 600 former CNDP rebels who had defected from the Congolese Armed Forces in April 2012 (BBC News, 27 June 2012).[17] The defection was allegedly led by 'The Terminator' Bosco Ntaganda against whom the International Criminal Court (ICC) has issued an arrest warrant for alleged war crimes including the recruitment of child soldiers (BBC News, 28 May 2012; BBC News, 15 May 2012). Ntaganda turned himself over to the US embassy in Kigali in March 2013 and appeared before the ICC later that month. The case against him was set to move to trial in July 2015 to face 18 counts of war crimes and acts against humanity (Reuters Africa, 9 June 2014; ICC, 22 April 2015).

Rwandan Foreign Minister Louise Mushikiwabo responded to the report draft leaked in mid June 2012 with a warning: 'In our corner of the world, words quickly become deeds and anti-Rwanda rhetoric carries grave consequences ... More hateful attacks can be feared as calls for Congolese worldwide to "kill the Tutsis" are being propagated over the internet' (*New Times*, 28 June 2012). Tension continued to rise between Kabila's government and the RPF amid further accusations of Rwandan and Ugandan support for the M23 rebels. In October 2012, a second report by a panel of UN experts accused Rwanda of partially funding the rebellion with profits acquired through smuggling and exporting Congolese minerals (Reuters, 16 October 2012). The RPF has faced long-standing accusations of benefiting from the plunder of minerals conducted by Rwandan soldiers and militias fighting inside DRC. The 2010 UN 'Report of the mapping exercise' describes an instance in Walikale territory when Rwandan soldiers are alleged to have purchased coltan from FDLR rebels

17 The CNDP was integrated into the Congolese Army following a peace agreement between Rwanda and DRC in 2009 (BBC News, 28 May 2012).

against whom they were at war (UN, 2010, p. 352).[18] This account and the October 2012 UN report reflect accusations of 'predatory behaviour' made by the international NGO, Global Witness, regarding Rwanda's alleged history of benefiting from plundering and exporting hundreds of millions of dollars worth of Congolese minerals (Reuters, 18 September 2012).[19]

M23 rebels entered Goma and seized the capital of North Kivu Province in mid November 2012 (BBC News, 21 November 2012). In Uganda, several days later, President Kabila met with the presidents of Tanzania, Kenya and Uganda, together with Foreign Minister Mushikiwabo. The leaders urged the rebels to withdraw from Goma and cease their threats of seizing power from Kabila (BBC News, 24 November 2012). The rebels withdrew from Goma, but later reentered. Approximately 800,000 civilians were displaced amid violent clashes between the M23 rebels, rival factions within the group and the Congolese Armed Forces (BBC News, 31 July 2013; BBC News, 25 February 2013). In late July 2013, 3,000 UN soldiers attempted to calm clashes of various rebel groups including M23 in eastern DRC. The UN gave the groups in Goma until 31 July to disarm, at which time it would use force if necessary (BBC News, 31 July 2013). The M23 rebellion ended on 5 November 2013 when the group surrendered following a joint mission between the Forces Armées de la République Démocratique du Congo and the Force Intervention Brigade, a specialised contingent of MONUSCO troops (UNSC, 2014a, p. 6). President Kabila authorised an amnesty law in March 2014 for acts of insurgency, war and political crimes committed by members of armed groups in DRC between 18 February 2006 and 20 December 2013. The law excludes cases of genocide, crimes against humanity, war crimes and gross human rights violations. Former M23 rebels in Rwanda would need to return to DRC to receive this amnesty (UNSC, 2014b, p. 4; BBC News, 5 June 2014).

Accusations made about the RPF having supported the M23 rebels resulted in limited suspensions of aid by international donors. The EU part-suspended aid to Rwanda in late September 2012 following similar actions by the US, Sweden, Germany and the Netherlands (*The Guardian*, 27 September 2012). The fact that major benefactors partially and temporarily suspended aid between 1999 and 2009, and again in 2012, may be explained by growing

18 See the UN 'Report of the mapping exercise' for further discussion of the relationship between the economic agendas of Congolese and Rwandan rebels, as well as Rwandan, Ugandan and Congolese government forces, and continuing violence related to the control of mineral mines in DRC (2010).

19 In November 2011, Rwanda returned 82 tonnes of minerals that had been smuggled out of DRC over the previous five months. Although this handover indicates that minerals were being smuggled across the border between both countries, the Rwandan deputy director of natural resources, Michael Biryabarema, denied allegations of plunder and illegal trade of minerals by the RPF (BBC News, 3 Nov. 2011).

consensus in the international community that regional instability is a primary threat to financial investments and diplomatic relations made in Rwanda in the post-conflict period (Zorbas, 2011, p. 112). Since these aid restrictions and suspensions have been applied inconsistently, they have had little effect overall (ibid.). For instance, in September 2012 the UK resumed its donation of £16 million to Rwanda after temporarily suspending aid in July 2012 following the accusations made in the leaked UN report that the RPF had supported the M23 rebels (BBC News, 13 November 2012). Justine Greening, the international development secretary, froze the £21 million budget payment due to be delivered in December 2012, citing Rwanda's breach of the principles which underline its donor partnership with the UK (Reuters, 30 November 2012).[20] President Kagame responded to a question about the suspension following his keynote address at the Said Business School, Oxford, by denying Rwanda's involvement in the conflict and asking, 'How long will Rwanda be made responsible for problems in another country?' (speech, 18 May 2013). Rwanda has since been accused of protecting 500 former M23 members in a camp inside the country. Those ex-combatants who have been in the camp for more than a year must return to DRC to be eligible for amnesty for crimes committed during the rebellion (BBC News, 5 June 2014).

'Victor's narrative', 'national reconciliation' and development

The RPF's reaction to the leak and subsequent release of the UN 'Report of the mapping exercise' demonstrates a decisive attempt to protect the political image it has created of Rwanda and its leadership. Accusations of RPF war crimes allegedly committed in DRC, and the use of the term 'genocide' with reference to these crimes, contradict the RPF's stated commitment to both technocratic and political 'good governance'.[21] These allegations may question the portrayal of Rwanda as safe, stable and ready for foreign investment. The RPF's vehement condemnation of the report also signifies the propagation of a single narrative about its role during the 1994 genocide and in the post-conflict period: 'On the international scene, we don't negotiate. On Rwanda we don't negotiate' (Rugwabiza interview, 14 July 2010). Kagame attempted to preserve the image of 'good governance' inside Rwanda by lashing out against critical voices from the international community, particularly human rights activists

20 Britain's Department for International Development has stated a commitment to disbursing £83 million per year to Rwanda until 2015 (Reuters, 30 Nov. 2012).

21 The 'Report of the mapping exercise' does not directly accuse the RPF of committing genocide against Hutu civilians in DRC, but rather states that, 'the apparent systematic and widespread attacks described in this report reveal a number of inculpatory elements that, if proven before a competent court, could be characterised as crimes of genocide' (UNHCR, 2010, p. 24).

and international NGOs. In a speech at the National Dialogue Council, Kigali, on 15 December 2011, he stated,

> There are voices that originate from outside the country where you hear people say that there is progress in Rwanda but at the end, they add 'but'. Where does the 'but' come from? The most common accusation from these people is that there is no freedom of speech in Rwanda. This can only mean three things; that Rwandans are mute, or someone is physically preventing them from speaking, or they have nothing to say. ...
>
> People say that there is no political space – there is no bigger space than this one. Actually, the only space lacking is the one that is occupied by these intruders. This nonsense from outside is occupying our space. These teachers of political space, press freedom are the same ones who give freedom to murderers of our people. It has taken 17 years for them to try Bagosora[22] and try the case so badly. They also have been letting those who worked with him to kill our people go scot free and yet they come here to lecture us on freedoms? They are jokers. ...
>
> We cannot be seen to be making all this progress and at the same time be so bad in terms of democratic government or freedoms – it doesn't add up. These people have their own problems that they need to address.

The image projected to the international community mirrors that disseminated to the Rwandan people. In the international context, however, the RPF's portrayal as the 'good guy' who ended the 1994 genocide and is actively 'reconciling' the people of Rwanda functions to promote development through donorship and direct foreign investment (Reyntjens, 2004, p. 179). In the development context, the RPF's 'good guy' image is portrayed through its stated commitment to high standards of technocratic governance (Marysse et al., 2006, p. 25). This type of 'good governance', unlike the form of political governance discussed at the beginning of this chapter, is not an RPF construction. It does not exist in opposition to the 'bad governance' of earlier regimes, nor does it serve the same political function. Instead, it represents a criterion of governance that seemingly appeals to international donors and investors (ibid.).

Wil Hout defines the technocratic approach to governance as 'the way in which the public sector is managed' (2004, as cited by Marysse et al., 2006, p. 25). In particular, Hout draws attention to government policies' positive features: legality, accountability and transparency (ibid.). Paul Collier emphasises how important excellent governance and economic policies are in helping governments of developing countries to make the most of opportunities and capabilities within their reach, such as bilateral aid (2007, p. 64). Although aid as a percentage of total government spending dropped from

22 See chapter 2 for an account of Théogene Bagosora's role in the 1994 genocide.

85 per cent in 2000 to 45 per cent in 2010, Rwanda remains highly dependent on international donors (ActionAid, 2011, p. 8). The country's dependence on aid is compounded by structural and geographical constraints to development, which include a history of conflict, a landlocked location between neighbouring countries with slow rates of economic growth, and resource-scarcity (Collier, 2007). Arguably, the most vital opportunity available to Rwanda is attracting donorship and foreign investment (Collier, Growth Week Conference, 21 September 2010).

According to Marysse et al., the RPF's high standard of technocratic governance successfully reestablished the provision of aid shortly after the 1994 genocide and has continued to attract interest from foreign donors and investors (2006, p. 17). Part of this attraction may stem from what Hayman describes as the RPF's ability 'to speak the language of international development' (2007, p. 18). She points to the government's stated commitment to pursue neoliberal development strategies and poverty reduction projects, as well as participatory programmes such as gacaca (ibid.).[23] Vision 2020 exemplifies this obligation as it outlines the RPF's stated goals of stabilising the economy by implementing macroeconomic reforms and wealth-creation projects, transforming the agrarian economy into one that is primarily knowledge-based, and fostering entrepreneurship and a flourishing middle class (Minecofin, 2000). The stated goal for the period 2014–20 includes a focus on creating jobs through economic and agricultural sector reform (Kagame speech, 11 March 2014).

This commitment to 'good governance' and rapid development is repeated in the Economic Development and Poverty Reduction Strategy 2 (EDPRS 2), which outlines the government's plans for transforming the private sector and alleviating constraints to growth over five years (2013–18). The EDPRS 2 is described as the final push towards achieving goals set out in Vision 2020 (Minecofin, 2013, pp. viii, 1). This document follows the first iteration of the strategy, EDPRS 1, which resulted in a 'perfect developmental "hat trick" ... of sustained economic growth, poverty reduction and lower levels of income inequality' (ibid., p. ix). The EDPRS 2 promulgates the government's commitment to new strategies and older policies such as the 'National Human Settlement Policy', launched in 1996,[24] which was mandated to guide the resettlement of refugees returning from the Great Lakes Region amidst a land scarcity crisis created by the 1994 genocide (IRIN, 5 October 2004). It stated that all Rwandans living in rural homesteads must move into government-constructed *imidugudu* or village settlements. HRW criticised the programme

23 See Harvey for a detailed historical description of the development of neoliberalism. Harvey contends that neoliberal economic reforms function to restore or enhance class power of the ruling elite. He rejects the 'failed utopian rhetoric' of neoliberalism and posits the alternatives of open democracy, social equality, and economic, political and cultural justice (2005, p. 206).

24 This policy was amended in 2004, 2006 and 2009 (Minaloc, 2013, p. 1).

in 2001 for benefiting some returnees and survivors while forcing others, both Hutu and Tutsi, to leave their homes, some of which were destroyed without compensation (2001, p. 2). It is described as a key strategy in EDPRS 2 as it promotes quality housing, a strong regulatory framework and the resettlement of families living in high-risk zones. In 2012, 53.1 per cent of households in rural areas were living in this type of village (Minaloc, 2013, p. 2).

The EDPRS 2's overarching goals of speeding progress towards middle-income status and improving quality of life for all Rwandans will purportedly be met by achieving sustained growth of 11.5 per cent and by reducing the percentage of the population living in poverty to less than 30 per cent (ibid., p. 1). Private sector growth is key to meeting these targets (Kagame speech, 11 March 2014). As such, the RPF has paid particular attention to fostering a 'pro-business environment' for the benefit of investors interested in Rwanda's development: 'We are painstakingly building the confidence of domestic and foreign investors to put their money into our hotels, energy projects, agriculture, the construction industry, and ICT on the basis of transparent government and predictability' (Kagame speech, 21 September 2009). This stated commitment to transparency and predictability is being pursued through institutional reforms aimed at bolstering technocratic 'good governance' and public services through the anti-corruption agenda, Public Sector Reform and the National Decentralisation Policy (UNDP, 2007, p. 66). Adopted in 2000, the latter policy outlined the process through which district mayors would be made responsible for implementing the government's development programme,[25] and which was informed by the same commitments to good technocratic governance seen in related documents. Meanwhile, it seeks to maintain transparency and political stability with the addition of giving local populations more say in government programming.

Imihigo, a purportedly pre-colonial practice in which leaders publicly stated their commitment to achieving particular goals, was reinvented in 2006 in the form of performance contracts to ensure mayoral accountability (Scher and MacAuley, 2014, p. 1). The contracts follow consultations with community council and vice mayors and the development of one-, three- and five-year action plans that seek to meet imihigo targets for economic growth, governance and social welfare (ibid., p. 5). Each mayor's achievement of these targets is analysed according to performance metrics resulting in an individual score. The accountability promoted by this form of measurement and evaluation is redoubled by public scrutiny. District mayors and President Kagame publicly sign the imihigo in a televised broadcast and all documents related to the

25 District leadership plays an important role in local government. These financially and legally independent entities oversee local-level development projects, such as agriculture and medium-sized enterprises, and coordinate the delivery of services including hospitals (Chemouni, 2014, p. 248).

targets are available online (ibid., p. 6), a process that has been commended for encouraging the delivery of results locally and ensuring that state-level policies are implemented at the lowest levels (Chemouni, 2014, p. 251). It has, however, been criticised for resulting in 'cooked' numbers that falsely meet strict imihigo targets, retaining state control over local objectives and creating non-partisan local elite who remain loyal to the RPF (ibid., p. 253).

With regard to promoting investment, the RPF has significantly reduced the barriers that businesses once faced in Rwanda. Reforms related to acquiring construction permits, protecting investors and paying taxes, among others, resulted in Rwanda's ranking in the 'Ease of doing business worldwide' category in the World Bank's 2014 'Doing Business Report' improving from 54th position the previous year to 32nd. The report also named Rwanda as the second most improved country and the second easiest African country in which to do business (World Bank, 2014; Rwanda Development Board, 2013). Rapid reforms over the past several years have translated into direct investment by several large international companies including Visa and Heineken NV, which owns 75 per cent of Rwanda's largest beer maker, Bralirwa (*The Economist*, 25 February 2012; *Bloomberg News*, 15 March 2012). Global chief economist at Renaissance Capital, Charles Robertson, explains the benefits of foreign investment for Rwandans: 'the Rwandan government is producing growth and that's very positive for the Rwandan people and eventually for Rwandan human rights and Rwandan democracy' (ibid.).

Robertson's prediction of the long-term benefits is ambitious, given the uneven nature of the development it promotes. 'Uneven development' is defined here as the inequitable distribution of 'intentional development' benefits to citizens such as international aid, direct foreign investment, and the implementation of development projects, policies and programmes (Cowen and Shenton, 1998, p. 50, as cited by Bebbington, 2004, p. 726). Development in Rwanda has been particularly uneven with regard to the least advantaged. For instance, 'pro-poor growth', a stated commitment articulated in Vision 2020, has been negatively impacted by issues of land scarcity, institutional constraints facing small-scale peasant farmers, and enhanced opportunities for larger commercial farms (Ansoms, 2007). Vision 2020 describes development as a common interest and benefit to all Rwandans yet, as Zorbas argues, the RPF's development strategy 'does not fundamentally improve the lot of the poor and vulnerable, nor does it alter the conditions of structural violence' (2011, p. 114). This failure is reflected in inequality levels in Rwanda. Whereas they have fallen in recent years with the gini coefficient – the measurement of the degree of inequality in the distribution of family income in a country – shifting from 0.52 to 0.49 between 2005–6 and 2010–11, Rwanda was labelled East Africa's most unequal country by the Society for International Development (SID). According to SID's *State of East Africa* report, published in November 2013, in

2011, the richest 10 per cent of the population earned 3.2 times more income than the poorest 40 per cent (2013, p. 83).[26]

It is encouraging that, in 2012, the RPF set new targets for Vision 2020 that include reducing poverty by 20 per cent by 2020 (*Rwanda Focus*, 12 March 2012).[27] However, this revised goal does not detract from the damaging consequences of uneven development for genocide survivors. Although they receive support from several non-governmental advocacy groups including: the Association of Widows of the Genocide; IBUKA (meaning 'remember' in Kinyarwanda); and the Survivors Fund (SURF), many continue to face significant challenges. In January 2012, HRW reported that survivors continued to have limited access to economic and social services across Rwanda. For instance, the *ubuhede* income-generating programme did not create sufficient opportunities for survivors in need of financial support. Most families of survivors did not have adequate housing or safe drinking water. Survivors faced 'discrimination' with regard to accessing bank loans and economic opportunities. Many of them also feared violent reprisals as several victims in Northern Province who had testified at gacaca had been attacked (HRW, 2012, p. 3). The progress Rwanda has made in the past 20 years was commended in SURF's 2013/14 annual report, although it does raise concerns that justice will never be fully served since the compensation awarded at gacaca has still not been delivered to survivors (2014a, p. 4).

The problems outlined above have not deterred international aid or foreign direct investment. High standards of technocratic governance often outweigh good political governance in attracting donor interest. Kauffman et al. argue that international benefactors are far less sensitive to issues of 'voice and accountability' with regard to those to whom they allocate aid (Kauffman et al., 2005, as cited by Marysse et al., 2006, p. 26).[28] The insignificance of those issues is particularly evident in the Rwandan context since the country continues to receive significant foreign aid amidst restricted civil and political rights and impunity for RPF crimes allegedly committed against civilians in Rwanda and DRC.[29]

26 The report was met with criticism from Kigali. The government is reported to have questioned the methodology and the data, which dates from 2006–11 and was collected from several government agencies including the Rwanda National Bureau for Statistics and the Ministry of Education (*The East African*, 7 Mar. 2014).

27 Other revisions include increasing life expectancy to age 66, which is 11 years greater than the previous target set in 2000 (*Rwanda Focus*, 12 Mar. 2012).

28 'Voice and accountability' is one of the six Worldwide Governance Indicators against which countries are ranked according to their levels of technocratic good governance. The others are: political stability and absence of violence; government effectiveness; regulatory quality; rule of law; and control of corruption (Clark et al., 2008, as cited by M.A. Thomas, 2009, p. 33).

29 Rwanda's net Official Development Assistance (ODA) amounted to US$1,081.10 million in 2013 (OECD-DAC, 2015).

Donors' readiness to overlook issues of impunity and alleged human rights violations takes us back to the relationship between the RPF's vision of 'national reconciliation' and development in Rwanda. The RPF has justified the silencing of domestic and international NGOs, political opponents and journalists as an appropriate approach to eradicating 'divisionism' and 'genocide ideology' inside the country. The elimination of both 'negative ideologies' appear as stated goals of the National Unity and Reconciliation Programme, with particular reference to the promotion of national unity (NURC, 2007, p. 3). Impunity, on the other hand, was guaranteed at gacaca for crimes against humanity allegedly committed by the RPF in Rwanda. Gacaca is integrally connected to the promotion of justice within the RPF's official reconciliation programme and has received significant funding and support from the international community with regard to coordination and monitoring.

The political image at the centre of the relationship between the RPF and the international community of donors and investors depicts a secure and stable country guided by strong leadership. The National Unity and Reconciliation Programme has several functions within this relationship. The first is to attract donors through stated commitments to 'national reconciliation' and the creation of a pro-business environment. The second is to provide a framework through which donors as well as NGOs fund and participate in the coordination and monitoring of specific projects inside the country, such as gacaca. The intricacy of this association supports the construction and dissemination of an image promoting development, and overshadows the negative effects of the RPF's official reconciliation programme on the freedom of speech, association, press and political participation.

Conclusion: the impact of national and international political images of Rwanda

The National Unity and Reconciliation Programme was created and implemented during a period of transition and transformation in Rwanda. The top-down political construction that emerged has been shaped by government priorities, power dynamics, and the evolving relationship between the RPF and the international community. It has produced differing, but interconnected political images of Rwanda for the domestic population and the international audience of donors, NGOs and investors. Their construction and dissemination have had similar impacts in both the national and international context. Inside Rwanda, the utilisation of the official reconciliation programme to portray the country as safe, stable and prosperous has yielded both legitimising and constraining results. It has bolstered political support, legitimised government policy and programming, and pushed forward the nation-building agenda. However, it has greatly restricted free speech and media and provided a framework through which opposition members and NGOs deemed to be 'divisionist' or purveyors of 'genocide ideology' have been silenced.

The image of Rwanda and the RPF projected to the international community, like that disseminated to the national audience, is informed by the 'victor's narrative' of history and shaped by the prioritisation of development that is primarily uneven. The 'victor's narrative' and international guilt have been used to silence criticism and awkward questions inside and outside of the country, albeit somewhat unsuccessfully with regard to the release in 2010 of the UN 'Report of the mapping exercise in DRC'. It has succeeded, however, in attracting donor and investor interest through high standards of technocratic governance. This dynamic image is underpinned by the relationship between the RPF and the international community and the inaction of donor countries and multilateral organisations during the 1994 genocide.

As with the image projected at the national level, its most severe effects have been upon the people of Rwanda. For instance, the international community's grossly inadequate response during the 1994 genocide has limited its capacity to publicly criticise RPF leadership about its alleged role during the 1994 genocide, and also in the violent conflict in DRC (Reyntjens, 2004, p. 199). Moreover, donor support and international NGO participation in constructing and implementing gacaca supported an institution that ensured RPF impunity for crimes allegedly committed against civilians. Lastly, international donors and investors have participated in advancing the uneven development that has failed to benefit the most marginalised. As such, the National Unity and Reconciliation Programme has succeeded in constructing and disseminating political images of Rwanda that do not reflect its social, political or economic reality. Images of the RPF as a government pursuing an official reconciliation programme that promotes a singular narrative, limited freedom of expression and uneven development would certainly be more fitting.

Chapter 7

Conclusion

Constructing a national reconciliation programme was not an early priority of the Rwandan Patriotic Front (RPF), which governed under the guise of the transitional Government of National Unity (GNU). After the genocide ended in July 1994, the GNU sought to prosecute all citizens suspected of having committed acts of genocide and crimes against humanity, a pursuit which led to the mass arrest of more than 120,000 civilians and officials in former President Habyarimana's government. Despite pressure from the UN to create a formal process, the GNU did not pursue any form of official reconciliation until a 'comfortable' environment had been created following military interventions in eastern Zaire and the arrest and expatriation of Hutu political opponents (Reyntjens and Vandeginste, 2005, p. 103).

The official National Unity and Reconciliation Programme that emerged followed a growing trend of countries shifting away from traditional conflict resolution mechanisms focused on retributive justice (Kritz, 1996, p. 128). The programme includes mechanisms that promote this form of justice, but is also shaped by projects mandated to promote restorative justice, civic education, development and 'national reconciliation'. It is a complex socio-political process, shaped by the political interests, actions and dynamics of the government that constructed it and continues to oversee it. The RPF government has stated multiple commitments to advancing its 'national reconciliation' vision including: eradicating 'divisionism' and 'genocide ideology'; educating Rwandans about unity; and promoting a culture of peace, 'good governance', national pride and human rights. These obligations are repeated in legislation, official discourse, radio broadcasts and presidential speeches, but the National Unity and Reconciliation Programme is far from an exercise in equality and engagement with legacies of past violence. Instead, it promotes the current RPF government's continued dominance, the manipulation of historical discourse, and impunity for the ruling party. In essence, the RPF's official reconciliation programme functions as a nation-building and state-legitimisation project that secures the current RPF regime's political control.

This concluding chapter outlines the analysis and summarises the research findings presented throughout the book, results which shed light on how the National Unity and Reconciliation Programme functions in social and political practice. The programme's 'internal logic' informs the analysis, as dictated by the GNU's and RPF's stated commitments to promoting 'national reconciliation'. This 'logic' is also informed by policy, legislation and official documents related to the National Unity and Reconciliation Programme. The chapter brings together three major themes pertinent to the official programme – justice, nation-building and the 'victor's narrative' – considering relevant concepts including 'genocide ideology', 'divisionism', ethnicity and national identity. This discussion also highlights concepts in the broader literature relevant to the RPF's vision of 'national reconciliation'. Finally, a brief overview is given of the particular contribution this book makes to the wider sociological studies of reconciliation and human rights.

Concepts and themes

The RPF's vision of 'national reconciliation' is shaped by a variety of concepts, many of which were constructed by the GNU and RPF. The RPF government did not formally define the terms 'national unity' and 'reconciliation' until the National Policy of Unity and Reconciliation was published in 2007. As chapter 4 demonstrated, this definition, although relatively unclear, outlines the attributes purportedly shared by all Rwandans, including a single shared nationality, which in this context relates to the Banyarwanda's singular national identity. The concept is particularly salient in official reconciliation discourse as it supersedes the ethnic identities that purportedly divided the nation prior to and during the 1994 genocide. More specifically, the shared identity of the Banyarwanda is an integral part of the RPF's conception of national unity and its wider nation-building agenda. The latter theme pervades the entire National Unity and Reconciliation Programme. For instance, Vision 2020, published in 2000, declares that all Rwandans share a common vision of the future. It also points to the perceived necessity of constructing a singular identity when it asks, '[h]ow do Rwandans envisage their future? What kind of society do they want to become? How can they construct a united and inclusive Rwandan identity?' (Minecofin, 2000, p. 1).

The national identity of the Banyarwanda is posited as a safeguard against a return to genocide (chapter 4). The government devised this association between ethnicity, 'divisionism' and 'genocide ideology'. As a result of the vilification of ethnicity the ethnic terms Hutu, Tutsi and Twa were de facto banned from public discourse and official documents. Integral to the RPF's official reconciliation programme's 'internal logic' are the concepts of 'genocide ideology' and 'divisionism'. This logic is shaped by the programme's overarching aim to eradicate history's 'bad' elements that purportedly led to the 1994 genocide, and to promote the 'good' ones of unity and 'national reconciliation'. The bad elements include 'bad governance', ethnicity, 'sectarianism', 'divisionism' and 'genocide ideology', the latter three of which have been codified as criminal offences punishable by significant fines and prison sentences (chapter 2). The good elements the government has identified include truth, justice, commonality, 'good governance' and national identity. The 'good' and 'bad' constituents of Rwandan history are described in great detail in the 'victor's narrative', one that includes events from the pre-colonial period to the present-day. It highlights social cohesion's alleged existence prior to the arrival of colonial rulers, the 'divisionism' and 'genocide ideology' of previous regimes, and the current government's attempts to promote its vision of 'national reconciliation'. The commitment to disseminate this narrative is clearly stated in the textbook, *Histoire du Rwanda: des origines à la fin du xxe siècle,* published by the NURC in 2011 (chapter 5). This book exemplifies the National Unity and Reconciliation Programme's education remit: to *correct* the 'mindset, bad behaviour, bad practices' of the Rwandan people (NURC, 2011a, p. 1).

The 'victor's narrative' had a significant impact on the pursuit of justice at community gacaca courts. As chapter 3 showed, the theme of justice shaped the early post-conflict period since it led to gacaca courts being restored to speed the prosecution of these cases. The 'victor's narrative' states that the RPF did not commit acts of genocide or crimes against humanity. As such, gacaca promotes a type of victor's justice as it prevents crimes perpetrated against Hutu civilians by RPF members being prosecuted and fosters a sense of collective guilt among the Hutu population.

The analysis

This book seeks to provide a detailed, theoretical and empirical analysis of the National Unity and Reconciliation Programme in post-conflict Rwanda from a broad sociological perspective. The overarching aim of the research was to shed light on how the programme functions in social and political practice. I attempted to meet this aim by examining how the official reconciliation programme was constructed and implemented in the social, economic and political contexts in which it was created and continues to function. I also considered the wider historical context that informs the normative and legal framework of the RPF's official reconciliation programme, with particular emphasis on the concepts of social cohesion, 'divisionism' and 'genocide ideology' (see chapters 2 and 6). This context includes the arrival of colonial rulers, the 1959 Social Revolution, the 1990 RPF invasion, and the events of the civil war and 1994 genocide. As Rwanda is a landlocked country, influenced by events outside its borders, I have discussed several pertinent conflicts in the Great Lakes Region, focusing on the impact of political and military interventions led by the RPF, and the effects of violence and refugee movement on political stability in Rwanda. Relevant conflicts include the

1972 genocide in Burundi, anti-Tutsi violence in Uganda, the Second Congo War and ongoing violence in DRC's North and South Kivu provinces.

In order to uncover the function of the National Unity and Reconciliation Programme, it was vital to understand the RPF's 'national reconciliation' vision. In doing so, I evaluated the official programme's 'internal logic', as depicted by stated commitments, policy and legislation related to it. I used Crocker's spectrum of 'thin' to 'thick' concepts to dissect and examine the RPF's stated commitments to 'national reconciliation'. Crocker describes 'thin' reconciliation as resembling little more than peaceful coexistence. The middle range includes such elements as representation of both sides of the conflict in national debate and public policy as well as communication between perpetrators and survivors of the conflict. The 'thickest' conception, most commonly pursued by truth commissions, includes acts of mutual forgiveness, healing, restoration and creating a shared vision of the future (Crocker, 2000, p. 108).

This evaluative tool was particularly useful for analysing individual concepts that shape the Rwandan government's stated obligations. It also facilitated the discovery of contradictions inherent in the government's description of 'national reconciliation' theory and practice as well as the analysis of changing priorities over time. As the introduction demonstrated, the GNU prioritised reintegration and non-violence in the early years after the 1994 genocide, priorities that can be located at the 'thin' end of the spectrum. Reintegration and non-violence are a far cry, however, from the stated objective to create a shared vision of the future, as outlined in Vision 2020. The latter conception of reconciliation merges stated commitments to promoting national unity, national identity and development, and most closely resembles Crocker's definition of 'thick' reconciliation (2000, p. 108).

This analysis was also informed by a number of relevant positions in the wider body of reconciliation literature. For instance, Lederach's description of it as a peacemaking paradigm was fundamental to my understanding of 'national reconciliation' as both a theory and a practice in post-conflict Rwanda. Lederach also describes reconciliation as the 'meeting point between realism and innovation' (1997, p. 25). So too is the RPF's official programme. This 'meeting point', as it were, is evident in the National Unity and Reconciliation Programme's mix of pragmatic and ideological goals, which include: fighting 'genocide ideology' and 'divisionism'; prioritising citizenship and the common interests of all Rwandans over ethnicity, family relationships and religious groups; respecting the law and human rights; healing moral wounds by revealing the truth, asking and giving pardon; and preventing the recurrence of genocide (NURC, 2007, pp. 4–5).

The literature about post-conflict reconciliation converges on three concepts representing dominant responses to collective violence: truth, justice and forgiveness (chapter 1). Several authors, including Allen (1999), Borer (2006), Lederach (1997) and Minow (1998), argue that truth is an integral element of reconciliation as a peacemaking paradigm, an argument which formed the framework for my examination of the role of dialogue between survivors and perpetrators in the process of rebuilding relationships in Rwanda (chapter 3). I also utilised it to analyse the opportunities for discussion about issues related to identity, unity and experiences of the 1994 genocide at ingando and itorero ry'igihugu camps (chapter 5).

As discussed above, the RPF's vision of 'national reconciliation' is shaped by a number of different concepts that it has constructed. Two of these were devised to describe relationship rebuilding in the post-conflict context. 'Vertical' reconciliation refers to rebuilding trust between civilians and the state and 'horizontal' reconciliation relates to the rebuilding of connections between citizens (introduction and chapter 3). Lederach's account of the role of rebuilding relationships after mass conflict informed my analysis of the reconciliation theory, both 'vertical' and 'horizontal'. Lederach states that acknowledging the past through acts of telling and hearing the truth validates the emotions of those who experienced the conflict, acts which represent the first steps in rebuilding associations damaged by violence (1997, p. 2).

Like Lederach, Clark argues that rebuilding relationships is vital to reconciliation after mass conflict, discussing this process in the context of gacaca. He asks, '[t]o what degree then should Rwanda pursue reconciliation and what degree of reconciliation is possible through gacaca?' (2010a, p. 334). Clark's definition of reconciliation between individuals and groups closely resembles that of the RPF's 'horizontal' concept. He does not, however, include an analysis of connections between individuals, groups and the state. As such, I built on his initial question, to analyse whether gacaca did in fact promote the government's vision of 'horizontal' and 'vertical' reconciliation.

The analysis of gacaca's potential to promote both forms of reconciliation was shaped by the work of a number of different authors (introduction). The examination of the government's pursuit of justice at gacaca in this book is informed by Kiss's conception of restorative justice as a process that includes both restorative and retributive elements such as compensation for victims and accountability for crimes committed during the conflict. She also argues that restorative justice provides victims with an opportunity to share their experiences of the conflict (2000, p. 83). Although gacaca did give victims the chance to tell their story, this dialogue was often 'forensic' in nature as it was guided by case parameters (Wilson, 2001, pp. 36–7).

I also engaged with the concept of forgiveness in the context of gacaca courts (see chapter 3), analysing the potential impact of the perceived pressure to forgive on the rebuilding of damaged relationships between victims and defendants. Minow (1998) and Arendt's (1958) descriptions of forgiveness as being unpredictable informed my understanding of the concept. The perceived expectation of being forgiven at gacaca is antithetical to Minow's argument that others cannot claim forgiveness as a right. Instead, those who have been wronged ought to have the freedom to choose whether they will forgive those who have perpetrated crimes against them (Minow, 1998, p. 17). Beyond the confines of gacaca, forgiveness does not feature prominently in official discourse – it does not appear in the official definition of national unity and reconciliation in the 2007 Reconciliation Policy or in the government's definitions of 'vertical' and 'horizontal' reconciliation. As such, this book's conception of forgiveness is similar to Worthington Jr.'s, who states that it is not necessary in order to rebuild relationships damaged by conflict (2006, p. 221).

As outlined in the introduction, Wilson argues that an examination is necessary of the ways in which state strategies guide the politics of punishment and the construction of a new official memory towards creating a new hegemony after conflict (2001, p. xvi). In the Rwandan context, it is vital to understand how state strategies shape the National Unity and Reconciliation Programme. As such, I employed a social constructionist lens to my analysis of the RPF's stated commitments to promote 'national reconciliation' within their social, economic, and political contexts. This particular approach allowed me to be critical of the ways in which political interests, dynamics and actions inform the National Unity and Reconciliation Programme.

Official reconciliation discourse is repeated at live-in ingando and itorero ry-igihugu camps, radio broadcasts, presidential speeches and in the history textbook *Histoire du Rwanda: des origines à la fin du xxe siècle* (chapter 5). In order to distinguish between rhetoric and reality, I examined whether the official programme meets its own stated commitments and goals, an evaluation which helped to identify the gaps between the political representations of Rwanda projected by the RPF and reality on the ground. Such images are projected to the national population as well as to the international community of NGOs, donors and foreign investors (chapter 6). I also applied a wider framework of international human rights standards to determine who does and does not benefit from the official programme. I looked closely at the violation of civil and political rights, as they are particularly relevant to the political landscape in Rwanda (chapter 5). Furthermore, I examined the implications of the RPF's stated commitment to development on one of the most marginalised groups in society: genocide survivors.

The results

A number of different aims shaped this research. Its primary aim was to determine how the RPF's official reconciliation programme functions in social and political practice. In order to meet this overarching objective, the research examined a number of other issues related to the programme's function. As discussed above, one of these aims was to determine how the RPF government conceives of 'national reconciliation', which the research suggests is not straightforward. Official discourse, policy, legislation and interviews depict it as both a theory and a practice. The former describes 'national reconciliation' as the rebuilding of relationships between citizens, as well as between citizens and the state ('horizontal' and 'vertical' reconciliation). As chapter 4 showed, the definition of national unity and reconciliation outlined in the 2007 Reconciliation Policy conflates the two terms. However, they refer to separate concepts, with national unity being closely related to the RPF's nation-building agenda. 'National reconciliation' is also conceived as a practice shaped by a number of stated commitments and priorities that have developed and changed over time including the pursuit of justice, civic education and development combined with eradicating 'bad' elements of history, and promoting the 'good elements' of national unity and reconciliation. This process is put into practice through the de facto banning of ethnic identities from official documents and public discourse, reeducating the population about the RPF's conceptions of national unity and 'national reconciliation', restoring gacaca courts and promoting development.

The research met its aim of contextualising the construction and implementation of the official reconciliation programme by examining how it was informed by the RPF's military and political role during the civil war, 1994 genocide and post-conflict period. The findings suggest that the RPF's role during the civil war and 1994 genocide impacted this process in several ways. The RPF's invasion in 1990 and the ensuing civil war added to economic strife and political tension gripping Rwanda in the late 1980s and early 1990s. Both events incited anti-Tutsi propaganda and added to growing violence in the run-up to the 1994 genocide (chapter 2). The 1990 'liberation invasion' continues to play an important role in official reconciliation discourse, which is used to depict the RPF's role in 1990, the civil war and during the 1994 genocide. As chapter 6 demonstrated, reference to the group as 'liberators' in official discourse, transforms the current government into a symbol of valour, morality and peace (Edelman, 1988, p. 2). In practical terms, the RPF's 'liberation' of the capital in July 1994 ended the violence of the 1994 genocide and led to a mass exodus of Hutu into neighbouring Zaire.

The RPF's political and military endeavours in the early post-conflict period had a significant impact on the official reconciliation programme's design and implementation. An executive presidency was created, which consolidated the RPF's power within the GNU and ensured that RPF interests and actions guided the National Unity and Reconciliation Programme. The mass expatriation of Hutu civilians, discussed above, created a need to implement a repatriation and reintegration programme shortly after the 1994 genocide ended. The stated commitment to preventing invasions by Hutu militias hiding in eastern Zaire legitimised the RPF's two military interventions across the border. Inside Rwanda, the GNU's pursuit of maximal justice after the 1994 genocide put tremendous pressure on the country's judicial system.

Consequently, the inability to process cases quickly led to the restoration of gacaca community courts.

Gacaca represented a major element of the National Unity and Reconciliation Programme. As discussed in chapter 3, gacaca was mandated to: reveal the truth about 1994 genocide events; speed genocide trials along; eradicate impunity; promote unity and reconciliation; and prove that Rwandans can solve their own problems (NSGJ, n.d.(b), p. 1). As such, the book has assessed the potential of gacaca to promote 'vertical' and 'horizontal' reconciliation, as defined by the government. It suggests that gacaca's ability to do so may have been impeded by the 'victor's narrative' of the 1994 genocide, RPF impunity, failure to adequately compensate survivors, and unrealistic expectations of forgiveness perceived by both survivors and defendants. The analysis does suggest, however, that gacaca may have created the opportunity for continued dialogue between individuals by providing a forum in which perpetrators, survivors and community members could discuss experiences of the civil war and 1994 genocide through testimonies and rebuttals.

The 'victor's narrative' had a significant impact on gacaca and the National Unity and Reconciliation Programme more generally. As such, the research sought to determine the implications of this narrative on the RPF's vision of national unity and 'national reconciliation'. This book has examined the ways in which this narrative is disseminated at live-in ingando and itorero camps as well as in *Histoire du Rwanda: des origines à la fin du xxe siècle* (chapter 5). The research found that the camps missed valuable opportunities to promote critical analysis and open discussion about such issues as identity, ethnicity and experiences of the 1994 genocide – stated commitments made by the NURC. One interpretation is that the pursuit of pro-RPF indoctrination rendered the camps unable to promote dialogue. The research also found that the NURC's history textbook (2011a) did little other than serve to legitimise the RPF's approach to governance in the post-conflict context.

Itorero camps are particularly pertinent to the study of 'national reconciliation' as they actively promote the RPF's nation-building and development agendas. The former is closely related to the RPF's conception of national unity. The research suggests that this agenda and the government's conception of national unity create a highly prescriptive path that dictates how both priorities ought to be pursued (chapter 4). This path transforms the National Unity and Reconciliation Programme into a conduit through which the government constructs its own vision of the people and the Rwandan nation, one which depicts the country as a prosperous and united nation ruled by the RPF. The government achieves this by promoting the programme's end goals before they have been achieved, thus precluding it from being analysed and criticised. Interestingly, this attempt to build the nation and unite the people limits the possibility of achieving the government's own conceptions of 'vertical' and 'horizontal' reconciliation by failing to provide the time and space necessary to rebuild relationships damaged by the conflict. These may be further damaged by the RPF's failure to fulfil its stated commitments to promoting social welfare, equal rights and open dialogue, as outlined in the 2003 Constitution. Amidst these obstacles, the nation-building agenda successfully secures RPF political control by constructing a singular national identity that legitimises state programming and equates political opposition and criticism of the regime with 'divisionism' and 'genocide ideology'.

The research also suggests that the National Unity and Reconciliation Programme produces two interrelated images of Rwanda and the RPF government, one of which is projected to the domestic population, while the other is aimed at the international community of NGOs, donors and foreign investors. The one constructed for the domestic audience portrays the country as safe, stable and developing rapidly, while the image projected to the international community is shaped by the relationship between that audience and the RPF government. This association attracts donorship and investment while quashing international criticism of the RPF's actions during the civil war, the 1994 genocide and interventions in DRC.

The RPF's economic reforms and technocratic approach to governance have garnered numerous accolades from both investors and donors. The innovation and speed of this development overshadows the inadequate social welfare and civil and political rights, a major obstacle in the RPF's pursuit of 'national reconciliation'. There is still value in the notion of reconciliation, however, amidst these inequalities, much of which stems from individual ingredients that comprise not only the RPF's vision of 'national reconciliation', but also the broader concept as discussed in the wider literature.

Speaking and hearing the truth, addressing conflict experiences and achieving justice have moral and legal import after violence. Some of these actions - confession, apology, truth-telling and rebuilding relationships - may have taken place without the formal establishment of an official reconciliation programme in Rwanda. Although I argue that we ought to be sceptical of the political interests, dynamics and actions that guide how programmes are constructed, reconciliation is still a useful paradigm through which we may analyse how individuals, groups, communities and nations move forward after conflict and genocide. With this in mind, my analysis of the social and political functions of the RPF's official programme leads to the conclusion that it is best understood as a nation-building and state-legitimisation project that secures the continued political dominance of the RPF government under Paul Kagame's presidency.

Contribution

This book makes a significant contribution to the broad sociological study of reconciliation and human rights. It provides a case-specific analysis of the National Unity and Reconciliation Programme according to its own logic, international human rights standards, and the theory and practice of reconciliation as a peacemaking paradigm using such evaluative tools as Crocker's spectrum of reconciliation (2000). In so doing, it applies a social constructionist framework to the complex socio-political programme in an attempt to uncover the dynamics, interests and interactions that shape how it is constructed by its creators and how it functions in social and political practice. This framework may be useful for further analyses of the social construction of human rights and reconciliation. The book will be beneficial to existing research on reconciliation theory and practice as it considers the complexity of constructing and implementing a government-led programme following the civil war and genocide in Rwanda. It will also contribute to the study of other post-conflict reconciliation processes as it analyses the particularly salient concepts of unity, identity and development in the context of post-conflict governance.

This book opens the door to several new directions for research including comparative studies of official reconciliation programmes in Burundi and Rwanda. The analysis could examine the stark differences in official discourse and the construction of ethnic identities in these neighbouring countries. Furthermore, the book may also support the analysis of recent conflicts in the Great Lakes Region, including the M23 rebellion in eastern DRC, from a broad sociological perspective. This particular direction may facilitate in-depth investigations of the social and political functions of such conflicts. Furthermore, it may also assist in examining the potential impact of foreign aid to Rwanda being partially frozen, and in assessing how the violence and political uncertainty in DRC has affected the RPF's efforts to promote its development programme and vision of 'national reconciliation'.

Bibliography

Abed, M. (2006) 'Clarifying the concept of genocide', *Metaphilosophy* 37 (3–4), pp. 308–30.

Abu-Nimer, M. (2001) 'Education for coexistence in Israel: potential and challenges in reconciliation, justice, and coexistence: theory and practice', in M. Abu-Nimer (ed.), *Reconciliation, Justice, and Coexistence: Theory and Practice* (Oxford), pp. 235-54.

Adelman, H. (2005) 'Rule-based reconciliation', in E. Skaar, S. Gloppen and A. Suhrke (eds.), *Roads to Reconciliation* (Oxford), pp. 287-308.

Allen, J. (1999) 'Balancing justice and social unity: political theory and the idea of a Truth and Reconciliation Commission', *University of Toronto Law Journal* 49 (3), pp. 315-53.

Andersen, R. (2000) 'How multilateral development assistance triggered the conflict in Rwanda', *Third World Quarterly* 21 (3), pp. 441-56.

Anderson, B. (1983) *Imagined Communities: Reflections on the Origin and Spread of Nationalism*, 1st edn. (London and New York).

— (2006) *Imagined Communities: Reflections on the Origin and Spread of Nationalism*, 2nd edn. (London and New York).

Ansoms, A. (2007) 'Striving for growth, bypassing the poor? A critical review of Rwanda's rural sector policies', www.ua.ac.be/objs/00152940.pdf (accessed 4 Mar. 2015).

Anyidoho, H.K. (1998) *Guns over Kigali: the Rwandese Civil War – 1994 (A Personal Account)* (Kampala).

Arendt, H. (1958) *The Human Condition*, 2nd edn. (Chicago, IL and London).

Balibar, E. (1996) 'The nation form: history and ideology', in G. Eley and R.G. Suny (eds.), *Becoming National: a Reader* (New York and Oxford), pp. 86-106.

Banton, M. (2000) 'Ethnic conflict', *Sociology* 34 (3), pp. 481-98.

Bar-Siman Tov, Y. (2004) 'Introduction: Why reconciliation?', in Y. Bar-Siman Tov (ed.), *From Conflict Resolution to Reconciliation* (Oxford), pp. 3-10.

Bar-Tel, D. and G.H. Bennink (2004) 'The nature of reconciliation as an outcome and as a process', in Y. Bar-Siman Tov (ed.), *From Conflict Resolution to Reconciliation* (Oxford), pp. 11–38.

Bebbington, A. (2004) 'NGOs and uneven development: geographies of development intervention', *Progress in Human Geography* 28 (6), pp. 725–45.

Berger, P.L. and T. Luckmann (1966) *The Social Construction of Reality: a Treatise in the Sociology of Knowledge* (Harmondsworth).

Bianchini, P. (2012) 'Une tâche problématique: enseigner l'histoire au Rwanda après le génocide', in *L'Ecole en situation postcoloniale: entre Africanisation et constructions nationales* (Paris), pp. 217–43.

Biggar, N. (2001) 'Making peace or doing justice: must we choose?', in N. Biggar, (ed.), *Burying the Past: Making Peace and Doing Justice After Civil Conflict* (Washington DC), pp. 3–24.

Bloomfield, D., et al. (2003) *Reconciliation After Violent Conflict: a Handbook* (Stockholm).

Boal, A. (1979) *Theatre of the Oppressed* (London).

— (1995) *The Rainbow of Desire: the Boal Method of Theatre and Therapy* (London).

— (1998) *Legislative Theatre: Using Performance to Make Politics* (New York).

Borer, T.A. (2006) 'Truth-telling as a peace-building activity: a theoretical overview', in T.A. Borer (ed.), *Telling the Truths: Truth-Telling and Peace Building in Post-Conflict Societies* (Notre Dame, IN), pp. 1–58.

Boyce, B.P. (1999) 'Nation-building discourse in a democracy', in M. Palmberg (ed.), *National Identity and Democracy in Africa* (Cape Town), pp. 231–43.

Bradfield, P. (2011) 'ICTR appeal judgements rendered in Bagosora & Nsengiyumva and Ntawukulilyayo', 19 Dec., www.internationallawbureau.com/index.php/archive/ (accessed 11 Mar. 2015).

Bruguière, J.-L. (2006) 'Issuance of international arrest warrants (no. P106–0046(E)). Tribunal de Grande Instance de Paris', www.taylor-report.com/Documents/BrugiereReport-English.pdf (accessed 4 Mar. 2015).

Buckley-Zistel, S. (2006) 'Dividing and uniting: the use of citizenship discourses in conflict and reconciliation in Rwanda', *Global Society* 20 (1), pp. 101–13.

— (2009) 'Nation, narration, unification? The politics of history teaching after the Rwandan genocide', *Journal of Genocide Research* 11 (1), pp. 31–53.

Burr, V. (2003) *Social Constructionism*, 2nd edn. (London).

Card, C. (2003) 'Genocide and social death', *Hypatia* 18 (1), pp. 63–79.

Chalk, F. (1999) 'Radio propaganda and genocide'. Occasional paper presented at the Montreal Institute of Genocide Studies (MIGS).

Chemouni, B. (2014) 'Explaining the design of the Rwandan decentralization: elite vulnerability and the territorial repartition of power', *Journal of East African Studies* 8 (2), pp. 246–62.

Chrétien, J-P., R. Verdier and E. Decaux (1995) *Rwanda. Un génocide du XXe siècle* (Paris).

Clark, P. (2008) 'The rules (and politics) of engagement: the Gacaca Courts and post-genocide justice, healing and reconciliation in Rwanda', in P. Clark and Z.D. Kaufman (eds.), *After Genocide: Transitional Justice, Post-Conflict Reconstruction and Reconciliation in Rwanda and Beyond* (London), pp. 297–319.

— (2010a) *The Gacaca Courts, Post-Genocide Justice and Reconciliation in Rwanda: Justice without Lawyers* (Cambridge).

— (2010b) 'Rwanda: Kagame's power struggle' (for *The Guardian*), www.theguardian.com/commentisfree/libertycentral/2010/aug/05/rwanda-kagames-power-struggle (accessed 18 Mar. 2015).

— (2014) 'Bringing the peasants back in, again: state power and local agency in Rwanda's *gacaca* courts', *Journal of East African Studies*, 8 (2), pp. 193–213.

Clark, P. and Z.D. Kaufman (eds.) (2008) *After Genocide: Transitional Justice, Post-Conflict Reconstruction and Reconciliation in Rwanda and Beyond* (London).

Collier, P. (2007) *The Bottom Billion: Why the Poorest Countries are Failing and What Can Be Done About It* (Oxford).

Crocker, D.A. (2000) 'Truth Commission, transitional justice, and civil society', in R.I. Rotberg and D. Thompson (eds.), *Truth v. Justice: The Morality of Truth Commissions* (Princeton, NJ and Oxford), pp. 99–121.

— (2003) 'Reckoning with past wrongs: a normative framework', in C.A.I. Prager and T. Govier (eds.), *Dilemmas of Reconciliation: Cases and Concepts* (Waterloo, ON), pp. 39–64.

Daly, E. and J. Sarkin (2007) *Reconciliation in Divided Societies: Finding Common Ground* (Philadelphia, PA).

Daye, R. (2004) *Political Forgiveness: Lessons from Africa* (New York).

De Jonge, K. (2010) 'PRI's gacaca research: Klaas de Jonge's commentary', www.penalreform.org/resource/pris-gacaca-research-klaas-de-jonges/ (accessed 5 Mar. 2015).

Des Forges, A. (1999) *Leave None to Tell the Story: Genocide in Rwanda* (London and New York).

Des Forges, A. and T. Longman (2004) 'Legal responses to genocide in Rwanda', http://faculty.vassar.edu/tilongma/justice.html (accessed 5 Mar. 2015).

Development Assistance Committee (1997) 'OECD guidelines for peace, conflict and development cooperation', www.conflictsensitivity.org/node/55 (accessed 5 Mar. 2015).

Dubois, O. (1997) 'Rwanda's national criminal courts and the International Tribunal', *International Review of the Red Cross* 321, https://www.icrc.org/eng/resources/documents/misc/57jnza.htm (accessed 20 May 2015).

Dwyer, S. (2003) 'Reconciliation for realists', in C.A.I. Prager and T. Govier (eds.), *Dilemmas of Reconciliation: Cases and Concepts* (Waterloo, ON).

Edelman, M. (1988) *Constructing the Political Spectacle* (Chicago, IL and London).

— (2001) *The Politics of Misinformation* (Cambridge).

Eltringham, N. (2004) *Accounting for the Horror: Post-Genocide Debates in Rwanda* (London).

— (2009) '"We are not a Truth Commission": fragmented narratives and the historical record at the International Truth and Reconciliation Commission', *Journal of Genocide Research* 11 (1), pp. 55–79.

Fisher, J. and B. Shelton (2001) *Face to Face: Making Dance and Theatre in Community* (Melbourne).

Freedman, S.W. et al. (2004) 'Confronting the past in Rwandan schools', in E. Stover and H.M. Weinstein (eds.), *My Neighbor, My Enemy: Justice and Community in the Aftermath of Mass Atrocity* (Cambridge), pp. 248–66.

— (2008) 'Teaching history after identity-based conflicts: the Rwanda experience', *Comparative Education Review* 52 (4), pp. 663–90.

— (2011) 'Teaching history in post-genocide Rwanda', in S. Straus and L. Waldorf (eds.), *Remaking Rwanda: State Building and Human Rights after Mass Violence* (Madison, WI), pp. 297–315

Freeman, M. (2002) *Human Rights: an Interdisciplinary Approach* (Cambridge).

Friere, P. (1972) *Pedagogy of the Oppressed* (London).

Fujii, L.A. (2009) *Killing Neighbors: Webs of Violence in Rwanda* (Ithaca, NY and London).

Galtung, J. (2001) 'After violence, reconstruction, reconciliation, and restitution: coping with visible and invisible effects of war and violence', in M. Abu-Nimer (ed.), *Reconciliation, Justice, and Coexistence: Theory and Practice* (Oxford), pp. 3–23.

Gatwa, T. (2005) *The Churches and Ethnic Ideology in the Rwandan Crises 1900–1994* (Oxford).

Gloppen, S. (2005) 'Roads to reconciliation: a conceptual framework', in E. Skaar, S. Gloppen and A. Suhrke (eds.), *Roads to Reconciliation* (Oxford), pp. 17–50.

Govier, T. (2003) 'What is acknowledgement and why is it important?', in C.A.I. Prager and T. Govier (eds.), *Dilemmas of Reconciliation: Cases and Concepts* (Waterloo, ON), pp. 65–90.

Govier, T. and W. Verwoerd (2002) 'Trust and the problem of national reconciliation', *Philosophy of the Social Sciences* 32 (22), pp. 178–205.

Graybill, L. and K Lanegran (2004) 'Truth, justice, and reconciliation in Africa: issues and cases', *African Studies Quarterly* 8 (1), pp. 1–18.

Hacking, I. (1999) *The Social Construction of What?* (Cambridge, MA.).

Harvey, D. (2005) *A Brief History of Neoliberalism* (Oxford).

Hayman, R. (2007) 'Milking the cow: negotiating ownership of aid and policy in Rwanda', www.esrc.ac.uk/my-esrc/grants/PTA-026-27-1383/outputs/read/cde6d93f-8e8b-45bf-a1d6-e8dfc6a18ec3 (accessed 5 Mar. 2015).

— (2009) 'From Rome to Accra via Kigali: "aid effectiveness" in Rwanda', *Development Policy Review* 27 (5), pp. 581–99.

— (2011) 'Funding fraud? Donors and democracy in Rwanda', in S. Straus, and L. Waldorf (eds.), *Remaking Rwanda: State Building and Human Rights after Mass Violence* (Madison, WI), pp. 118–31.

Hayner, P.B. (1994) 'Fifteen Truth Commissions – 1974 to 1994: a comparative study', *Human Rights Quarterly* 16 (4), pp. 597–655.

— (2011) *Unspeakable Truths: Transitional Justice and the Challenge of Truth Commissions*, 2nd edn. (New York and London).

Herman, E.S. and D. Peterson (2010) *The Politics of Genocide* (New York).

Hermann, T. (2004) 'Reconciliation: reflections on the theoretical and practical utility of the term', in Y. Bar-Siman Tov (ed.), *From Conflict Resolution to Reconciliation* (Oxford), pp. 39–60.

Hintjens, H. (2008) 'Reconstructing political identities in Rwanda', in P. Clark and Z.D. Kaufman (eds.), *After Genocide: Transitional Justice, Post-Conflict Reconstruction and Reconciliation in Rwanda and Beyond* (London), pp. 77–99.

Hippler, J. (2005) *Nation-Building: a Key Concept for Peaceful Conflict Transformation?* (London).

Immigration and Refugee Board of Canada (2001) 'Rwanda: information on Rwandan ID cards for the period following the 1994 Genocide', www.refworld.org/docid/3df4bea424.html (accessed 5 Mar. 2015).

Ingelaere, B. (2007) '"Does the truth pass across the fire without burning?" Transitional justice and its discontents in Rwanda's gacaca courts', www.ua.ac.be/objs/00167435.pdf (accessed 5 Mar. 2015).

Jones, A. (2006) *Genocide: a Comprehensive Introduction* (New York and London).

— (2010) *The Courts of Genocide: Politics and the Rule of Law in Rwanda and Arusha* (Abingdon).

Kagame, P. (2008) Preface, in P. Clark and Z.D. Kaufman (eds.), *After Genocide: Transitional Justice, Post-Conflict Reconstruction and Reconciliation in Rwanda and Beyond* (London), pp. xxi–xiv.

Karekezi, A. (2001) 'Juridictions gacaca: lutte contre l'impunité et promotion de réconciliation national', in E. Ntaganda (ed.), *Les juridictions gacaca et les processus de réconciliation nationale* (Butare), pp. 9–20.

Kayigamba, J.B. (2008) 'Without justice, no reconciliation: a survivor's experience of genocide', in P. Clark and Z.D. Kaufman (eds.), *After Genocide: Transitional Justice, Post-Conflict Reconstruction and Reconciliation in Rwanda and Beyond* (London), pp. 33–42.

Kayitesi-Blewitt, M. (2006) 'Funding development in Rwanda: the survivors' perspective', *Development in Practice* 16 (3–4), pp. 316–21.

Kiss, E. (2000) 'Moral ambition within and beyond political constraints: reflections on restorative justice', in R.I. Rotberg and D. Thompson (eds.), *Truth v. Justice: The Morality of Truth Commissions* (Princeton and Oxford), pp. 68–98.

Kiwuwa, D.E. (2007) 'Post-ethnic conflict reconstruction and the question of national identity in Asia and Africa', in S.C. Saha (ed.), *The Politics of Ethnicity and National Identity* (New York), pp. 7–27.

Klinghoffer, A.J. (1998) *The International Dimension of Genocide in Rwanda* (New York).

Kritz, N. (1996) 'Coming to terms with atrocities: a review of accountability mechanisms for mass violations of human rights', *Law and Contemporary Problems* 59 (3), pp. 127–52.

Kuperman, A.J. (2004) 'Provoking genocide: a revised history of the Rwandan Patriotic Front', *Journal of Genocide Research* 6 (1), pp. 61–84.

Lederach, J.P. (1997) *Building Peace: Sustainable Reconciliation in Divided Societies* (Washington DC).

— (2005) *The Moral Imagination: the Art and Soul of Building Peace* (Oxford).

Lemarchand, R. (1970) *Rwanda and Burundi* (London).

— (1998) 'Genocide in the Great Lakes: Which genocide? Whose genocide?', *African Studies Review* 41 (1), pp. 3–16.

— (2008) 'The politics of memory in post-genocide Rwanda', in P. Clark and Z.D. Kaufman (eds.), *After Genocide: Transitional Justice, Post-Conflict Reconstruction and Reconciliation in Rwanda and Beyond* (London), pp. 56–76.

— (2009) *The Dynamics of Violence in Central Africa* (Philadelphia, PA).

Lemarchand, R. and M. Niwese (2007) 'Mass murder, the politics of memory and post-genocide reconstruction: the cases of Rwanda and Burundi', in S. Chesterman, A. Schnable and B. Poulgny (eds.), *After Mass Crime: Rebuilding States and Communities* (New York), pp. 165–89.

Llewellyn, J.J. (2006) 'Restorative justice in transitions and beyond: the justice potential of truth-telling mechanisms for post-peace accord societies', in T.A. Borer (ed.), *Telling the Truths: Truth-Telling and Peace Building in Post-Conflict Societies* (Notre Dame, IN), pp. 83–114.

Long, W.J. and P. Brecke (2003) *War and Reconciliation: Reason and Emotion in Conflict Resolution* (The MIT Press, Cambridge and London).

Longman, T. (2006) 'Justice at the grassroots? Gacaca trials in Rwanda', in N. Roht-Arriaza and J. Mariezcurrena (eds.), *Transitional Justice in the Twenty-First Century, Beyond Truth Versus Justice* (Cambridge and New York), pp. 206–28.

— (2011a) 'Limitations to political reform: the undemocratic nature of transition in Rwanda', in S. Straus and L. Waldorf (eds.), *Remaking Rwanda: State Building and Human Rights after Mass Violence* (Madison, WI), pp. 25–47.

— (2011b) 'Countries at the crossroads 2011 – Rwanda', www.unhcr.org/refworld/docid/4ecba645c.html (accessed 5 Mar. 2015).

Lukes, S. (2005) *Power: a Radical View*, 2nd edn. (London).

Mamdani, M. (1996) 'From consent to conquest as the basis of state formation: reflections on Rwanda', *New Left Review* I (216), pp. 3–36.

— (2001) *When Victims Become Killers: Colonialism, Nativism, and the Genocide in Rwanda* (Princeton).

Mannheim, K. (1952) *Essays on the Sociology of Knowledge* (London).

Marshall, G. and J. Scott (eds.) (2005) 'Social constructionism', in *A Dictionary of Sociology*, 3rd rev. edn. (Oxford).

Marysse, S. et al. (2006) 'The aid "darlings" and "orphans" of the Great Lakes Region in Africa', www.ua.ac.be/objs/00152962.pdf (accessed 5 Mar. 2015).

McLean Hilker, L. (2010) 'The role of education in driving conflict and building peace – the case of Rwanda'. Background paper for Education for All Global Monitoring Report 2011, http://unesdoc.unesco.org/images/0019/001913/191301e.pdf (accessed 5 Mar. 2015).

— (2011) 'Young Rwandans' narratives of the past (and present)', in L. Waldorf and S. Straus (eds.), *Remaking Rwanda: State Building and Human Rights after Mass Violence* (Madison, WI), pp. 316–30.

Melvern, L. (2000) *A People Betrayed: the Role of the West in Rwanda's Genocide* (London and New York).

Melvin, J. (2010) 'Reconstructing Rwanda: balancing human rights and the promotion of national reconciliation', *International Journal of Human Rights* 14, pp. 932–51.

— (2012) 'Beyond the veneer of reconciliation: human rights and democracy in Rwanda'. Opinion piece for the Commonwealth Advisory Bureau, Institute of Commonwealth Studies, School of Advanced Study, http://sas-space.sas.ac.uk/4835/ (accessed 5 Mar. 2015).

Mgbako, C. (2005) 'Ingando solidarity camps: reconciliation and political indoctrination in post-genocide Rwanda', *Harvard Human Rights Journal* 18, p. 201.

Minow, M. (1998) *Between Vengeance and Forgiveness: Facing History after Genocide and Mass Violence* (Boston, MA).

— (2001) 'Innovating responses to the past: human rights institutions', in N. Biggar (ed.), *Burying the Past: Making Peace and Doing Justice after Civil Conflict* (Washington DC), pp. 87–100.

Morris, L. (2006) 'Sociology and rights: an emergent field', in L. Morris (ed.), *Rights: Sociological Perspectives* (London), pp. 1–16.

Moses, D. (2008) 'Toward a theory of critical genocide studies', *Online Encyclopedia of Mass Violence*, www.massviolence.org/Toward-a-Theory-of-Critical-Genocide-Studies (accessed 3 Feb. 2015).

Nabudere, W.D. (2004) 'Africa's First World War: mineral wealth, conflicts and war in the Great Lakes Region', *African Association of Political Science* 8 (1).

Ndahinda, F.M. (2011) *Indigenousness in Africa: a Contested Legal Framework for Empowerment of 'Marginalized' Communities* (The Hague).

Nesiah, V. (2005) 'Coming to terms with irreconcilable truths', in E. Skaar, S. Gloppen and A.Suhrke (eds.), *Roads to Reconciliation* (Oxford), pp. 271–86.

Newbury, C. (1983) 'Colonialism, ethnicity, and rural political protest: Rwanda and Zanzibar in comparative perspective', *Comparative Politics* 15 (3), pp. 253–80.

Newbury, C. and D Newbury (1999) 'A Catholic mass in Kigali: contested views of the genocide and ethnicity in Rwanda', *Canadian Journal of African Studies* 33 (2/3), pp. 292–328.

Newbury, C. and H. Baldwin (2000) 'Aftermath: women in postgenocide Rwanda', in Working Paper no. 3, Centre for Development Information and Evaluation US Agency for International Development, Washington DC, pp. 1–12.

Oomen, B. (2005a) 'Donor-driven justice and its discontents: the case of Rwanda', *Development and Change* 36, pp. 887–910.

— (2005b) 'Rwanda's gacaca: objectives, merits and their relation to supranational criminal law', in R. Haveman et al. (eds.), *Sentencing in Supranational Criminal Law* (The Hague), pp. 161–84.

Pankhurst, D. (1999) 'Issues of justice and reconciliation in complex political emergencies: conceptualising reconciliation, justice and peace', *Third World Quarterly* 20 (1), pp. 239–56.

Paris, R. (2004) *At War's End: Building Peace after Civil Conflict* (Cambridge).

Peskin, V. (2008) *International Justice in Rwanda and the Balkans: Virtual Trials and the Struggle for State Cooperation* (Cambridge).

Philpot, R. (2003) *Ça ne s'est pas passé comme ça à Kigali* (Boisbriand).

Pottier, J. (2002) *Re-imagining Rwanda: Conflict, Survival and Disinformation in the late 20th Century* (Cambridge).

Powell, C. (2011) *Barbaric Civilization: a Criminal Sociology of Genocide* (Montreal and Kingston).

Prunier, G. (1995) *The Rwanda Crisis: 1959–1994: History of a Genocide* (London).

— (2002) *From Genocide to Continental War: the Congo Conflict and the Crisis of Contemporary Africa* (London).

Ranger, T. (1999) 'The nature of ethnicity: lessons from Africa', in E. Mortimer and R. Fine (eds.), *People, Nation and State: The Meaning of Ethnicity and Nationalism* (New York and London), pp. 12–28.

Renton D., D. Seddon and L. Zeilig (2007) *The Congo: Plunder and Resistance* (New York and London).

Reyntjens, F. (1990) 'Le gacaca ou la justice du gazon au Rwanda', *Politique Africaine* 40, pp. 31–41.

— (1998) 'Procès d'intention et faux-fuyants au sujet du Rwanda: une mise en point', www.africamuseum.be/research/libraries/contemporary_history/reference/15848/africa_museum (accessed 9 Mar. 2014; not available for download).

— (2004) 'Rwanda, ten years on: from genocide to dictatorship', *African Affairs* 103, pp. 177–210, http://afraf.oxfordjournals.org/content/103/411/177.short (accessed 9 Mar. 2015).

— (2010) 'Constructing the truth, dealing with dissent, domesticating the world: governance in post-genocide Rwanda', *African Affairs* 110, pp. 1–134, http://afraf.oxfordjournals.org/content/110/438/1.short (accessed 9 Mar. 2015).

— (2011) 'Waging (civil) war abroad: Rwanda and the DRC', in S. Straus and L. Waldorf (eds.), *Remaking Rwanda: State Building and Human Rights after Mass Violence* (Madison, WI), pp. 132–51.

Reyntjens, F. and S. Vandeginste (2005) 'Rwanda: an atypical transition', in E. Skaar, S. Gloppen and A. Suhrke (eds.), *Roads to Reconciliation* (Oxford), pp. 101–28.

Rigby, A. (2001) *Justice and Reconciliation: After the Violence* (London).

Sarkin, J. (2001) 'The tension between justice and reconciliation in Rwanda: politics, human rights, due process and the role of the gacaca courts in dealing with the genocide', *Journal of African Law* 45, pp. 143–72, http://journals.cambridge.org/action/displayAbstract?fromPage=online&aid=91433&fileId=S0221855301001675 (accessed 9 Mar. 2015).

Schaap, A. (2006) 'The proto-politics of reconciliation: Lefort and the Aporia of Forgiveness in Arendt and Derrida', *Australian Journal of Political Science* 41 (1), pp. 615–30.

Scharf, M.P. (2008) 'Statute of the International Criminal Tribunal for Rwanda', http://legal.un.org/avl/pdf/ha/ictr/ictr_e.pdf (accessed 10 Mar. 2015).

Scher, D., and C. Macaulay (2014) 'How tradition remade Rwanda', *Foreign Policy*, www.foreignpolicy.com/articles/2014/01/28/how_tradition_remade_rwanda (accessed 10 Mar. 2015).

Schweisfurth, M. (2006) 'Global and cross-national influences on education in post-genocide Rwanda', *Oxford Review of Education* 32 (5), pp. 697–709.

Shaw, M. (2003) *War and Genocide: Organized Killing in Modern Society* (Cambridge).

Short, D. (2005) 'Reconciliation and the problem of internal colonialism', *Journal of Intercultural Studies*, 26 (3), pp. 267–82.

— (2008) *Reconciliation and Colonial Power: Indigenous Rights in Australia* (Aldershot).

— (2009) 'Sociological and anthropological approaches', in M. Goodhart (ed.), *Human Rights: Politics and Practice* (Oxford), pp. 91–106.

Sibomana, A. (1999) *Hope for Rwanda: Conversations with Laure Guilbert and Hervé Deguine* (London and Sterling).

Simon, D.J. (2012) 'The challenge of social reconciliation in Rwanda: identity, justice, and transformation', in A. Jones (ed.), *New Directions in Genocide Research* (London and New York), pp. 254–69.

Sosnov, M. (2008) 'The adjudication of genocide: gacaca and the road to reconciliation in Rwanda', *Denver Journal of International Law & Policy* 36, pp. 125–53.

Stearns, J. and F. Borello (2011) 'Bad karma: accountability for Rwandan crimes in the Congo', in L. Waldorf and S. Straus (eds.), *Remaking Rwanda: State Building and Human Rights after Mass Violence* (Madison, WI), pp. 152–72.

Straus, S. (2006) *The Order of Genocide: Race, Power and War in Rwanda* (Ithaca, NY and London).

Tavuchis, N. (1991) *Mea Culpa: a Sociology or Apology and Reconciliation* (Palo Alto, CA).

Taylor, P. (2003) *Applied Theatre: Creating Transformative Encounters in the Community* (Portsmouth).

Thomas, M.A. (2009) 'What do the World Governance Indicators measure?', *European Journal of Development Research* 22, pp. 31–54.

Thomson, S. (2011) 'Reeducation for reconciliation: participant observations on ingando', in S. Straus and L. Waldorf (eds.), *Remaking Rwanda: State Building and Human Rights after Mass Violence* (Madison, WI), pp. 331–42.

Tiemessen, A.E. (2004) 'After Arusha: gacaca justice in post-genocide Rwanda', *African Studies Quarterly* 8 (1), pp. 57–76.

Twagiramungu, F. (2006), 'Environmental profile of Rwanda', www.vub.ac.be/klimostoolkit/sites/default/files/documents/rwanda-environmental-profile.pdf (accessed 10 Mar. 2015).

Uvin, P. (1999) 'Ethnicity and power in Burundi and Rwanda: different paths to mass violence', *Comparative Politics* 31 (3), pp. 253–71.

— (2000) *The Introduction of a Modernized Gacaca for Judging Suspects of Participation in the Genocide and the Massacres of 1994 in Rwanda* (Brussels).

— (2001) 'Reading the Rwandan genocide', *International Studies Review* 3 (3), pp. 75–99.

Van de Meeren, R. (1996) 'Three decades in exile: Rwandan refugees 1960–1990', *Journal of Refugee Studies* 9 (3), pp. 252–67.

Van der Merwe, H. (2001) 'National and community reconciliation: competing agendas in the South African Truth and Reconciliation Commission', in N. Biggar (ed.), *Burying the Past: Making Peace and Doing Justice after Civil Conflict* (Washington DC), pp. 101–24.

Van Erven, E. (2001) *Community Theatre: Global Perspectives* (London and New York).

Vandeginste, S. (1998) 'A truth and reconciliation approach to the genocide and crimes against humanity in Rwanda', Institute of Development Policy and Management (Antwerp).

— (1999) 'Justice, reconciliation and reparation after genocide and crimes against humanity: the proposed establishment of popular gacaca tribunals in Rwanda' (Antwerp).

— (2001) 'Rwanda: dealing with genocide and crimes against humanity in the context of armed conflict and failed political transition', in N. Biggar (ed.), *Burying the Past: Making Peace and Doing Justice after Civil Conflict* (Washington DC), pp. 251–86.

Villa-Vicencio, C. (2000a) 'Getting on with life: a move towards reconciliation', in C. Villa-Vicencio and W. Verwoerd (eds.), *Looking Back Reaching Forward: Reflections on the Truth and Reconciliation Commission of South Africa* (Cape Town), pp. 109–209.

— (2000b) 'Restorative justice: dealing with the past differently', in C. Villa-Vicencio and W. Verwoerd (eds.), *Looking Back Reaching Forward: Reflections on the Truth and Reconciliation Commission of South Africa* (Cape Town), pp. 68–76.

— (2005) 'The politics of reconciliation', in T.A. Borer (ed.), *Telling the Truths: Truth-Telling and Peace Building in Post-Conflict Societies* (Notre Dame, IN), pp. 59–82.

Waldorf, L. (2007) 'Rwanda's failing experiment in restorative justice', in D. Sullivan and L. Tifft (eds.), *Handbook of Restorative Justice* (London and New York), pp. 422–34.

— (2009) 'Revisiting Hotel Rwanda: genocide ideology, reconciliation, and rescuers', *Journal of Genocide Research* 11 (1), pp. 101–25.

— (2010) '"Like Jews waiting for Jesus": posthumous justice in post-genocide Rwanda', in R. Shaw, L. Waldorf and P. Hazan (eds.), *Localizing Transitional Justice: Interventions and Priorities after Mass Violence* (Palo Alto, CA), pp. 183–204.

Waugh, C.M. (2004) *Paul Kagame and Rwanda: Power, Genocide and the Rwandan Patriotic Front* (Jefferson, NC and London).

Weber, M. (1968) *Economy and Society: an Outline of Interpretive Sociology* (New York).

Williamson, J.A. (2006) 'An overview of the international criminal jurisdictions operating in Africa', *International Review of the Red Cross* 88 (861), https://www.icrc.org/eng/resources/documents/article/review/review-861-p111.htm (accessed 20 May 2015).

Wilson, R.A. (1997) 'Human rights, culture and context: an introduction', in R.A. Wilson (ed.), *Human Rights, Culture and Context: Anthropological Perspectives* (London), pp. 1–27.

— (2001) *The Politics of Truth and Reconciliation in South Africa: Legitimizing the Post-Apartheid State* (Cambridge).

Worthington Jr., E.L. (2006) *Forgiveness and Reconciliation: Theory and Application* (New York).

Zorbas, E. (2004) 'Reconciliation in post-genocide Rwanda', *African Journal of Legal Studies* 1 (1), pp. 29–52.

— (2009) 'What does reconciliation after genocide mean? Public transcripts and hidden transcripts in post-genocide Rwanda', *Journal of Genocide Research* 11, pp. 127–47.

— (2011) 'Aid dependence and policy independence: explaining the Rwandan paradox', in S. Straus and L. Waldorf (eds.), *Remaking Rwanda: State Building and Human Rights after Mass Violence* (Madison, WI), pp. 103–17.

News sources

AFP, 'Rwanda loses German aid over DRC unrest' 29 July 2012, http://mg.co.za/article/2012-07-29-rwanda-loses-german-aid-over-drc-unrest (accessed 12 Mar. 2015).

BBC News, 'Behind DR Congo's war games', 19 Oct. 2007, http://news.bbc.co.uk/1/hi/world/africa/7053567.stm (accessed 19 Mar. 2015).

— 'Genocide hatred lingers', 19 Feb. 2008, http://news.bbc.co.uk/1/hi/world/africa/7246985.stm (accessed 19 Mar. 2015).

— 'Rwanda arrests Congo rebel leader', 23 Jan. 2009, http://news.bbc.co.uk/1/hi/7846339.stm (accessed 11 Mar. 2015).

— 'Ex-army chief Nyamwasa shot in Johannesburg', 19 June 2010, www.bbc.co.uk/news/10358171 (accessed 11 Mar. 2015).

— 'Rwandan opposition politician found dead', 14 July 2010, www.bbc.co.uk/news/10633500 (accessed 11 Mar. 2015).

— 'Vote counting begins in Rwanda's presidential election', 9 Aug. 2010, www.bbc.co.uk/news/world-africa-10908087 (accessed 19 Mar. 2015).

— 'Kagame wins election with 93% of vote', 11 Aug. 2010, www.bbc.co.uk/news/world-africa-10935892 (accessed 19 Mar. 2015).

— 'Rwanda threatens UN over DR Congo "Genocide" report', 29 Aug. 2010, www.bbc.co.uk/news/world-africa-11122650 (accessed 19 Mar. 2015).

— 'UN relief as Rwanda "drops Darfur peacekeeping threat"', 27 Sep. 2010, www.bbc.co.uk/news/world-africa-11417721 (accessed 19 Mar. 2015).

— 'Rwanda terror charge for opposition's Victoire Ingabire', 25 Oct. 2010, www.bbc.co.uk/news/world-africa-11623454 (accessed 18 Mar. 2015).

— 'Rwanda sentences dissident exiles to long jail terms', 4 Mar. 2011, www.bbc.co.uk/news/world-africa-12190699 (accessed 19 Mar. 2015).

— 'Rwandan exiles in London "threatened by hitman"', 21 May 2011, www.bbc.co.uk/news/world-africa-13475635 (accessed 19 Mar. 2015).

— 'Call to stop Rwandan aid over death threats to exiles', 2 Aug. 2011, www.bbc.co.uk/news/uk-14217337 (accessed 19 Mar. 2015).

— 'Rwanda gives back tonnes of DR Congo minerals', 3 Nov. 2011, www.bbc.co.uk/news/world-africa-15570648 (accessed 17 Mar. 2015).

— 'Rwanda genocide: Kagame "cleared of Habyarimana crash"', 10 Jan. 2012, www.bbc.co.uk/news/world-africa-16472013 (accessed 17 Mar. 2015).

— 'ICC seeks warrants for rebel leaders', 15 May 2012, www.bbc.co.uk/news/world-africa-18065792 (accessed 19 Mar. 2015).

— 'Rwanda supporting DRC mutineers', 28 May 2012, www.bbc.co.uk/news/world-africa-18231128 (accessed 17 Mar. 2015).

— 'Rwanda helped launch DR Congo rebels, say UN experts', 27 Jun 2012, www.bbc.co.uk/news/world-africa-18612612 (accessed 19 Mar. 2015).

— 'Rwandan aid: Greening to reflect "very carefully" before continuing UK support', 13 Nov. 2012, www.bbc.co.uk/news/uk-politics-20309859 (accessed 19 Mar. 2015).

— 'UN condemns DR Congo rebel seizure of Goma', 21 Nov. 2012, www.bbc.co.uk/news/world-africa-20422053 (accessed 19 Mar. 2015).

— 'DR Congo conflict: M23 urged to stop war', 24 Nov. 2012, www.bbc.co.uk/news/world-africa-20476677 (accessed 19 Mar. 2015).

— 'Rebels in DR Congo withdraw from Goma', 1 Dec. 2012, www.bbc.co.uk/news/world-africa-20565711 (accessed 19 Mar. 2015).

— 'DR Congo: M23's Makenga and Runiga factions "clash"', 25 Feb. 2013, www.bbc.co.uk/news/world-africa-21578357 (accessed 19 Mar. 2015).

— 'DR Congo unrest: Rwanda recruiting for M23 rebels', 31 July 2013, www.bbc.co.uk/news/world-africa-23519330 (accessed 19 Mar. 2015).

— 'Victoire Ingabire: Rwanda leader's jail term raised', 13 Dec. 2013, www.bbc.co.uk/news/world-africa-25371874 (accessed 19 Mar. 2015).

— 'Rwanda "protecting M23 DR Congo rebels"', 5 June 2014, www.bbc.co.uk/news/world-africa-27714346 (accessed 19 Mar. 2015).

Bloomberg News, 'Rwanda gets business reformer tag', 15 Mar. 2012, www.bloomberg.com/news/2012-03-14/kagame-s-rwanda-earns-business-reformer-tag-as-opponents-jailed.html (accessed 19 Mar. 2015).

IRIN News, 'Rwanda: focus on helping former child soldiers', 22 Jan. 2004, www.irinnews.org/report/48199/rwanda-fosuc-on-helping-former-child-soldiers (accessed 14 May 2015).

— 'Government implements low-cost housing for returnees', 5 Oct. 2004, www.irinnews.org/report/51581/rwanda-government-implements-low-cost-housing-for-returnees (accessed 19 Mar. 2015).

Jeune Afrique, 'Rwanda: La France annule sa participation aux commémorations du génocide', 5 Apr. 2014, www.jeuneafrique.com/Article/ARTJAWEB20140405193338/ (accessed 18 Mar. 2015).

Kangura, 'The Ten Commandments' (6), Dec. 1990, www.trumanwebdesign.com/~catalina/commandments.htm (accessed 21 May 2015).

New Times, 'Embrace itorero, Rwandans urged', 13 Jan. 2008, www.newtimes.co.rw/Section/Archives/ (accessed 19 Mar. 2015).

— 'Kabarebe, Kayonge head to Goma as tensions mount', 28 June 2012, www.newtimes.co.rw/Section/Archives/ (accessed 19 Mar. 2015).

— 'World joins "Global Umuganda"', 28 Mar. 2014, www.newtimes.co.rw/Section/Archives/ (accessed 17 Mar. 2015).

Pomfret, J., 'Rwandans led revolt in Congo' (for the *Washington Post* Foreign Service), 9 July 1997, www.washingtonpost.com/wp-srv/inatl/longterm/congo/stories/070997.htm (accessed 18 Mar. 2015).

Reuters, 'Bizimungu free from jail' (online video), 6 Apr. 2007, www.reuters.com/video/2007/04/06/bizimungu-free-from-jail?videoId=47878 (accessed 11 Mar. 2015).

— 'France and Rwanda agree to restore relations', 29 Nov. 2009, http://af.reuters.com/article/topNews/idAFJOE5AS09920091129 (accessed 17 Mar. 2015).

— 'Rwanda's Kagame wins election by landslide', 11 Aug. 2010, www.reuters.com/article/2010/08/11/us-rwanda-election-idUSTRE67A2EZ20100811 (accessed 19 Mar. 2015).

— Rwanda grenade attack kills two people, wounds 28', 29 Jan. 2011, www.reuters.com/article/2011/01/29/us-rwanda-explosion-idUSTRE70S28I20110129 (access 19 Mar. 2015)

— 'Congo calls for embargo on Rwandan minerals', 18 Sep. 2012, www.reuters.com/article/2012/09/18/congo-democratic-rwanda-minerals-idUSL5E8KIM6920120918 (accessed 14 May 2015).

— 'Mineral traders in Rwanda helping fund Congo rebels', 16 Oct. 2012, www.trust.org/alertnet/news/exclusive-mineral-traders-in-rwanda-helping-fund-congo-rebels-un-panel (accessed 19 Mar. 2015).

— 'UK freezes aid to Rwanda over Congo rebel claims', 30 Nov. 2012), http://uk.reuters.com/article/2012/11/30/uk-britain-rwanda-aid-idUKBRE8AT0JU20121130 (accessed 17 Mar. 2015).

Rwanda News Agency, 'Rwanda doesn't belong to Hutu, Tutsi, or Twa', 4 Aug. 2010, www.rnanews.com/ele-2010/3949-rwanda-doesnt-belong-to-hutu-tutsi-or-twa-says-kagame (accessed 18 Mar. 2015).

— 'Statement by the Government of Rwanda leaked draft UN report on DRC', 27 Aug. 2010, http://rnanews.com/politics/4080-statement-by-the-government-of-rwanda-on-leaked-draft-un-report-on-drc- (accessed 19 Mar. 2015).

— 'Official Government of Rwanda comments on the draft UN Mapping Report on the DRC', 30 Sep. 2010, www.rnanews.com (accessed 17 Mar. 2015).

— 'Dramatic revelations in Nyamwasa trial', 19 Mar. 2012, www.rnanews.com (accessed 19 Mar. 2015).

The East African, 'Govt faults report ranking Rwanda as most unequal', 7 Mar. 2014, www.theeastafrican.co.ke/Rwanda/News/Govt-faults-report-ranking-Rwanda-as-most-unequal-/-/1433218/2235162/-/14ix0ewz/-/index.html (accessed 17 Mar. 2015).

The Economist, 'Africa's Singapore', 25 Feb. 2012, www.economist.com/node/21548263 (accessed 19 Mar. 2015).

The Guardian, 'Peter Erlinder arrest a blow to international law', 30 June 2010, www.guardian.co.uk/law/2010/jun/29/peter-erlinder-arrest-international-law (accessed 19 Mar. 2015).

— 'Why we're prosecuting Peter Erlinder', 3 July 2010, www.guardian.co.uk/law/2010/jul/03/why-prosecute-peter-erlinder (accessed 19 Mar. 2015).

— 'Genocide report exonerates Kagame', 11 Jan. 2012. Article has been removed from website, see http://kagame15.rssing.com/chan-5486065/all_p1.html (accessed 17 Mar. 2015).

— 'EU partially freezes aid to Rwanda', 27 Sep. 2012, www.guardian.co.uk/world/2012/sep/27/eu-partially-freezes-aid-to-rwanda (accessed 19 Mar. 2015).

The New York Times, 'US lawyer is barred from Rwandan tribunal', 27 Apr. 2011, www.nytimes.com/2011/04/28/world/africa/28rwanda.html (accessed 19 Mar. 2015).

The Rwanda Focus (Kigali), 'Vision 2020 national targets revised', 12 Mar. 2012, http://allafrica.com/stories/201203121336.html (accessed 12 Mar. 2015).

— 'Clearer genocide ideology law to be more lenient', 5 Aug. 2013, www.focus.rw/wp/archives/ (accessed 19 Mar. 2015).

The Telegraph, 'DR Congo warlord Laurent Nkunda seized by Rwandan army', 23 Jan. 2009, www.telegraph.co.uk/news/worldnews/africaandindianocean/rwanda/4325623/Dr-Congo-warlord-Laurent-Nkunda-seized-by-Rwandan-army.html (accessed 19 Mar. 2015).

— 'Rwanda joins Commonwealth', 29 Nov. 2009, www.telegraph.co.uk/news/worldnews/africaandindianocean/rwanda/6685316/Rwanda-joins-the-Commonwealth.html (accessed 16 Mar. 2015).

— 'Rwandan police arrest opposition leader', 14 Oct. 2010, www.telegraph.co.uk/news/worldnews/africaandindianocean/rwanda/8064420/Rwandan-police-arrest-opposition-leader.html(accessed 19 Mar. 2015).

Reports from international NGOs

ActionAid (2011) 'Real aid: ending aid dependency' (situation report), www.actionaid.org.uk/doc_lib/real_aid_3.pdf (accessed 19 Mar. 2015).

Africa Watch (1992) 'Rwanda: talking peace and waging war. Human rights since the October 1990 invasion', vol. 4, no. 3 (situation report), 17 Feb., www.hrw.org/reports/pdfs/r/rwanda/rwanda922.pdf (accessed 11 Mar. 2015).

African Rights (1995) *Rwanda: Death, Despair and Defiance* (human rights report), 2nd edn., June (African Rights, London).

— (2003) 'Gacaca justice: a shared responsibility' (situation report), African Rights, London, http://reliefweb.int/report/rwanda/rwanda-gacaca-justice-shared-responsibility (accessed 18 Mar. 2015).

Amnesty International (AI) (1995) 'Rwanda: arming the perpetrators of the genocide' (situation report), www.eldis.org/go/home&id=22762&type=Document#.VQlsTqNFBCo (accessed 18 Mar. 2015).

— (1996) 'Rwanda and Burundi: the return home: rumours and realities' (situation report), 29 Feb., http://amnesty.org/en/library/info/AFR02/001/1996/en (accessed 18 Mar. 2015).

— (2007) 'Rwanda abolishes death penalty' (news report), 2 Aug., www.amnesty.ie/content/rwanda-abolishes-death-penalty (accessed 11 Mar. 2015).

— (2010a) 'Rwanda: opposition leader must receive fair trial' (press statement), 28 Apr., www.amnesty.org.uk/press-releases/rwanda-opposition-leader-must-receive-fair-trial (accessed 31 Mar. 2015).

— (2010b) 'Safer to stay silent: the chilling effects of Rwanda's laws on "genocide ideology" and "sectarianism"' (human rights report), 21 Aug., http://amnesty.org/en/library/info/AFR47/005/2010/en (accessed 19 Mar. 2015).

— (2011) 'Unsafe to speak out: restrictions on freedom of speech in Rwanda' (situation report), 3 June, http://amnesty.org/en/library/info/AFR47/002/2011/en (accessed 16 Mar. 2015).

— (2012) 'Rwanda: prisoner of conscience released after decade in detention' (news report), 1 Mar., https://www.amnesty.org/en/documents/AFR47/002/2012/en/ (accessed 16 Mar. 2015).

Avocats sans Frontières (2008) 'Monitoring of the gacaca courts judgement phase, analytical report no. 3, October 2006–April 2007' (monitoring and evaluation), www.asf.be/publications/Publication_rwanda_Rapport_analytique_GacacaIII_EN.pdf (accessed 18 Mar. 2015).

Commonwealth Human Rights Initiatives (CHRI) (2009) 'Rwanda's application for membership in the Commonwealth' (situation report), www.humanrightsinitiative.org (accessed 16 Mar. 2015).

COPORWA (n.d.) 'Coporwa – the Rwandese Community of Potters' (historical background), http://coporwa1en.wordpress.com/coporwa/history/ (accessed 18 Mar. 2015).

— (2009) Annual Report, http://coporwa.files.wordpress.com/2011/08/coporwa-annual-report-2009-anglais.pdf (accessed 18 Mar. 2015).

Human Rights Watch (HRW) (1995) 'Rwanda: the crisis continues (situation report) vol. 7, no. 1, Apr., www.hrw.org/legacy/reports/1995/Rwanda.htm (accessed 11 Mar. 2015).

— (2001) 'Uprooting the rural poor in Rwanda' (situation report), www.unhcr.org/refworld/docid/3bd540b40.html (accessed 18 Mar. 2015).

— (2009) '"You will be punished": attacks on civilians in Eastern Congo' (situation report), 13 Dec., www.hrw.org/reports/2009/12/13/you-will-be-punished (accessed 16 Mar. 2015).

— (2010) 'Rwanda: silencing dissent ahead of elections' (situation report), 2 Aug., www.hrw.org/news/2010/08/02/rwanda-attacks-freedom-expression-freedom-association-and-freedom-assembly-run-presi (accessed 16 Mar. 2015).

— (2011a) *Justice Compromised: the Legacy of Rwanda's Community-Based Gacaca Courts* (evaluation), www.hrw.org/sites/default/files/reports/rwanda0511webwcover_0.pdf, (accessed 11 Mar. 2015).

— (2011b) 'World Report 2011: Rwanda', www.hrw.org/world-report-2011/rwanda (accessed 17 Mar. 2015).

— (2012) 'World Report 2012: Rwanda', www.hrw.org/world-report-2012/world-report-2012-rwanda (accessed 19 Mar. 20125).

— (2014) 'World Report 2014', www.hrw.org/sites/default/files/wr2014_web_0.pdf (accessed 17 Mar. 2015).

— (2015) 'DR Congo: Arrest Rebel Leader Wanted by ICC' (situation report), 13 July, www.hrw.org/news/2015/07/13/dr-congo-arrest-rebel-leader-wanted-icc (accessed 18 Sept. 2015).

Human Rights Watch Africa (1994) 'A new catastrophe? Increased international efforts required to punish genocide and prevent further bloodshed' (situation report), www.hrw.org/reports/pdfs/r/rwanda/rwanda94d.pdf (accessed 19 Mar. 2015).

International Criminal Court (ICC) (2015), 'Ntaganda case' (press release), 22 Apr., www.icc-cpi.int/en_menus/icc/press%20and%20media/press%20releases/Pages/pr1105.aspx (accessed 14 May 2015).

International Federation of Human Rights (2005) 'Observatory for the Protection of Human Rights Defenders Annual Report 2004 – Rwanda', Apr., www.refworld.org/docid/48747c8d97.html (accessed 22 Sept. 2015).

Jackson, D. (2003) 'Twa women, Twa rights in the Great Lakes Region' (Minority Rights Group International report), www.minorityrights.org/1066/reports/twa-women-twa-rights-in-the-great-lakes-region-of-africa.html (accessed 11 Mar. 2015).

Lewis, J. (2000) 'The Batwa Pygmies of the Great Lakes Region' (Minority Rights Group international report), www.unhcr.org/refworld/pdfid/469cbf89d.pdf (accessed 11 Mar. 2015).

Minority Rights Group International (MRGI) (2012) 'Twa' (situation report), Apr., www.minorityrights.org/4952/rwanda/twa.html (accessed 16 Mar. 2015).

Penal Reform International (PRI) (2004) 'From camp to hill: the reintegration of released prisoners' (situation report), www.essex.ac.uk/armedcon/story_id/000872.pdf (accessed 12 Mar. 2015).

— (2010) 'Eight years on … a record of gacaca monitoring in Rwanda' (monitoring and evaluation document), www.penalreform.org/resource/years-ona-record-gacaca-monitoring-rwanda/ (accessed 14 Mar. 2015).

SURF (2008) 'Survivor's Fund: financial statements and report', http://survivors-fund.org.uk/who-we-are/our-reports/annual-reports/surf-annual-report-2008/ (accessed 18 Mar. 2015).

— (2012) 'Survivors' concerns over closure of gacaca courts' (online news), 15 June, http://survivors-fund.org.uk/news/what-we-do/gacaca/ (accessed 18 Mar. 2015).

— (2014a) 'Annual Report 2013/14', http://survivors-fund.org.uk/who-we-are/our-reports/annual-reports/surf-annual-report-201314/ (accessed 19 Mar. 2015).

— (2014b) 'Rwanda genocide: why the victims are not paid compensation', Compensation section, 4 March, http://survivors-fund.org.uk/news/compensation-4/ (accessed 2 Jan. 2015).

Reports and documents published by or on behalf of the Rwandan government

Government of Rwanda (2013) 'Rwanda's GDP rises' (press release), 20 Mar., www.gov.rw/newsdetails2/?tx_ttnews%5Btt_news%5D=101&cHash=0755ec7fb6d09304232458a458849f2e (accessed 17 Mar. 2015).

Minaloc (Ministry of Local Government) (2013) 'Progress made and main achievements registered from 2009 to 2013' (report), www.minaloc.gov.rw/fileadmin/documents/Minaloc_Documents/PROGRESS_MADE_AND_MAIN_ACHIEVEMENTS_REGISTERED_FROM_2009_TO_2013_RSTF.pdf (accessed 17 Mar. 2015).

Minecofin (Ministry of Finance) (2000) Vision 2020 (financial plan), www.minecofin.gov.rw/fileadmin/General/Vision_2020/Vision-2020.pdf (accessed 12 Mar. 2015).

— (2013) 'Economic development and poverty reduction strategy 2 (2013–2018)', www.unpei.org/sites/default/files/e_library_documents/Rwanda_Economic_Development_and_Poverty_Reduction_Strategy_2013-2018.pdf (accessed 18 Mar. 2015).

Minijust (Ministry of Justice) (2014), 'The Ministry of Justice signed a MoU with the International Organisation for Migration (IOM)', 29 May, www.minijust.gov.rw/media-center/news/news-details/?tx_ttnews%5Btt_news%5D=243&cHash=170c716c1c29a8b195300bbb410136a5 (accessed 19 May 2015).

MOD (Ministry of Defence) (2003) 'Constitution of the Republic of Rwanda' (document), www.rwandahope.com/constitution.pdf (accessed 12 March 2015).

Mugabe Shyaka, A. (2004) 'The Rwandan conflict: origin, development, exit strategies' (historical report commissioned by NURC) (NURC, Kigali).

— (2007) 'Community conflicts in Rwanda: major causes and ways to solutions' (evaluation commissioned by the NURC) (NURC, Kigali).

National Service of Gacaca Jurisdictions (NSGJ) (n.d. (a)) 'Historical background' (document).

— (n.d.(b)) 'Objectives' (document), http://gacaca.rw/about/ (accessed 26 May 2015).

National Unit and Reconciliation Commission (NURC) (n.d.) 'A summary of lectures used in solidarity camps and other workshops in six chapters' (syllabus).

— (1999) 'Nation-wide grassroots consultations report: unity & reconciliation initiatives in Rwanda' (NURC, Kigali), http://repositories.lib.utexas.edu/bitstream/handle/2152/4198/3309.pdf?sequence=1 (accessed 19 Mar. 2015)

— (2001) 'Report on the evaluation of national unity and reconciliation' (NURC, Kigali), https://repositories.lib.utexas.edu/bitstream/handle/2152/5515/2805.pdf?sequence=1 (accessed 19 Mar. 2015).

— (2003) 'General and specific goals of courses designed for authority seminaries' (syllabus) (NURC, Kigali).

— (2005) 'The role of women in reconciliation and peace building in Rwanda: ten years after genocide 1994–2004' (evaluation) (NURC, Kigali), www.africaknowledgeproject.org/index.php/jenda/article/view/574 (accessed 19 Mar. 2015).

— (2006) 'Impact of the solidarity camps/ingandos on unity and reconciliation of Rwandans: 1996–2006' (progress report) (NURC, Kigali), www.nurc.gov.rw (accessed 19 Mar. 2015).

— (2007) National Policy of Unity and Reconciliation (NURC, Kigali), www.nurc.gov.rw (accessed 19 Mar. 2015).

— (2008a) 'Social cohesion in Rwanda: an opinion survey 2005–2007' (NURC, Kigali), www.nurc.gov.rw (accessed 19 Mar. 2015).

— (2008b) *The Causes of Violence after the 1994 Genocide in Rwanda* (situation report), www.rwandahope.com/thecausesofviolence.pdf (accessed 18 Mar. 2015).

— (2008c) 'Training manual on genocide ideology' (NURC, Kigali).

— (2009a) 'Itorero ry'igihugu: policy note and strategic plan' (policy), www.nurc.gov.rw/ (accessed 19 Mar. 2015).

— (2009b) 'Reconciliation work in Rwanda' (evaluation) (NURC, Kigali), www.nurc.gov.uk (accessed 19 Mar. 2015)

— (2010) 'Rwanda reconciliation barometer' (survey) (NURC, Kigali), www.nurc.gov.rw/fileadmin/Documents/RWANDA_RECONCILIATION_BAROMETER.pdf (accessed 19 Mar. 2015).

— (2011a) *Histoire du Rwanda: des origines á la fin du XXe siècle*, 1st edn., (history textbook) (Kigali).

— (2011b) 'Understanding itorero ry'igihugu' (document) (NURC, Kigali), www.nurc.gov.rw (accessed 19 Mar. 2015).

— (2011c) 'Itorero ry'igihugu: its objectives, participants, structures and functioning' (policy) (NURC, Kigali).

Ndangiza, F. (2003) 'Community sensitization: case of "ingando" in Rwanda'. Presentation on behalf of the NURC at the International Conference on Security and Lasting Peace in the Great Lakes Region of Africa, Kigali (NURC, Kigali).

Office of the President (1999) 'The unity of Rwandans before the colonial period and under the colonial rule, under the First Republic (historical report) (Government of Rwanda, Kigali).

Rwanda Development Board (2013) 'Rwanda rated world's fastest reformer in the World Bank's Doing Business 2014 Report' (press release), www.rdb.rw/news-pages/news-details/article/rwanda-rated-worlds-fastest-reformer-in-the-world-banks-doing-business-2014-report.html (accessed 18 Mar. 2015)

United Nations (UN) reports

UN (1945) Charter of the United Nations, www.un.org/en/documents/charter/ (accessed 18 Mar. 2012).

— (1948) Convention on the Prevention and Punishment of the Crime of Genocide, www.hrweb.org/legal/genocide.html (accessed 17 Mar. 2015).

— (1995) World Summit on Social Development programme of action (summit report), http://social.un.org/index/Home/WorldSummitforSocialDevelopment1995.aspx (accessed 16 Mar. 2015).

UN Development Programme (UNDP) (2007) 'Turning Vision 2020 into reality: from recovery to sustainable human development' (national human development report), http://hdr.undp.org/sites/default/files/rwanda_2007_en.pdf (accessed 12 May 2015).

— (2011) 'Poverty reduction' (report), www.undp.org/content/undp/en/home/librarypage/results/fast_facts/poverty-reduction.html (accessed 18 Mar. 2015).

UN General Assembly (UNGA) (1996) 'Situation in Rwanda: international assistance for a solution to the problems of refugees, the restoration of total peace, reconstruction and socio-economic development in Rwanda' (situation report), www.un.org/documents/ga/docs/51/plenary/a51-353.htm (accessed 23 Mar. 2015).

UN Refugee Agency (UNHCR) (1995) International Colloquium on Post-Conflict Reconstruction Strategies, Stadt Schlaining/Austria, 23–24 June 1995 (memorandum), www.metafro.be/grandslacs/grandslacsdir300/2413.pdf (accessed 6 May 2015).

— (2010) 'DRC: mapping human rights violations 1993–2003' (human rights report), www.ohchr.org/en/Countries/AfricaRegion/Pages/RDCProjetMapping.aspx (accessed 17 Mar. 2015).

UN Secretary General (UNSG) Kofi Annan (1999) 'Letter to the President of the Security Council' (official letter), 16 Dec., www.securitycouncilreport.org/atf/cf/%7B65BFCF9B-6D27-4E9C-8CD3-CF6E4FF96FF9%7D/POC%20S19991257.pdf (accessed 17 Mar. 2015).

UN Security Council (UNSC) (1994) Resolution 995, www.un.org/Docs/scres/1995/scres95.htm (accessed 18 Mar. 2015).

— (1995) 'Report of the Secretary-General on the United Nations assistance mission for Rwanda (no. 1995/457)' (situation report), www.refworld.org/docid/3ae6aed88.html (accessed 18 Mar. 2015).

— (2012) 'Letter dated 26 June 2012 from the Chair of the Security Council Committee established pursuant to Resolution 1533 (2004) concerning the Democratic Republic of the Congo addressed to the President of the Security Council' (addendum to Group of Expert's interim report), www.un.org/ga/search/view_doc.asp?symbol=S/2012/348/Add.1 (accessed 19 Mar. 2015).

— (2014a) 'Letter dated 22 January 2014 from the Coordinator of the Group of Experts on the Democratic Republic of the Congo addressed to the President of the Security Council' (official letter), www.securitycouncilreport.org/atf/cf/%7B65BFCF9B-6D27-4E9C-8CD3-CF6E4FF96FF9%7D/s_2014_42.pdf (accessed 23 Mar. 2015).

— (2014b) Resolution 2147 (2014), www.securitycouncilreport.org/atf/cf/%7B65BFCF9B-6D27-4E9C-8CD3-CF6E4FF96FF9%7D/s_res_2147.pdf (accessed 19 Mar. 2015).

Financial reports

OECD-DAC (2012) 'Rwanda', www.oecd.org/countries/rwanda/aid-at-a-glance.htm (accessed 22 Sept. 2015).

Society for International Development (2013) 'State of East Africa 2013', www.sidint.net/content/state-east-africa-report-series (accessed 17 Mar. 2015).

World Bank (2009) 'Rwanda: from post-conflict reconstruction to development', http://siteresources.worldbank.org/IDA/Resources/ida-Rwanda-10-02-09.pdf (accessed 19 Mar. 2015).

— (2014) *Doing Business Report 2015: Going Beyond Efficiency, Economy Profile, Rwanda*, www.doingbusiness.org/~/media/GIAWB/Doing%20 Business/Documents/Annual-Reports/English/DB14-Full-Report.pdf (accessed 19 May 2015).

— (2015) 'Per capita GDP' (report), http://data.worldbank.org/indicator/ NY.GDP.PCAP.CD (accessed 14 May 2015).

Speeches given by President Paul Kagame (see www.paulkagame.com - accessed 18 Mar. 2015)

Speech given at the Nelson Mandela Foundation's Promise of Leadership dialogue, 20 Mar. 2009.Speech given at the 15th Commemoration of the Rwandan Genocide, 7 Apr. 2009.

Liberation Day speech, 4 July 2009.

Speech given at the International Peace Institute, 21 Sep. 2009.

Speech given at the Leadership Summit on Private Equity in Africa, 2 Nov. 2009.

Speech given at the 16th Commemoration of the Rwandan Genocide, 7 Apr. 2010.

Speech given at the International Institute for Strategic Studies entitled 'The challenges of nation-building in Africa: the case of Rwanda', 16 Sep. 2010.

Opening address for the 9th National Dialogue Council, 15 Dec. 2011.

Statement made when receiving the US Special Envoy, 11 Mar. 2014.

Speech given at Tufts University, 22 Apr. 2014.

Speech given at Gen Next event, 28 Apr. 2014.

Legal texts and statutes

Parliament (2001) Law no. 47/2001, 'Prevention, suppression and punishment of the crime of discrimination and sectarianism', www.unhcr.org/refworld/pdfid/4ac5c4302.pdf (accessed 18 Mar. 2015).

— (2003) Law no. 33 of 6/9/2003, 'Repressing the crime of genocide, crimes against humanity and war crimes', www.refworld.org/docid/46c4597c2.html (accessed 10 Mar. 2015).

— (2004) 'Organic Law no. 16/2004 of 19/6/2004 establishing the organisation, competence and functioning of Gacaca Courts charged with prosecuting and trying the perpetrators of the crime of genocide and other crimes against humanity, committed between October 1, 1990 and December 31, 1994', http://repositories.lib.utexas.edu/bitstream/handle/2152/4582/3677.pdf?sequence=1 (accessed 18 May 2015).

— (2006) 'Organic Law no. 28/2006 modifying and complementing Organic Law no. 16/2004 of 19/06/2004 of 19/06/2004 establishing the organisation, competence and functioning of Gacaca Courts charged with prosecuting and trying the perpetrators of the crime of genocide and other crimes against humanity, committed between October 1, 1990 and December 31, 1994', www.refworld.org/pdfid/452e391c4.pdf (accessed 18 Mar. 2015).

— (2007) 'Organic Law no. 10/2007 modifying and complementing Organic Law no. 16/2004 of 19/6/2004', www.geneva-academy.ch/RULAC/pdf_state/2007-Gacaca-Crts-Organic-Law-10-2007-3-languages-.pdf (accessed 18 May 2015).

— (2008a) 'Organic Law no. 13/2008 of 19/05/2008 modifying and complementing Organic Law no. 16/2004 of 19/06/2004 establishing the organisation, competence and functioning of Gacaca Courts with prosecuting and trying the perpetrators of the crime of genocide and other crimes against humanity, committed between October 1, 1990 and December 31, 1994 as modified and complemented to date' www.geneva-academy.ch/RULAC/pdf_state/2008-Gacaca-Courts-Organic-Law-13.2008.pdf (accessed 12 May 2015).

— (2008b) Law no. 18/2008, 'The punishment of the crime of genocide ideology', www.unhcr.org/refworld/type,LEGISLATION,,RWA,4acc9a4e2,0.html (accessed 18 Mar. 2015).

The Prosecutor v. Ferdinand Nahima, Jean-Bosco Barayagwiza, Hassan Ngeze (2003), case no. ICTR-99-52-T, www.refworld.org/docid/48b5271d2.html (accessed 23 Mar. 2015).

The Prosecutor v. Jean-Paul Akayesu (1998), case no. ICTR-96-4-T, www.unictr.org/sites/unictr.org/files/case-documents/ictr-96-4/trial-judgements/en/980902.pdf (accessed 17 Mar. 2015).

The Prosecutor v. Théoneste Bagosora et al., (2008), case no. ICTR-98-41-T, www.haguejusticeportal.net/Docs/Court%20Documents/ICTR/Bagosora_Judgement_Summary_EN.pdf (accessed 17 Mar. 2015).

Transitional National Assembly (TNA) (1996) 'Organic Law no. 08/96 of August 30 1996 on the Organisation of Prosecutions for Offences Constituting the Crime of Genocide or Crimes against Humanity committed since October 1, 1990', www.geneva-academy.ch/RULAC/pdf_state/Offences-genocide-cah-prosecutions-Rwanda-ORGANIC-LAW-08-96.pdf (accessed 18 May 2015).

— (2001) 'Organic Law no. 40/2000 of 26/01/2001 setting up gacaca jurisdictions and organizing prosecutions for offences constituting the crime of genocide or crimes against humanity committed between October 1, 1990 and December 31, 1994', www.refworld.org/cgi-bin/texis/vtx/rwmain/opendocpdf.pdf?reldoc=y&docid=52f2349c4 (accessed 11 Mar. 2015).

Interviews conducted by the author that are cited in the text

Bikesha, D., then the director of training, mobilisation, and sensitisation at gacaca, 9 June 2009 and 20 July 2010.

Rwandan respondent, 19 July 2010.

Augustin, 7 Apr. 2009.

Angélique, 8 Apr. 2009.

Bakusi, A., then the director of the NURC's civic education department, 23 July 2010.

Bawaya, S., then the head of syllabus development and training, 30 May 2009.

Ingando official, 15 June 2009.

Kabayiza, E., then the coordinator at TIG camp in Rebero, 19 June 2009.

Kanyambo, J., then the assistant centre manager at Mutobo Demobilization and Reintegration Centre, 27 June 2009.

Lliberwaax (no initial), staff member at Mutobo Demobilization and Reintegration Centre, 28 June 2009.

Mukajiranga, L., then the acting director, peace-building and conflict management at the NURC, 9 June 2009.

Ndoli, P., then the coordinator of TIG camp in Kicukiro, 19 June 2009.

Son of returnee, 6 Apr. 2009.

Son of returnee, 7 Apr. 2009.

Rugwabiza, L., then the director general of national development, planning, and research in the Finance and Economic Planning department (Minecofin), 14 July 2010.

Victim at gacaca, 3 May 2009.

Victim at gacaca, 17 July 2010.

Volunteer in student-led religious reconciliation project, 21 July 2010.

Interviews conducted by the author that are not included in the text

Actor, 26 June 2009.

Actor, 28 June 2009.

Actor, 30 June 2009.

Bartender, 15 Apr. 2009.

Mugabire, J., then the nurse at TIG camp in Nyanza, 19 June 2009.

Runiga, P.C., then the legal and legislative translation coordinator at Ministry of Justice (Minijust), 30 June 2009.

Survivor, 4 Feb. 2009.

Theatre director, 19 May 2009

Theatre director, 11 June 2009.

Volunteer in 'Reconciliation Club', 21 July 2010.

Youth, 20 July 2010

Events attended that are cited in the text

15th Commemoration of the Genocide against the Tutsi, Amahoro Stadium, Kigali, 7 Apr. 2009.

Growth Week Conference, London School of Economics, 21 Sep. 2010.

Gacaca trial, Burema, Kigali Province, 12 Feb. 2009.

Gacaca trial, Burema, Kigali Province, 5 May 2009.

Gacaca trial, Butare, Southern Province, 11 Feb. 2009.

Gacaca trial, Butare, Southern Province, 5 May 2009.

Kagame, P., keynote address, the 5th Oxford Africa Business Conference, Oxford, 18 May 2013.

Lecture at ingando for students entering university, Peace and Leadership Centre, Ruhengeri, 3 June 2009.

Lecture at ingando for students entering university, Peace and Leadership Centre, Ruhengeri, 15 June 2009.

RPF Election Rally, Amahoro Stadium, Kigali, 18 July 2010.

Waldorf and Clark debate, Oxford University, 3 Mar. 2010.

Events attended that are not included in the text

'Africa's Hope', play performed by Mashirika Creative and Performing Arts Group, Greenwich, 4 Nov. 2008.

Forum Theatre workshop led by J. Melvin, Kigali, Rwanda, 15 May 2009.

Gathering for Forgiveness at La Palisse Hotel, Kigali, 10 Feb. 2009.

Gacaca trial, Burema, Kigali Province, 7 May 2009.

Gacaca trial, Burema, Kigali Province, 21 May 2009.

Gacaca trial, Burema, Kigali Province, 28 May 2009.

Gacaca trial, Butare, Southern Province, 17 June 2009.

Genocide memorial, Murambi, southern Rwanda, 10 July 2009.

Gisozi Genocide memorial, Kigali, 7 Apr. 2009.

Littoral, play performed by Isoko Theatre, Kigali, 24 May 2009.

The Monument, play performed by Isoko Theatre, Kigali, 4 Feb. 2009.

Index

www.ingramcontent.com/pod-product-compliance
Lightning Source LLC
LaVergne TN
LVHW012052300826
846742LV00017B/60

* 9 7 8 0 9 9 3 1 1 0 2 0 7 *